to dear Carmen –

from Betty

(the author) with

love –

The Art of
German Cooking

The Art of
GERMAN
COOKING

Betty Wason

Doubleday & Company, Inc., Garden City, New York

Acknowledgments

Had I not revisited West Germany recently, I would not have been able to appreciate the diversity and creativity of today's German cuisine, for in a period of fabulous prosperity, when they are able to make use of imported food delicacies from all over the world, the people of West Germany are today cooking in a way that would have astonished the solid burghers of a century ago. In many respects, the German cuisine has changed in the same way and for the same reasons as the American cuisine.

It was thanks to the hospitality of the German National Tourist Association that I had this insight into the Art of German Cooking, for in each of the fourteen cities I visited, I was wined and dined and introduced both to professional chefs and home cooks who showered me with recipes. Frequently I was taken on tours of markets and shopping centers and on my own wandered through markets making note of the foods displayed for sale. My hosts in each city were so charming and friendly I shall long treasure the opportunity to have made their acquaintance.

Like most Americans today, I chose to fly to Germany in order to spend all my available time in the country itself, using the speedy transatlantic services of Trans World Airlines between New York and Frankfurt. Later, taking a cruise on the North German Lloyd's luxurious new motor ship *Europa,* I realized how lovely it would be to have the leisure once again to cross the Atlantic by ship. At least, during the Caribbean cruise, I was able to talk with Chef Herbert Burmeister several times and to get from him recipes for some of the superb German specialties served on the *Europa* and on other North German Lloyd ships.

To advise which is the best time of year to visit West Germany is difficult, for each season has its own special attractions. My last visit was in autumn when the hills were bright with autumn foliage and the air crisp and dry. It was during the period of the grape harvest and I was interested in seeing how the vineyard workers gather the clusters of grapes which go into the making of Germany's wonderful wine. Yet it was too late in the season to take a boat trip down the Rhine, one of the most delightful of all diversions for the tourist, and the great summer fun festivals were over.

On the other hand, by late November, shop windows were being decorated for Christmas and it was a thrill to see the wonderful German toys on display and the fabulous marzipan candies sculptured in the most extraordinary forms. Then, too, there were the *Zwetschgenmännchen,* the prune men, of Nuremberg, gay figures fashioned from figs, prunes, peanut shells, raisins and other simple grocery items. German cooks express their artistry in many ways.

One can only appreciate the great diversity of West Germany— from its towering Black Forest mountains to the nautical atmosphere of its lovely coastal cities—by traveling through the country, in either the comfortable and reliable German trains, by rented car over the autobahns, or by plane from city to city. And one can only learn how intriguingly different the food specialties of the various provinces are by tasting regional dishes in the cities of their origin. To have had this privilege, I am indeed grateful.

Contents

CONTENTS

Recipes for ingredients marked with an asterisk (*) may be found by consulting the Index

The Changing Cuisine
of Germany

The cities of West Germany today are a-bustle with building activity; beautiful sparkling shopping centers have sprung up and window-shopping is one of the great attractions for the tourist, whether it's to ogle furs and other fashions displayed on manikins, or to look at the enchanting toys which the Germans make with such skill and imagination, or to gaze at the fabulous array of sausages draped enticingly in butcher-shop windows. In many cities, traffic-free shopping streets have been set aside in the very heart of the downtown districts, so that shoppers can wander from one dazzling store to another without having to dodge honking cars. West Germany is enjoying a period of prosperity such as Germans have never known before.

Yet beautiful as the new buildings are, the Germans point with pride to the reconstruction of treasured old buildings, rebuilt stone by stone exactly as they were before. Here is a street that was 75 per cent destroyed in World War II, they will tell you, but the street is full of sixteenth-, seventeenth- or eighteenth-century architecture which differs from the original buildings only in its pristine newness.

A comparable thing has happened to the German cuisine.

I was astonished to learn how frequently the German cooks of today use curry powder to season sauces and seafood dishes, to find tomato catsup used as an ingredient in many sauces and stews, and to discover that one of the most delicious of all German ways of preparing sauerkraut is with canned pineapple imported from Hawaii. Yet dumplings and red cabbage and sausages are just as popular as ever, and just as much treasured, and the

Konditoreien, the pastry shops which are such an important part of German life, display if anything more elaborate pastries and coffee cakes than ever before.

Some purists may contend that these recent changes in the German cuisine are merely the adaptation of foreign dishes by a people who have always traveled a great deal and whose traveling today, both for business and pleasure, has reached an all-time peak. But in adapting foreign dishes, they add their own distinguishing characteristics. Hollandaise sauce in Germany, for example, is quite different from the French hollandaise; it is really a white sauce to which egg yolks and additional butter are added. And a curried shrimp dish I enjoyed in Bremen, while oriental in inspiration, contained such purely occidental ingredients as catsup and Worcestershire sauce.

Besides, even sauerkraut and potatoes are recent innovations in the German cuisine, if one is to be literal about it. Sauerkraut was not known in Germany before the thirteenth century, and potatoes not until the seventeenth century. In fact, when King Frederick of Prussia tried to make his peasants grow potatoes, he met with such resistance, he announced that those peasants who refused to plant the tubers would have their noses and ears cut off. Frederick the Great in the late eighteenth century was more subtle; he distributed seed potatoes free along with instructions on how to plant them, and with this persuasion, the people of Germany finally came to admit that this curious importation from South America could be very good to eat indeed. Today, the Germans do more interesting things with potatoes than probably any other people in the world, and it is hard to imagine what the German cuisine was without them.

The one food that has always been a staple of the German diet is pork, for as far back as there are records of the Germanic peoples, the wild boar figures. In Cologne, I saw the mosaic floor of a banqueting hall in a Roman villa from the time when this city was the Roman Colonia, the most important northern outpost of the far-flung Roman Empire, and the home-town of Agrippina, wife of the Emperor Claudius and mother of Nero. The location of the villa is a recent discovery; it was during World War II when an air raid shelter was being dug here that the remains of the two-thousand-year-old Praetorium, the "town hall" of the Roman city, were unearthed, and not far away, the foundations of what had been an exceptionally large villa built in the Mediterranean style. Probably the villa belonged to a wealthy merchant, or it could have been the governor's mansion. Today, directly above the Roman Praetorium stands the rebuilt town hall of Cologne, and all around the area which surrounds the glorious Cologne cathedral are superb restaurants whose menus still offer some of the same foods the Romans enjoyed, to judge from the pictorial record of what is called the Dionysian mosaic, the floor of the ancient banqueting hall. The floor in a sense is a Roman menu, starting with oysters, and proceeding with small birds, duck, pears, cherries and plums, and finally a wild boar. There is also the picture of a dog chewing on bones! In the very center, Dionysus, the wine god (or Bacchus, as the Romans called him), is obviously in a very inebriated state, his wine glass broken on the floor beside him.

The wild boar whose meat was so prized by the ancient Germanic tribes is also immortalized in stone in a Roman archway in the Rhineland town of Remagen, a village which still has Roman street names in the section bordering the river. (The street just beyond the well-preserved Roman archway carries a sign *Via Principalis,* and the ancient stone church which stands here began life as a Roman temple.)

Besides pork, and the meat of deer and rabbits, the Germanic tribes of that period ate mostly "fruits, nuts and sour milk," according to Tacitus the Roman historian, whose book *Germania* was written in the first century A.D. Fruit, nuts, buttermilk and sour cream still play an important part in the German cuisine. I was particularly impressed with the extraordinary use of fruit in every part of the Roman menu—apples, especially. Apples are used in soup, cooked with potatoes (the *Himmel und Erde* of the Rhineland), dried apples are simmered with meat in stews, apples are made into wine and used in every sort of pastry. Pears, too, as the Roman banqueting floor revealed, have always been enjoyed, and today one of the most interesting of German dishes is a mixture of pears, berries and bacon baked in pastry. Modern uses of fruit are still more imaginative: peaches with shrimp, pineapple with veal, prunes with fish.

When fruit is not cooked with meat, fruit preserves are served as a relish. Fruit sauces are often spooned over dumplings to be served as a luncheon entree. Mixed fruit and nut salads are the most frequently served desserts. A most delicious first course served at the Hotel Eisenhut in the medieval city of Rothenburg ob der Tauber was a melon shell filled with a mixture of shrimp, walnuts, melon and pineapple, tossed with what we would call Russian dressing (mayonnaise blended with a little tomato catsup).

As always, in the cuisine of any country, it is the indigenous products that are used most frequently. In this northern climate, where the hardier fruits do best and even the growing season for vegetables is comparatively brief, those fruits and vegetables that store well over a long period are inevitably the most used. It is this that makes cabbage, turnips, dried split peas and lentils such staples of the diet.

Climate, too, affects appetites and living habits. It was autumn, and I was impressed by the vigor of those who walked through the large parks which are an important part of every German city. There was none of the casual strolling one sees in Mediterranean parks, none of the flirtatious dalliance between young men and maids. When Germans go for a walk in the park, they walk briskly and purposefully, and their faces become ruddy with exertion in the crisp air. In this age of motor travel, people even drive to the country on weekends, park their cars at the edge of woodland areas and march under the trees at a steady pace. No wonder when they find a restaurant in the heart of the park, they order thick soups and dumplings, and fall to with a will on plates piled high with sauerkraut, potatoes and plump sausages or fat-rimmed *Eisbein*.

But this is changing, too. Germans have become weight-conscious. Berlin has Europe's only institution devoted solely to the study of nutrition, and literature is published here for the edification of Germans in all walks of life—children, truck drivers, pregnant women, and the overweight who want to slim down. On quite a few restaurant menus, I noted a special section listing low-calorie dishes and I picked up a magazine full of magnificent food pictures only to find the pictures were in illustration of a forty-four-day reducing diet. While I was in Berlin, an interview was arranged for me with the woman who directs this institute, and she gave me a breakdown of the rules for weight control that the institute recommends. Germans are advised to have fruit for snacks instead of cookies, or when they go to their favorite *Konditorei* in the afternoon, to have only one or two cookies instead of five or six. The Berliners who had arranged the interview for me joked about this. "People will listen, then eat five or six cookies just the same as before," they predicted. But before we left, the two men asked if they could take with them some of the information on weight control, and went away carrying almost as much literature as I.

Another factor which has affected the German cuisine is the prevalence of modern gas and electric ranges today in German kitchens. During my stay in Berlin, interviews were also arranged for me with the home economists at the gas and electric power companies, each of whom gave me cookbooks printed by their companies for the use of customers. Because so many homes were destroyed during the war, the majority of city dwellers today live in apartment buildings, and the kitchens in these buildings are equipped with the same sort of automatic appliances as we enjoy. With modern ovens and broilers, German cooks do a great deal more broiling and roasting of meats than formerly, and because women must learn to adapt old cooking habits to the new equipment, they are receptive to new recipes, too, and recipes carefully tested by German home economists are widely disseminated.

It was in the late thirties, on the eve of World War II, when I visited Germany the first time as a journalist. During the Hitler era, elegance was frowned upon, at least for the people as a whole. The women were not permitted to use make-up and their clothes looked as if they had been designed to make every woman as dowdy and shapeless as possible. Since most of the women I saw on the streets seemed to be pregnant, perhaps there was good reason for such fashions, but the impression this made on me was of a stodgy, unimaginative people who got little enjoyment out of life. I was in Germany twice during the war years, before Pearl Harbor, and again in 1950 I visited Munich, Frankfurt and Stuttgart when those cities still had the rubble of aerial bombardments cluttering their streets and most shops offered only the barest necessities of life. To visit the richly prosperous, gay West Germany of today is almost like seeing another country altogether. One is staggered by the change.

For me, the most revealing indications about a people are to be found in little things. I always love wandering through markets, looking at the foods on display as a way of learning what kinds of foods go into home cooking. It's not surprising that supermarkets have sprung up in Germany. Here is a kind of efficiency dear to German hearts, packaged foods stacked in neat piles, labeled clearly, separated into distinctive categories. And what variety and abundance their supermarkets offer! Thanks to the Common Market, French, Dutch, Belgian and Italian products are in plentiful supply, but so are canned goods and frozen products from the United States, and in a Munich market, I noted an entire counter given over to Italian pastas of all sorts. The reason for the latter is the growing number of Italian workers in labor-short Germany. In one restaurant, the waiter serving our table could not even speak German!

Germans still shop in open markets, and farmers bring their garden-crisp vegetables, country-baked bread and farm-fresh eggs to the big municipal markets. The municipal market of Frankfurt serves not only local *Hausfrauen,* but has an international clientele, as well. At least, I talked with one TWA pilot who, whenever he has a few hours' stopover in Frankfurt, makes a bee-line for the market to buy *Bauernbrot,* a curiously shaped big loaf baked in a country *Steinofen* (stone oven), which has that wonderful crunchy wheaty flavor that only slow-baked European breads seem to possess. As he is on the regular TWA New York to Frankfurt run, the American pilot manages to pick up his *Bauernbrot* once a week, to the great delight of his family back in New York.

One of the most difficult things about studying the German cuisine is the language. I once had the naïve idea that Germans all spoke the same language. Not a bit of it. If you live in the Rhineland, you call potato pancakes *Reibekuchen,* literally, "grated cakes." If you live in other parts of Germany, you call potato pancakes *Kartoffelpuffer,* "puffed potatoes." But you don't call them *Pfannkuchen,* which means "pancake," even though they are cooked in much the same way as *Pflaumenpfannkuchen* (plum pancakes).

In Berlin, a *Pfannkuchen* is a jelly doughnut. But in Bavaria, a jelly doughnut is a *Krapfen.*

Cabbage is *Kraut* to some Germans, *Kohl* to others. Sauerkraut is "sour cabbage." This leads to considerable confusion, because

Champagnerkraut sometimes means green cabbage cooked in champagne (or white wine), or it can mean sauerkraut cooked in champagne—there's no way of knowing which until it is set before you.

The words *Kuchen* and *Torte* are impossible to define, since a *Kuchen* may be made with pastry dough (as an *Apfelkuchen*) or with grated potatoes as a *Reibekuchen,* or with yeast-raised dough, as *Zwiebelkuchen* (onion cake) often is. Still more confusing to the non-German-speaking tourist is the fact that a *Küken* is neither pastry nor cake of any kind, but a chicken. Dumplings are variously called *Knödel, Klösschen, Klösse* and *Klopse; Dampfnudeln,* literally "steamed noodles," are dumplings raised with yeast.

As I learned to find my way through this language maze, I became increasingly surprised and delighted by the subtle irony of German wit. I had never thought of the Germans as a particularly witty people; in fact, I shall confess that I had considered German humor to be rather on the heavy side, if not actually pompous. Yet after viewing several scintillating performances of light opera where the acting was superb, frothy and deft, and the stage productions no less than magnificent, I came to see there were aspects of the German character I had never fully appreciated. The curious names Germans sometimes give to pet dishes were an equal delight.

Take the *Halve Hahn* of Cologne. Literally this means "half a chicken," but really it is nothing more than a slice of Dutch (Edam) cheese in a rye roll! The name goes back to the Middle Ages, I was told, when the monks in the monasteries ate very well, indeed, and the half-starved people nibbling on dry bread with a thin piece of cheese inside would mockingly remark, "Can't you see how well off we are, this is a half chicken!" Similarly, "Cologne caviar" is a common name for *Blutwurst,* blood sausage topped with sliced onion.

Something of the same irony explains why a puree of potatoes and apples, the lowliest of garden produce, should be called "Heaven and Earth" (*Himmel und Erde*). The Silesian Heaven (*Schlesisches Himmelreich*), on the other hand, is a stew of pork cooked with dried fruit, a much more substantial repast. *Himmel* in Westphalia has a still different connotation. There it refers to the big open hearths where the Westphalian hams used to be smoked in the days when such a hearth was the heart of every farm kitchen.

If "caviar" is the name given by the people of Cologne to blood sausage topped with chopped onions, a topping of raw onion mixed with oil and vinegar is called "music" elsewhere. *Handkäs mit Musik* is a delightful snack with beer, and the kind of music it immediately suggests is the *oompah, oompah* of a German band.

There are a dozen stories to explain the origin of the name *Pumpernickel* for the slow-baked black bread of Westphalia, but none very convincing, and most likely the word stems from a local dialect now long forgotten. For one of the things that must be remembered about Germany is that until Bismarck's time the land consisted of many independent states and even free cities which refused to accept the sovereignty of any king, and the local language differed from province to province and state to state. At the time of the American Revolution, the language spoken by the Hessian soldiers who fought in the American Army was probably as different from that of the Pomeranians in the northeast and the Bavarians in the southeast as English today is different from modern German. People of Frankfurt even today cannot understand Swabians when they talk among themselves, and Berliners are completely baffled by the Bavarian dialect. During a performance of *Der Rosenkavalier* in Frankfurt when I asked my escort to explain what was happening on stage, he replied apologetically that he did not understand it himself because the opera was sung in the Viennese dialect!

The foods differ quite as much from region to region as the dialects. In north Germany, fruit, vegetables and meat are often cooked together. In the country districts of Schleswig-Holstein, buckwheat and rye are used not only in making breads, but for porridge to be topped either with milk or a fruit sauce. Fruit soups, too, are characteristic of the northern provinces. When I asked whether these were served as a first course or as dessert, a puzzled expression came over the faces of those queried. They are always served as entrees, a light meal in themselves! Not surprisingly, the foods of Schleswig-Holstein are very much like those of Denmark and Scotland, whereas many of the Bavarian dishes bear close resemblance to specialties of Austria just across the border. Swabia has its *Spätzle,* which is thicker and bitier than noodle paste, made into all sorts of shapes. The Swabians, too, like tricky food names. *Spätzle* means "little sparrows" and why such a name should be given to a flour dough, no one can explain. *Laubfrösche,* literally "tree frogs," is their name for meat-filled spinach rolls. *Landjäger,* which normally means a local policeman, actually is a kind of smoked sausage, quite dry and chewy.

I like the alliteration of German food names as much as the double meanings. *Küche, Kirche und Kinder* has its counterpart in *Birnen, Bohnen und Speck* (pears, beans and bacon), and what phrase could be more delightful for children to repeat than *Snuten und Poten,* the name of a Hamburg dish of pig's snout and sauerkraut.

Everyone knows that many of our American Christmas customs come straight from Germany, starting with the Christmas tree itself and the baubles used to decorate it. Many of our most beloved Christmas sweets and goodies are German, too, as is the custom of giving toys, which is such an important part of Christmas. The Germans are undoubtedly the world's most skillful and imaginative toy-makers. Where else in the world can one find such clever puppets, such cuddly stuffed animals with almost human faces, such whimsical jumping jacks and entrancing music boxes? The same fairy-tale skill is lavished on marzipan candies, sugar-plum fairies and the little men made of figs, raisins and peanut shells which are to be seen in every grocer's window during the Christmas season.

Nuremberg is the toy-making center of Germany and here the gingerbread houses in candy shop windows makes the story of Hansel and Gretel become very real. The sugar plum fairy and the king of the nutcrackers, too, are a part of Nuremberg magic, quite as much as the delicious *Lebkuchen* shipped out from Nuremberg to all parts of the world.

(When I realized how many nuts are used in the German cuisine, in appetizers, entrees, sauces and sweets, I could see why every German child wants a "king of the nutcrackers" as a doll. The number of nutcrackers in use during the hour before dinner in Germany must be formidable.)

I have attempted in this book to collect a cross-section of recipes from the German cuisine of today, both new specialties born of today's prosperity and old favorites which reflect customs and traditions of another age. Many recipes were given to me during the course of my recent trip to the country. Others I culled from the voluminous amount of printed material I brought home with me, including several cookbooks in German. Still others I worked out as best I could with the help of notes jotted down at the time of my visit. A few are recipes given to me by American friends of German background.

The Germans have a phrase which I like very much. Sauerkraut prepared in the Bavarian style is described as *"auf Bayrische Art";* a Florida-type fruit salad is listed on a menu as *"auf Florida Art,"* or if a sauce contains pineapple, it may be called *"Hawaiian Art."* The word *art* is a synonym for style, of course, yet the phrase has a ring to it which I find delightful.

Reading German restaurant menus is great fun, anyway. Some of the printed menus are perfectly enormous, illustrated with gay drawings in three colors. One which I brought home from the *Marktstuben* (Market Tavern) in Bremen has dishes listed according to these categories (to name a few):

> *Dishes for Mr. Hurry*
> *For Those Who Can't Decide*
> *What the Hen Gives and What We Add*
> *Cooked with Love*
> *For the Slim Figure*
> *To Finish the Meal*
> *What You Find on Every Menu*

The *Marktstuben* menu also contains special listings of non-alcoholic drinks, and special dishes for children. The back of the menu is covered with gay line drawings picturing German specialties. The sketch of *Schlesisches Himmelreich* (Silesian Heaven), for example, shows fruit falling down like stars from the sky into a big pot.

Restaurants in West German cities today cater to all tastes and all pocketbooks. There are modest little *Bäckereien,* pastry shops with a few tables where one can have a mid-morning breakfast (the second breakfast of the day, which is an old German custom), or mid-afternoon pastry with coffee. Then there are the *Molkereien* or dairy shops where cheeses of all kinds can be purchased to take out, or where customers can have a sandwich at a stand-up counter. And there are kiosks on street corners where hot sausages are dispensed much as we sell hot dogs.

For those with a hankering for Chinese, French, Indonesian or Italian food, there are restaurants specializing in all these cuisines. Oriental food is so popular with Germans that virtually every first-class restaurant lists *Nasi Goreng,* the Dutch-Indonesian rice dish, on its menu. Those who enjoy dining in the sky can gaze upon the city beneath them as they are served in the revolving pinnacle of Frankfurt's Henninger Turm Restaurant, or atop Stuttgart's radio-TV tower, or in Berlin at the Funkturm, also a radio tower, located on the city fairgrounds. Such restaurants offer foods of every nationality, and for those American tourists who do not read German, menus printed in English are available for the asking. These ultra-modern restaurants are not mere tourist spots; on the contrary, you will find yourself surrounded by German family groups, who are as much intrigued by restaurants with atmosphere as are Americans.

For sumptuous service and skillfully prepared food, there are many restaurants famous even beyond the borders of West Germany. Such is the dining room of the Erb Prinz Hotel in the town of Ettlingen which French gourmets rate as one of the ten best in Europe. The Hotel Sommerberg at Wildbad on the edge of the Black Forest is one of the most luxurious resort hotels to be found anywhere, commanding a breathtaking view from its mountaintop site and serving Swabian specialties so exquisitely prepared, every morsel is to be savored. Humplmayr's in Munich has an old-world elegance in a setting of dark-paneled walls, and nowhere is one likely to taste Bavarian dishes more skillfully seasoned or deftly served.

In Bremen, I dined in so many excellent restaurants, it is hard to single out which was the finest. It seemed to me the best food I tasted anywhere in Germany was in Bremen, with Cologne a close second, though Düsseldorf is generally considered the "gastronomic capital" of West Germany and others rave about the many superb restaurants in Munich. Among the renowned dining places in Hamburg is the dining room at the Hotel Four Seasons (*Vier Jahreszeiten*), whose chef, Oskar Behrmann, gave me his own recipes for outstanding Hamburg food specialties—and told me he was always glad to see Americans come into his dining room because Americans always appreciated good food.

(There were others who said quite the opposite, however. In

fact, so many different people expressed surprise that I was writing a cookbook because "most Americans don't seem to care what they eat," I began to wonder what sorts of Americans traveled in Germany!)

For *gemütlich* atmosphere, there are always charming low-raftered taverns in every German city, where strangers sit together at roughhewn tables and it is considered quite proper to talk to the person next to you even though you have never laid eyes on one another before. A tavern with a touch of elegance is the *Wirtshaus* in Cologne, a series of small intimate rooms delightfully decorated with wheels, buckets and gaskets retrieved from ancient wineries, which maintains a bowling alley on a lower level for the sportsminded, while still farther below, those with a historical bent may walk through a Roman sewer still completely intact after two thousand years. (The sewer has not been used as such for many hundreds of years, but it served as an excellent air raid shelter during World War II.)

One of the most attractive country restaurants I visited was in a moated castle in Westphalia, not far from the city of Münster. Havixbeck is the town, and the castle is the Burg Hülshoff whose owner, the Baron von Droste-Hülshoff, decided to open his family home to the public, transforming an unused quarter to a tavern-like restaurant, having tables and benches for the restaurant made from oaks grown on the property. His daughter, the Baroness, a tall, slim beauty who wears chic country tweeds, supervises the kitchen and serves as hostess.

Munich has dozens of beer halls, great and small, including what is self-proclaimed as "the largest beer hall in the world" (Bavarians are frequently described as "The Texans of Germany"), and one of the gayest of these *Bierstuben* is the Platzl, where a stage show is put on for the amusement of customers who may enjoy a very inexpensive and hearty meal washed down with huge steins of beer while laughing at bawdy Bavarian wit.

(Munich also has many superb wine restaurants of which the elegant Künstlerhaus, the Walterspiel Restaurant in Munich's Vier Jahreszeiten Hotel, and Zur Kanne are particularly noteworthy. Zur Kanne is a favorite after-theater spot; the specialty at the Walterspiel is smoked brook trout stuffed with caviar.)

For those who are enchanted with the past, there are cities and

towns where the medieval atmosphere has been painstakingly preserved (or re-created). Rothenburg, which in the height of its summer season sometimes entertains as many as two thousand American
tourists a week, has two exceptionally fine restaurants. The Eisenhut
Hotel boasts that its front door was once a part of the St. Nicholas
chapel built on this same spot in the year 1100. A huge hand-
written chronicle on display under glass in the lobby contains
records of the town since A.D. 419. Priceless antiques fill the public
rooms of the Eisenhut, including the armor of two fearsome-looking
medieval knights whose long swords nearly touch the hand-hewn
beams of the small dark lobby. But there is nothing antique about
the food served in the dining room, for one of Germany's most
skilled chefs rules in the kitchen, and each dish of the traditional
five-course dinner is likely to be memorable enough to write home
about.

Adams das Kleine Hotel is not competitive with the Eisenhut in
the matter of size, since it can accommodate only eight guests, but
its proprietor is one of West Germany's best-known chefs, for Hans
Karl Adam for several years conducted a TV cooking school and
is the author of a number of cookbooks. It was in this tiny hostelry
that I was introduced to the ceremony of *Der Meistertrunk* (The
Master Drink) which every visitor to Rothenburg sooner or later
witnesses. In the seventeenth century, in the course of the Thirty
Years' War, Rothenburg was under siege and might have been
razed to the ground if General Tilly, the enemy invader, had not in
a weak moment agreed to spare the town if the *Bürgermeister,* a
genial character named Nusch, could swallow an entire liter of
wine without removing the huge Rothenburg wine tankard from his
lips. Nusch drank the wine down without drawing a single breath,
and Rothenburg lived. In memory of this feat, a costumed character appears before the table of tourists, repeats the story, then
offers the huge tankard to be downed, while a photographer takes
shots of the ceremony. Visitors are not expected to equal *Bürgermeister* Nusch's feat, however; the tankard holds only a normal
wine glass of liquid.

The visitor to Germany should not be misled by the raucous
laughter and boisterous good humor in Bavarian beer halls (which
are to be found in every West German city, not just in Bavaria)
into thinking the Germans are as informal as Americans. It is a

paradox of the German character that only after wine or beer has loosened tongues and relaxed the stiff manners of sobriety do they let themselves go. When sober, there are no more proper people in all the world. It has always struck me as symbolic that in France one calls every waiter *garçon* (boy), but in Germany one addresses every waiter, regardless of his rank, as *Herr Ober* (Mr. Headwaiter). If a German has earned a Ph.D., he (or she) must always be addressed as *Herr Doktor,* or *Frau Doktor* as the case may be—it would be highly insulting to call such a distinguished person *Doktor* So-and-So, like calling our President "Mr. Johnson." And the number of *Herr Doktors* one meets in Germany is impressive, indeed. The etiquette of the table is equally strict. One must never, but *never,* lift a wine glass (or beer tankard) until one's host or hostess has first done so. There were times during my recent visit when I found my fingers about to lift a wine glass half a dozen times, and hastily I would have to bring my hand back to my lap as I noted my table companions had not yet lifted *their* glasses. When the host's glass is raised, there is always the hearty toast, *"Prosit,"* and then everyone clicks glasses, all around the table. Sometimes *Prosit* is followed by *zum Wohl* (to your health) or *auf Ihre Gesundheit* (which means the same thing). After glasses have been clicked, it is proper to start the first of the five courses that constitute a formal German meal. And of course you will wish everyone at the table *Guten Appetit.*

Notes on Wines, Beers and Other German Beverages

WINES

Say "German" to a thirsty American and his immediate response is likely to be "beer." Yet there are parts of Germany where the natives themselves drink more wine than beer and along the banks of the Rhine and Moselle (*Mosel* in German), some of the world's finest white wines are produced.

The storied castles along the Rhine, whose spires and turrets suggest the very stuff of fairy tales, are many of them vineyard castles whose names embellish the labels of particularly fine wines. Some of the castles date back to the Middle Ages when their high walls were erected to enclose monasteries. But the German wine industry was already centuries old when the monasteries were built, for the Romans planted the first vineyards along the Rhine two thousand years ago. A Roman vine-pruning knife is one of the most valuable of the artifacts in Rüdesheim's Wine Museum, an extraordinary display of wine memorabilia housed in an eleventh-century castle. At the other end of the Rhine, in Cologne, another museum contains a display of exquisite Roman wine goblets, some of them cut from solid blocks of crystal, with raised designs in vivid color. One such goblet, recently unearthed in a Cologne suburb, bears the legend in Latin on its rim, "Drink and live happily always."

With the collapse of the Roman Empire in the fifth century, the vineyards fell into neglect, but three hundred years later, Charlemagne revived the Rhineland wine industry and the Frankish king himself selected the hills above Rüdesheim as the spot on which to plant the first new vineyards, observing that these slopes remained free of snow throughout the winter. Even today this is the region where the finest of Rhine wines are made.

By the fourteenth century, Rhenish wines were the most prized in Europe, more in demand than those of France, for the white wines of this northern land aged better in the gigantic oaken tuns then used to store wines (before the use of corked bottles had been invented). Some of the tuns erected during the Middle Ages are still to be seen in Rhineland cities; the tun at Heidelberg is a favorite tourist spot, while one in the Palatinate city of Bad Dürkheim has been turned into a three-story restaurant with tables for five hundred patrons.

In the days of the Holy Roman Empire, when bishops were often more powerful than kings, Rhenish wines were used exclusively for ecclesiastical purposes, and this meant a brisk wine trade, much of it centered in the city of Bremen in the north, seat of the most important northern bishopric. To store the wine supplies for buyers who came to Bremen from all parts of Europe, huge underground vaults were built beneath the market square. Today these same damp cool underground chambers still are used to store German wines for one of the most remarkable wine cellars in Europe, the Bremen Ratskeller.

The German word *Rat* means government or parliament; the *Rathaus* is the government building. Because the city fathers in the Middle Ages were usually men of substance with an appreciation of the better things of life, Ratskellers in all German cities can be counted on as places where the finest food and the best wines are served, in dining rooms maintained especially for the convenience of city councilors. Bremen's Ratskeller, however, is primarily a retail establishment selling only German wines and only the finest of wines. Yet its vaults hold more than half a million bottles plus many more barrels of wine aging in wood, and the inventories list some eight hundred different wines, some going back to 1889, with one Rüdesheimer of 1727. In a chamber called the Rose Cellar two intricately carved wine barrels hold still older vintages, one a 1653 Rüdesheimer. I was permitted a sip of this three-hundred-year-old wine, standing in the candlelit dimness of the Rose Cellar, and before I put the glass to my lips, I sniffed at its heady bouquet in wonder. But the taste was acrid-bitter. Wines of this age are retained as a curiosity, not to be drunk. A few treasured German wines do remain drinkable for as long as fifty years—a vintner in Rüdesheim told me he had tasted a wine of this age and it was still golden-smooth. But such wines are rare, indeed. The two most valuable of the wines for sale in Bremen's Ratskeller are a 1921 Niersteiner from the Rheinhessen and a 1920 Schloss Vollrads, each costing 200 marks (about $50).

Just to wander through the damp cool wine vaults of the Ratskeller is an unforgettable experience. The older wine barrels are intricately carved and only candlelight is used in the rooms in which they are stored. This is because a wine's clarity can be tested only by holding the glass before the flame of a candle—no artificial light ever invented is so revealing. There is a sense of time standing still in these quiet, dark rooms lit only with the flickering soft light of candles, rooms perfumed by the penetrating essence of ancient wine dregs.

The *Kellermeister* must sample every wine he accepts for the Ratskeller (and on a tasting morning, I was told, his handwriting becomes successively more wobbly as one glass after another is placed before him!). Once a year, each of the wines stored for aging must be retasted and a record kept of how each is holding up. The finest are locked away in a vault called the Treasury, three bottles of each; once every ten years, one of the three bottles will be uncorked and tasted. If the wine is still holding up well, the bottles will be replaced in the vault for another ten years. Only an expert can judge when the wine has reached its prime and must be used immediately.

The Bremen Ratskeller survived all the bombings of World War II without mishap, thanks to its deep subterranean structure, but when the building became an Allied officers' club during the occupation, its huge stock of wines rather swiftly disappeared. When the Ratskeller was again restored to the city of Bremen, the *Kellermeister* was horrified to find stocks of precious thirty-, forty- and fifty-year-old wines wiped out, but in the years since, a small but precious selection of pre-1945 wines has been acquired from private vintners. Because American officers stationed in Germany are now some of the Ratskeller's best customers, the wine connoisseurs of Bremen have forgiven the looters.

Another renowned pre-war wine cellar was not so fortunate. The old Adlon Hotel on the Unter den Linden in what is now East

Berlin used to be famous throughout Europe for its fabulous selection of vintage wines, stored in vaults deep underground beneath the hotel's crimson-carpeted lounges. The Adlon miraculously survived all the Allied bombings of Berlin, but its end came ignominiously during the Russian occupation, when Russians took over the hotel as an officers' mess. One night, discovering the rare stocks of wines, the Soviet officers staged a drunken orgy of typical Russian proportions and in the course of the wild night which followed, fire broke out. In a city without water, nothing could be done to save the Adlon and the famed hotel burned to the ground. One lone wing survived the holocaust and it still stands, facing on the Wilhelmstrasse, but it has the appearance of a run-down third-rate hotel. The underground vaults themselves may still be intact, but their shelves are empty.

Learning to be selective about German wines is not easy. In this northern climate, where the growing season is short, a rainy cold summer can utterly destroy the vintage. Wines will be produced, but all the skill of the vintner cannot make them outstanding. For this reason, the connoisseur choosing German wines must have at least a smattering of knowledge about vintage years. The greatest year of all, the "year of the century," was 1959. There are not many '59s available now, and those that remain are treasured and costly—most of them, that is. A few have begun to turn, not living up to their early promise of greatness, and in German wine shops one may occasionally see '59s at bargain prices.

Here is a quick breakdown of the years since 1959:

1960: the poorest year on record in Germany.

1961 and 1962: poorer than average, though some of the *Kabinett* and *Original-Abfüllung* wines have developed better than expected.

1963: not a good year, for some wines a very poor year, though curiously some of the secondary (*verbessert*) wines of that year with aging came off better than the estate-bottled (*Original-Abfüllung*) wines.

1964: the best year since 1959, though many are not yet ready and will need several years more to reach their prime.

1965: a year of incessant summer rains, saved only by a late clear fall. Prospects are poor.

This breakdown may serve as a general guide, but there are many exceptions. For example, the 1964 Moselles did not measure up as well as the wines of the Saar and Ruhr, which ordinarily are not as good as the Moselles. And the Palatinate wines of 1964 were so outstanding, they are considered better than those of 1959. The *Kellermeister* at Bremen advised that no hard-and-fast rules of selection for German wines can be laid down, one must taste critically and when a superior wine comes along, note it and buy more of the same.

Quite as important as learning about vintages is to become acquainted with German wine geography. For the location of the vineyard tells much about the potential of the wine.

There are four principal wine-producing regions in Germany: the Rhine and Moselle valleys, Baden-Württemberg and Franconia. Of these, the Rhines and Moselles are by far the most important. The Franconian wines, traditionally bottled in flask-shaped stone bottles, are pleasant but undistinguished. A greater quantity of wine is produced in Baden-Württemberg than in any other region, but the people of this region drink more wine than other Germans, and nearly the entire production is locally consumed.

The finest of the Rhine wines come from the Rheingau, the section of the river lying between Rüdesheim and Wiesbaden, from vineyards growing on the river's north bank. The Weinstrasse, or Wine Road, a favorite tourist route, traverses the Rheinpfalz or Palatinate, a region of rolling hills where vineyards stretch on every side. Rheinhessen and the Middle Rhine are other sections of the Rhineland whose names are frequently listed on wine cards.

The Moselle is a corkscrew-twisting river which originates in France and winds leisurely north to empty into the Rhine at Koblenz. Its great vineyards begin at Trier, Germany's oldest city (legend says Trier was founded by an Assyrian prince in 2053 B.C.). Because of the peculiar way in which the river twists back and forth, the vineyard slopes receive an abundance of sunlight and many connoisseurs consider the wines produced in this region the greatest white wines in the world, lighter, drier and more delicate than the Rhine wines, the palest gold in color. Moselles usually (but not always) are put up in green bottles; Rhine wines are usually in brown-tinted bottles.

Besides a knowledge of wine *regions,* it is important to be familiar with wine *villages* and castles or vineyards (or both), for every reputable German wine will carry the name of its village on the label.

Before going to Germany, I thought I knew something about German wines. I always looked for the names Liebfraumilch or Moselblümchen on labels, believing these to be good samples of the German vintner's art. Quite the contrary is true. The two are mere merchandising labels, usually placed on blends of secondary wines. Still another name often to be found on wines from the Mosel-Ruhr region is Schwarze Katz (Black Cat), which is also a blend of lesser wines with a trace of sugar added in the processing. While this is not a connoisseur's wine, I have found a Schwarze Katz produced by Scholl & Hillebrand to be extremely pleasant, moderately dry, very good with fish.

The nicest way to become familiar with Germany's wine geography is to make a trip down the Rhine or up the Moselle, tasting as you go, then the names of towns and villages along the way will become forever indelible in memory. Next best is to drink enough German wines so that the place names become familiar from frequent perusal of labels. An "r" is always added to a village name: a wine of Rüdesheim is a Rüdesheimer, a wine of Bingen is a Binger, a wine of Hochheim is a Hochheimer, and so on.

In certain cases, only the name of the castle appears on the label, when the castle vineyards are that renowned. Schloss Johannisberg and Schloss Vollrads are the two most famous.

Here are some of the names to look for on wine labels:

Rheingau: Rüdesheim, Schloss Johannisberg, Steinberg, Eltville, Winkel, Schloss Vollrads.

Rheinhessen: Nierstein, Alsheim, Bingen, Oppenheim.

Rheinpfalz (Palatinate): Deidesheim, Dürkheim, Forst, Kallstadt.

Moselle: Bernkastel (Bernkasteler Doktor is world-famous), Piesport, Zeltingen, Urzig, Wehlen, Kasel, Trier.

Besides carrying the name of the region, the name of the village or vineyard or both, and the vintage year, German wine labels usually also indicate the grape variety. All Moselles and most Rheingau wines are produced from Riesling grapes; some Rhine wines may be produced from a mixture of Riesling and Sylvaner. Occasionally Traminer grapes are used.

Here are other German wine terms which are important to understand:

Kabinett: this means a wine of outstanding quality.
Original-Abfüllung: estate-bottled.
Spätlese: wine produced from selected grapes of late harvesting.
Auslese: wine from very ripe grapes, individually selected.
Beerenauslese: from grapes so ripe they have begun to shrivel so that the juice is concentrated and very sweet.
Trockenbeerenauslese: wine from grapes almost as dry as raisins, carefully selected one by one from the cluster. It takes ten men working all day long for ten days to gather grapes enough to make one hundred bottles of this wine, the costliest of all, a wine the owners of estate vineyards make for their own pleasure and satisfaction. Few are sold on the open market.
Eiswein: literally "ice wine," this is made from grapes picked after the frost; the wine is very sweet, meant to be served at tea-time with lacy crisp cookies.
Natur: This means no sugar has been added to the wine. It is only in Germany that the practice of adding sugar to any wine is condoned, and then only for secondary wines or in a year when climatic conditions have been so poor, well-balanced wines are all but impossible to produce.

It was by curious accident that the first *Trockenbeerenauslese* wines were produced. In the Middle Ages, when all viniculture was controlled by the monasteries, it was necessary to obtain permission of the Abbot of Fulda to proceed with the grape harvest. One year the Abbot's messenger was late in arriving at the Schloss Johannisberg and the worried monks watched the grapes shrinking and drying on the vines, and feared they would have no wine that year at all. To their amazement, the wine that resulted from this "dry harvest" proved to be exceptionally sweet and luscious. This marked a change in German wine-making procedures, and ever since certain vineyards or sections of vineyards have been set aside each year for late harvesting.

Usually *Auslese* or *Beerenauslese* wines are quite sweet and even the *Spätlese* wines tend to be sweeter than those of the regular harvest, though a memorable 1959 Ver Ziger-Würzgarten *Spätlese* which was served us at dinner in the Weinhaus Brückenkeller in Frankfurt on the last night before my departure was exquisitely dry. Frankfurt was blanketed with low fog that night, so intense there was a possibility my flight home next day by TWA might be canceled, but so lovely was the wine, and so charming this elegant restaurant located deep underground in a former wine cellar, I would not have minded staying longer in Frankfurt at all.

Superb as the Rheingau and Moselle wines are, there are no German red wines worthy of note, despite the fact that almost as much red as white wine is produced in the Württemberg region. German connoisseurs, when the meal demands a red wine, order a French Bordeaux or Burgundy.

It was no surprise to me to be told while in Germany that those seeking fine food should go to wine restaurants in preference to *Bierstuben*. Wine always makes good food taste better, and the elegance with which it is served helps the simplest meal to seem sumptuous. Still I was surprised when in Munich, the city often called the beer capital of the world, to be told by a young lady who was escorting me to markets and restaurants, that she had never visited a *Bierstube* in her life, because her father, a lifelong resident of Munich, was a wine drinker and gourmet. When the family dined out, she said, it was always at wine restaurants—a tip for the gourmet visiting West Germany.

It depends, of course, upon what kind of food you want. For hearty, no-nonsense sauerkraut-and-sausage fare, the beer restaurants and beer cellars offer big helpings of simple food at reasonable cost, and in a much more informal atmosphere.

Perhaps the difference between the wine restaurants of Germany and the beer taverns can be compared to the difference between the music of Beethoven and that of a stomping, horn-tooting Bavarian band. Those who find Beethoven too "long-haired" for their musical tastes may also feel uncomfortable in white-clothed wine restaurants where the wine steward waits respectfully to know whether the sample of wine he has just poured meets with the host's approval. For myself, I enjoy Beethoven and Bavarian music equally—for each creates its own mood. The ribald gayety of

German beer taverns is great fun. But what other music can be compared to that of Beethoven for pure rapture?

From the first of August until mid-October, there is always a wine festival going on somewhere in German wine country. Today these are staged primarily for the tourists, and while they are gay and colorful, no longer are they related to the pagan festivities which in ancient times accompanied the trampling of the grapes into must. The actual harvesting of the grapes does not begin until late October and reaches its prime in November.

I was a guest at the last of the wine festivals, one in the small town of Bockenheim in the Palatinate. As we approached this country town on a crisp cool October afternoon, after driving through mile after mile of vineyards, the breathless anticipation of festivity was in the air. Banners flew from flagpoles, the roadsides were thronged with people walking toward the big tents that had been set up for the *Winzerfest*. Yet, despite the air of celebration, when we first entered the largest of the tents, I feared the evening would be deadly dull. Inside, men and women sat sedately at long tables and while a band played foot-stomping German music, no one seemed to respond. Not until plump blonde country girls began to walk through the aisles with big pitchers of wine in their hands, filling tall glasses as they went, did things begin to liven up. The wine glasses each held a demiliter (about 17 ounces) and as each glass of wine cost something like 50 pfennigs, not surprisingly it was soon being tossed off like water. Ballons in the shape of bunnies floated near the tent's top, and as the music of the band became more insistent and the wine started loosening tongues, I noted that the bunny-balloons began to bob in time with the music. Before long, those sitting at the long tables were linking arms and swaying back and forth to the *oompah* of the band, singing lustily, then men and women began dancing over the hard earth floor, and before an hour had passed, there was nothing sedate about the atmosphere at all. Jovially, old friends embraced one another and then they began embracing strangers. The young men became bolder, the old men began to make like wolves. By the time we left the *Winzerfest*, the Bockenheimers were dancing on the tables.

Linking arms with those who sit next to you at the table is a custom one encounters everywhere in Germany, a custom guaranteed to break down all barriers of reserve very quickly indeed. In contrast to the preciseness and formality of Germans on other occasions, in the atmosphere of the tavern or the festival, anything goes. Dancing on the tables is also a favorite German way of expressing abandon. I tried it myself one night at a Bavarian-type night club in Hamburg's Reeperbahn, the sailors' street where there are probably more cabarets per square foot than on any other street in the world. On the stroke of midnight, everyone in this huge barnlike cabaret climbed on the tables and the band played a particularly lively number. I can report that it was an interesting experience, but except for the honor of the thing, I would just as soon sit down. Table-dancing does not allow for much fancy footwork.

BEERS

Bavaria is beer country, and Munich is its capital. There are 1600 breweries altogether in Upper Bavaria, 4000 in West Germany as a whole. It is claimed that the annual per capita consumption of beer in Bavaria is two hundred quarts and for the regular beer drinkers, this probably means more than a quart a day. The city of Munich accounts for 60 per cent of Bavarian beer production, in seven enormous breweries, each of which maintains a *Bierkeller* where people can enjoy an evening of fun at modest cost. Not only is food as well as beer inexpensive, those who wish to do so are encouraged to bring their own lunches in a paper bag and it's not unusual for customers to put away as much as two quarts of beer in a single evening.

For the convenience of Munich residents, door-to-door delivery of beer is made by means of carts that drive through the residential areas, much as we have milk delivered, except that the customers bring out their own jugs to be filled.

Germans have been drinking a barely-fermented brew similar to beer since time immemorial, for "barley wine" was already the regional drink when the Roman historian Tacitus first toured Germania. It is doubtful if hops were used in making the earliest of beers, though the Germans claim they were using hops in beer as far back as A.D. 700 and in 1516 a Purity Law was passed stipulating that only barley, hops and water could go into beer. (In England at that time hops were considered poisonous and some beers during the Middle Ages, even in Germany, were flavored with juniper, thyme and various other herbs.) The extraction of malt sugar to be fermented with yeast, the step that gives today's beer its bubbly, foaming quality, did not become a part of the brewing process until comparatively modern times. Pilsner beer, the type most commonly brewed in Germany today, originated in the city of Pilsen in Czechoslovakia.

But it was the Germans who invented the lagering process of making beer, which causes the yeast to settle to the bottom during brewing, creating a heavier, more stable brew and one which stores longer and better in the cask. (The word *lagern* means to store.) Lager beer ranges in color from pale gold to dark brown, from very light in alcohol to very potent. Light lager beers are called *hell,* darker ones *dunkel.*

The first court brewery was established in Bavaria in the year 1589 when Duke Wilhelm V grew tired of having to buy his beer from the monasteries and decided the royal treasury should pocket the profits. His *hofbrauerei* turned out mostly dark beer, chocolate-brown and rather sweet. It is called bock beer after Einbeck, the town where this type beer originated, but the spelling sometime during the ages changed from *beck* to *bock* and since bock means a young male goat, and goats are associated with Bacchus the Roman wine god, the traditional symbol of bock beer became a goat's head.

Bock beer is still the favorite of Bavarians who consume as much of this heavy dark beer as they do the more golden Pilsner.

By the time Ludwig I mounted the throne of Bavaria, beer had become such an important drink with Bavarian workers that when in 1848 the king raised the price one pfennig a drink, riots broke out that nearly cost the king his throne. It was an Irish dancer, Lola Montez, who drove the king to this extreme measure. Ludwig was quite a ladies' man as one can see by visiting the Gallery of Beauties at Schloss Nymphenburg where portraits of his many lady-loves still hang on the walls. After the beer riots, Lola was forced to flee the country, but she found refuge easily enough in the United States where tales of her royal romance were a decided asset to her stage career. She lies buried in a Brooklyn cemetery. I don't suppose anyone thought of using a keg of beer for her funeral urn, but it would have been appropriate.

Pilsner is the type of beer most Americans think of when German beer is mentioned, and this is probably the most popular of all beers among Germans, too, but it is not by any means the only one. There are some German beers which contain as little as 2 per cent alcohol (*Einfachbier*), others contain up to 28 per cent alcohol, and in between there is *Schankbier* (7 to 8 per cent), *Vollbier* (11 to 14 per cent) and *Starkbier* ("strong beer") with 16 per cent or more.

Bock is a *Starkbier* and South Germans can grow quite nostalgic about it. But while this dark sweet beer is popular in Bavaria, in north Germany a beer lighter in both alcoholic content and color is preferred. North Germans like their beer chilled; South Germans prefer it at room temperature.

In Cologne a beer called *Kölsch* is a popular hot-weather drink. It is very light in alcohol, tart, a most curious drink. *Weissbier* is made of wheat, not barley, and it is usually served with a slice of lemon. Münster favors *Altbier Bowle,* a light, almost sour beer which is usually blended with fruit juice or fresh fruit; it is served in summer floating with strawberries or peaches, in winter may be blended with orange or raspberry juice. *Berliner Weisse* is a light northern beer usually mixed with lemonade or red berry juice, a "nice drink after sailing," as one person described it.

While most of the German beer is produced in Bavaria, other cities are equally proud of their breweries. The Henninger Turm Restaurant in Frankfurt is located above Frankfurt's leading brewery, and anyone who wishes to do so may make a tour of the brewery installations. On the *Getränke* menu at the Henninger Turm are listed four kinds of beer, including *Diät-Pils* for the weight-conscious.

SPIRITUOSEN

(*Brandies and Schnaps*)

Weinbrand (literally "burnt wine") is the German name for brandy made from wine, and probably the best-known of German brandies is Asbach Uralt, whose distilleries are located in the wine village of Rüdesheim. Visitors are welcomed at the Asbach distilleries and some 100,000 of them go through its modern plant every summer, enjoying a free sip of this potent distillate at the end of the tour. The method of making brandy from wine in Germany is somewhat different from that of French cognac; the result is that the brandy has a less heady bouquet but a more decisive and lingering aftertaste. This makes it particularly effective (though rather costly) as a flavoring ingredient. The Asbach company also produces superb brandy-filled chocolates, a product which cannot be exported to the United States because according to American customs regulations, it contains too high a proportion of brandy to be classed as a candy. Visitors to West Germany take note: these luscious confections are worth searching for in confectionery shops.

Spirits are made from many other fruits in Germany besides grapes. *Kirschwasser,* or *Kirsch* as it is more commonly called, is one of the most delightful, a water-clear brandy made from the cherries which grow in the Black Forest. *Kirsch* is said to induce untroubled sleep if taken just before bedtime—much nicer than sleeping pills! *Kirsch* is a superb flavoring agent for fruit compotes and pastries, too.

Other brandies are made from pears, plums, raspberries, and blackberries. Most are only moderately sweet. There are also a number of liqueurs available, though none of world-renown.

Schnaps is a generic term for all strong spirits such as gin, aquavit, and *Korn* or *Doppelkorn,* a clear, potent beverage distilled from rye which Westphalians toss off with a beer chaser.

In Hamburg and Bremen, rum is popular and those who take the harbor tour in Hamburg may have a hot rum grog while viewing the immensely long harbor from the deck of the sightseeing boat, whatever the hour of day. (Hamburgers consider grog a suitable breakfast drink.)

OTHER DRINKS

Anyone who visits Frankfurt should plan to spend at least one evening in Sachsenhausen, the suburb across the river whose *Apfelwein* taverns are gay, warm places where everyone sings to the accompaniment of an accordion. As in most other German taverns, it's the custom for strangers to share tables, and when the singing starts, everyone links arms and sways in time to the music, a custom known in Germany as *Schunkeln.*

Apfelwein (or *Ebbelwoi* as it is spelled in the local dialect) is a tart drink, made from several kinds of apples with a goodly number of crabapples thrown in. It tastes much like a light home-brewed white wine and is low in alcoholic content. But don't let this fool you. It is always served in tall glasses and I was warned that more than seven glasses can be disastrous. I did not make that many. After the fifth, I suddenly noticed the room was spinning.

On first taste, the apple wine is too tart for most Americans, but the *gemütlich* atmosphere of the taverns is such fun, the drink seems to become better as the evening progresses. For those who insist, beer or Rhine wine can be obtained, but a frown is likely to be the response to such an order.

Traditionally with apple wine one has *Handkäs mit Musik* (hand cheese topped with an onion mixture), *Kasseler Rippchen* (smoked pork ribs) or *Schlachtplatte* ("butcher's plate," a selection of sausages with sauerkraut).

Non-alcoholic fruit drinks are also very popular with Germans, especially red currant juice and black raspberry juice, usually served in stemmed glasses tinkling with ice.

Nor should German mineral waters be forgotten. Every city in Germany which has a *bad* or *baden* in its name has a mineral spa somewhere nearby, and many of these centers have been famous for their waters since Roman times. Wiesbaden, for example, was once a Roman health center. Baden-Baden in the Black Forest gained its grandeur during the nineteenth century when it was one of the most famous of the fashionable "watering places" in Europe. The day I was in Stuttgart, I saw two women filling bottles with mineral water from a public spring. Bad Cannstadt, which lies just across the river from Stuttgart, proudly boasts of its two-thousand-year history when it, too, drew visitors from all over the Roman world to drink of its curative waters.

And how can one write of German beverages without mentioning coffee? Wasn't it the Germans who gave us the custom of the *Kaffeeklatsch*? And what would Germany's elegant *Konditoreien* be without cups of strong coffee to accompany those wonderful pastries? Coffee may be ordered topped with whipped cream, or blended with chocolate, or simply served with cream and sugar. Curiously, most Germans today prefer it with evaporated milk (a fact which struck me with horror). It is also possible to order decaffeinated coffee, for the first of all such coffees, Kaffee Hag, was invented in Germany. Most of Germany's coffee, shipped green from South America, is roasted in the city of Bremen and one of the delights of Bremen is the good odor of roasting coffee permeating its streets.

Germans enjoy mixing drinks as much as we do, and many current West German publications carry recipes for such American concoctions as Missouri Mule, Bloody Mary, Manhattan Cocktail, and Gin Fizz. We would do well to adapt a German specialty, a delightful mixture of wine, champagne and fresh fruit which the Germans call *Bowle*. Hot wine drinks are popular in winter, too, the famous *Glühwein*, as well as hot punches spiked with rum or brandy.

Ananasbowle
(PINEAPPLE WINE PUNCH)

½ cup superfine sugar	2 bottles Moselle wine
2 cups chopped fresh	1 half-bottle champagne
pineapple	or 1 split club soda

Add sugar to pineapple, let stand ½ hour. Add wine; chill 1 to 2 hours. Just before serving, add chilled champagne or club soda. Makes 20 servings, enough for 8 persons.

Pfirsichbowle (Peach Wine Punch). Use fresh peaches, cut up, instead of pineapple.

Erdbeerbowle (Strawberry Wine Punch). Use sliced fresh strawberries instead of pineapple.

Berliner Schlosspunsch
(BERLIN CASTLE PUNCH)

2 cups water	1 cup rum or brandy
2 cups sugar	10 to 12 lumps sugar
1 bottle Rhine wine	

Heat water and sugar together in chafing dish or in casserole; stir until sugar is dissolved. Add wine and ½ cup of the rum or brandy. Soak sugar lumps in remaining rum or brandy. When wine is steaming but not boiling, lower the rum-soaked lumps of sugar into the chafing dish bowl or the casserole, set aflame. When flame has died out, serve in punch cups or mugs. Makes 12 to 14 servings.

Glühwein

(GLOW WINE)

1 bottle red wine,	**Whole cloves**
Burgundy type	**1 orange, sliced**
½ cup sugar	

Place wine and sugar in casserole or chafing dish. Stick whole cloves into the orange slices, place orange slices in the wine. Heat until wine steams, but do not allow to boil. Serve hot in punch cups or mugs. Makes 8 punch cup servings, 4 to 6 servings if mugs are used. For a party, multiply ingredients according to number to be served, allowing 2 to 3 servings per person. Serve from large heatproof (not glass) punch bowl.

Maiwein Bowle

(MAY WINE)

The herb called woodruff is the secret ingredient in this provocative wine drink. It may be obtained from specialty food shops in neighborhoods catering to those of German, Austrian or central European background. Place a sprig of woodruff in a 1½-quart bowl, add one bottle (a fifth) of Moselle wine, chill thoroughly. Remove woodruff. Dissolve 2 tablespoons sugar in ½ cup water, add to wine along with one thinly-sliced orange. Serve chilled. Makes 8 servings.

Sellerie Bowle (Celery Punch). Instead of woodruff, place a sprig of celery leaves in bowl, add a bottle of Moselle and, if desired, a 1-ounce jigger of white rum. Remove celery when wine is thoroughly chilled; add orange slices.

Gurkenbowle

(CUCUMBER PUNCH)

Peel of 1 cucumber, cut in long spiral
1 orange, thinly sliced
1 to 2 tablespoons superfine sugar

¼ cup Curaçao liqueur
1 bottle (fifth) red wine, Burgundy type
Ice block or ice cubes
1 pint club soda

Place cucumber peel, orange slices, sugar and Curaçao in 2-quart (or larger) punch bowl. Let stand ½ hour. Add red wine. Chill thoroughly. Add ice and soda just before serving. Makes 10 to 12 servings.

Note: If more servings are desired, multiply ingredients, allowing 2 to 3 servings per person. Marinate cucumber, orange, sugar and Curaçao in advance to have mixture ready for refills.

Buttermilch

(SPICED BUTTERMILK)

This is a refreshing and nourishing drink which both children and adults will enjoy. For each quart buttermilk, add 2 tablespoons sugar, ½ teaspoon of cinnamon and ¼ teaspoon nutmeg. Beat with a wire whisk until frothy. Serve very cold. Makes 4 servings.

Vorspeisen

(HORS D'OEUVRES AND SNACKS)

The German word *Vorspeisen* means literally "before foods," or appetizers. But some *Vorspeisen* may also be served as between-meal snacks or after-theater snacks or as light meals in themselves. Some are nothing more than make-your-own spreads: soft cheese served surrounded by little mounds of chopped onions and seasonings to be mixed at the table and spread over slices of black bread or pumpernickel. Or *Vorspeisen* may consist of dainty canapés glazed with aspic, or hot bite-size morsels in puff paste shells, or spicy salad mixtures intricately seasoned.

I was astonished during my most recent visit at the number and variety of *Vorspeisen,* especially those to be purchased in supermarkets and delicatessens. True that *Delicatessen* is a German word, and our German-American delicatessens have always furnished a wide variety of cheeses, sausages and such things as potato and macaroni salads. But here were tongue salads, rice salads, complicated seafood salads, and others too numerous to mention, presented in cases so enticingly, one wanted to buy them all.

The most famous delicatessen in all of Germany is Dollmayr's in Munich, an elegant establishment where one must go before noon in order to buy canapés and salads for a party, for by one o'clock the fabulous array of hors d'oeuvres will be mostly gone. Dollmayr's offers more than canapés, salads and delicacies for a cold buffet. It sells complete meals, delivered ready to serve, plus fantastically elaborate pastries, coffee blends roasted to order, and every kind of fish, fresh and smoked, garnished cold meats and poultry, and fancy dressed meats, from suckling pigs and wild boar to filet mignon and dressed pheasant ready to be cooked. It has customers all over West Germany—all over the world, for that matter. The cable address of the establishment is *Lukullus.*

I had heard of Dollmayr's before going to West Germany and

was prepared from the description to expect a gourmet's paradise within its oak-paneled walls. But still more surprising were the delicatessen counters in the supermarkets, for most of the large department stores in West German cities now have entire floors given over to supermarkets much like ours, complete with carts which the customers push around from one counter to another. As in our supermarkets, there are many "fixings" for the making of hors d'oeuvres, but there are far more ready-to-serve appetizers than we offer.

Besides the delicatessen counters in the large markets, there are the individual fish stores which offer an enormous variety of smoked fish (I counted two dozen kinds of smoked fish in a Bremen fish shop), and the *Wurst* (sausages) in infinite variety in the butcher shops, and the salads and aspic-glazed goodies for take-out sale in *Konditoreien* (pastry houses).

This is a new development, such a selection of *Vorspeisen* was not known in Germany before World War II, and this trend in German eating habits is therefore an indication of how the art of German cooking is changing with the times.

Lachstüten mit Rahm

(SMOKED SALMON CONES WITH CREAM FILLING)

1½ teaspoons
(½ envelope) unflavored
gelatine
2 tablespoons cold water
¼ cup boiling water

1 teaspoon sugar
(optional)
½ cup heavy cream
2 tablespoons prepared
horseradish
12 slices smoked salmon

Soften the gelatine in cold water, add boiling hot water and sugar, if desired; stir until dissolved. Chill about 5 minutes. Beat the cream until stiff, blend in horseradish. Stir into cold gelatine. Roll the salmon into cones (or place flat on counter, spoon mixture into each slice of salmon, fold over into cone shape), spoon the whipped cream mixture into each, place overlapped side down on waxed-paper-lined pan or baking sheet until gelatine is set. Keep chilled until ready to serve. Makes 12. For a first course, allow 3 to each person. To make 24, double all ingredients.

Krabben Cocktail à la Adam
(SHRIMP COCKTAIL À LA ADAM)

This shrimp-and-peach cocktail is a creation of Hans Karl Adam, owner of Adams Kleine Hotel in the quaint medieval city of Rothenburg. The combination of fruit and seafood, served with a curry-spiced sauce, is typically German.

2 fresh peaches, or 1 cup sliced canned peaches, drained	1 teaspoon brandy
	1 pound small shrimp, shelled, cooked
¼ teaspoon lemon juice	Lettuce
Pinch of salt	

SAUCE

¾ cup mayonnaise
3 tablespoons heavy sweet cream or sour cream
Pinch of curry powder

Peel and stone peaches, cut into cubes. Sprinkle with lemon juice, salt and brandy. Cut shrimp into smaller pieces, combine with peaches. Spoon over lettuce in sherbet dishes, top each serving with 1 heaping tablespoon of the sauce. Makes 6 to 8 cocktail servings.

Krabben Canapés
(SMALL SHRIMP CANAPÉS)

1 pound tiny shrimp, shelled, cooked, or	1 boiled tongue, cut into ¼-inch slices
3 2¾-ounce jars Danish or California shrimp, drained	4 or 5 pimiento-stuffed olives, sliced
	Wine Aspic
	Remouladensosse*

Place overlapping tiny shrimp across thick slices of boiled tongue, trimmed to form a circle. In the center of each, place a sliced stuffed olive. Glaze with successive layers of aspic, chilling each layer until set. Keep chilled until time to serve. Serve with *Remouladensosse*. Makes about 12.

WINE ASPIC

1 cup chicken stock
⅛ teaspoon crushed
  fennel
⅛ teaspoon crushed dried
  thyme

1 envelope unflavored
  gelatine
¼ cup Rhine wine

Heat chicken stock (which may be made with powdered concentrate or bouillon cubes) with fennel and thyme. Soften gelatine in cold wine, add boiling stock, stir to dissolve. Cool. Spoon a thin film over each hors d'oeuvre, chill until set; repeat with two successive layers.

Hummersalat mit Gurken
(LOBSTER SALAD WITH CUCUMBER)

2 cups diced cooked
  lobster meat
2 large cucumbers, peeled,
  diced
½ cup mayonnaise
2 tablespoons tomato
  catsup
1 teaspoon mustard
2 tablespoons grated
  horseradish
2 tablespoons dry sherry

1 tablespoon brandy
Pinch of cayenne
¼ teaspoon salt, or to
  taste
¼ teaspoon crushed dried
  chervil, or 1 teaspoon
  minced celery leaves
¼ teaspoon crushed dried
  tarragon
1 tablespoon grated onion
  or onion juice

Toss lobster and cucumber with remaining ingredients. Makes 4 to 6 servings as a first-course cocktail.

Variation. Instead of fresh cucumber, use 1 large dill pickle, cubed, and 1 cup cooked diced potato. Serve mounded in high pyramid, garnished with meat from lobster claws, and capers arranged in a pattern over the top. Arrange cucumber cups around the bottom: cut cucumbers into 1-inch pieces, peel partially, scoop out seeds from center, leaving a cup shape. Fill each with Horse-radish Cream* to which minced fresh dill has been added.

Krebssalat Helgoländer Art

(CRAB SALAD HELGOLAND STYLE)

2 cups cooked lump crabmeat	2 hard-cooked eggs, chopped
1 cup cooked rice	Few drops lemon juice
2 teaspoons curry powder	¼ teaspoon salt
¾ cup mayonnaise	1 tablespoon minced dill or chives
¼ cup sour cream	

Toss crabmeat and rice together. Add curry powder to mayonnaise and sour cream, blend well, stir into crabmeat-rice mixture. Sprinkle chopped egg with lemon juice, salt and dill or chives, add this to salad mixture. Serve on lettuce as a seafood cocktail. Makes 6 cocktail servings.

With Avocado. Avocados, imported from the Caribbean, are just beginning to appear in German markets. This salad is sometimes garnished with avocado slices which have been marinated in an oil and vinegar dressing.

Note: The word *Krebs* refers to crayfish, but since these are available in only certain American markets, crabmeat or shrimp may be used instead.

With all the fancy new appetizers to whet German thirst, nothing can replace the beloved herring, which is served in numerous versions, though most often combined with apple and onion. Because it is so popular, and always available, herring is fresher and better in Europe than the herring we get in American markets. I was particularly taken with Matjes Herring which I found to be so delicate in flavor, I determined to try to find it after reaching home. When I saw in a supermarket counter a sign proclaiming "Matjest Herring," I promptly bought some—and was in for a shock. Instead of being more delicate and less salty, it was far more salty than other herring. The explanation apparently is that Matjes is the virgin herring, very young and perishable, and only when it can be consumed in or near the ports where brought in, is it possible to get it lightly salted. When packed for export, it must be more heavily salted than regular herring.

Marinierter Hering

(PICKLED HERRING)

4 salt herrings
4 large yellow onions, or 2 large Spanish onions, thinly sliced

VINEGAR MARINADE

2 teaspoons sugar
1 tablespoon mustard seed
1 tablespoon peppercorns

1 tablespoon juniper berries (optional)
2 bay leaves
1½ cups vinegar
½ cup water

Soak herrings 24 hours; skin and bone, cut into 2-inch pieces. Place in layers in wide-mouthed quart jar with sliced onions. Add sugar, mustard seed, peppercorns and juniper berries to the vinegar and water, bring to a boil, pour over herring. Leave in refrigerator 2 or 3 days. Makes 3 cups.

Rollmops

4 salt herrings
2 cups milk
4 to 6 sour gherkins, chopped
2 large onions, very thinly sliced
Capers
Düsseldorf mustard (or Dijon style)
Vinegar Marinade*
1 tablespoon pickling spices
2 bay leaves

Soak herrings 24 hours, changing water several times. Skin and bone carefully, keeping the two fillets intact. Lay out fillets flat, place some chopped gherkins, onion slices, capers and a dab of mustard on each, roll up and tie with thread or fasten with small skewers or toothpicks. Place in small crock or large wide-mouthed jar with remaining sliced onions between the layers. Heat Vinegar Marinade to boiling, pour over *rollmops,* add pickling spices and bay leaves. Leave in mixture 3 or 4 days. Makes 8 *rollmops.*

This version of Herring Salad is as important a part of Christmas Eve in the Rhineland as the Christmas tree and the carols.

Heringssalat Rheinischer Art

(RHINELAND HERRING SALAD)

1 jar pickled herring, drained
½ cup diced cooked or canned beets
1 large apple, cored and diced
2 medium potatoes, cooked and diced
1 small onion, minced
½ cup chopped walnuts
½ cup sour cream
½ cup mayonnaise
1 teaspoon sugar, or to taste
1 hard-cooked egg, sliced
6 to 8 small canned whole beets, drained
1 tablespoon minced parsley or dill (optional)

Combine herring with beets, apple, potatoes, onion and nuts. Toss with sour cream, mayonnaise and sugar. Arrange in a salad bowl or platter, place egg slices over top and whole beets around the edges for garnish. Sprinkle with minced parsley or dill just before serving, if desired. Makes 6 appetizer servings.

Salat von Geräuchertem Aal

(SMOKED EEL SALAD)

½ pound smoked eel, cut into ½-inch pieces
1 apple, peeled, cored and chopped
Grated rind and juice of ½ lemon
2 cups diced cooked potatoes
¼ cup olive oil
¼ teaspoon salt

¼ cup sour cream
¼ cup mayonnaise
1 tablespoon minced fresh or frozen dill
Lettuce
Freshly ground black pepper
Lemon wedges
Pumpernickel bread
Sweet butter

Place eel and apple in mixing bowl. Sprinkle with lemon rind and juice. Toss potatoes while still warm in olive oil, sprinkle with salt, add to eel and apple in mixing bowl. Combine sour cream, mayonnaise and dill, blend well, add to salad mixture, stir to coat salad with dressing. Transfer to salad platter, spoon over lettuce. Grind pepper over top. Arrange lemon wedges around salad. Serve salad with pumpernickel and sweet butter as a snack with beer or Moselle wine. Makes 6 to 8 hors d'oeuvre servings.

Schinkenröllchen mit Spargel
(HAM ROLLS WITH ASPARAGUS)

6 thin slices boiled ham
12 spears canned white
  asparagus, well drained
Pimiento strips
1 cup asparagus liquid
¼ teaspoon thyme
Pinch of salt

1½ teaspoons
  (½ envelope) unflavored
  gelatine
2 tablespoons cold water
Few drops lemon juice
Mayonnaise

Lay ham slices flat. Place 2 asparagus spears in each, roll ham around them in cone shape. Place a strip of pimiento over top of each. Heat asparagus liquid to boiling with thyme and salt. Soften gelatine in cold water; pour boiling-hot asparagus liquid through a strainer over gelatine, stir to dissolve. Add lemon juice. Cool; spoon a little of the cooled but still liquid gelatine over the top of each ham roll. Chill until it sets. Add another layer, chill again. Repeat with a third layer. Do not remove from refrigeration until shortly before serving. Serve with mayonnaise on the side. Makes 6. (Double all ingredients to make 12.)

Kalbsbraten mit Champignons in Aspik
(VEAL WITH MUSHROOMS)

Cooked roast veal sliced
  ¼-inch thick, cut into
  12 2 × 2-inch squares
1 6-ounce can sliced
  mushrooms

Yolks of 2 hard-cooked
  eggs, sieved
Capers
Wine Aspic*

The veal slices serve as a canapé base for the mushrooms. Arrange the mushrooms in overlapping slices over veal squares. Sprinkle sieved egg yolk over top of each and arrange a line of capers down the center of each. Spoon a thin layer of Wine Aspic over each, chill; repeat 3 times. Keep chilled until time to serve. Makes 12.

Sülze
(JELLIED VEAL LOAF)

6 scrubbed pig's knuckles
1 pound veal neck
  (or stewing veal with
  bone)
6 cups water
2 teaspoons salt
8 peppercorns
½ bay leaf
¼ teaspoon thyme
1 onion stuck with 2
  cloves

½ cup vinegar
1 teaspoon sugar
1 envelope unflavored
  gelatine
¼ cup cold water
3 hard-cooked eggs,
  sliced
Slivers of green pepper
  and pimiento
Thin-sliced cauliflower
  buds

Place pig's knuckles and veal neck in water, add salt, peppercorns, bay leaf, thyme, onion and vinegar. Cook, covered, for 2
hours, or until meat comes away from bone easily. Cut meat into
strips or small pieces. Discard bones. Strain broth, cool, then chill
in refrigerator until fat and scum from meat broth have risen to
top and congealed. Skim off fat. Reheat broth, measure, add liquid
to make 5½ cups altogether, and add sugar. Soak gelatine in cold
water, then add to hot broth. Pour a thin layer of the gelatinized
broth into bottom of 1½-quart mold. Chill until partially set. Arrange egg slices, green pepper and pimiento in a pattern over the
bottom. Chill until almost firm. To remaining broth, add cut-up
meat, chopped eggs and remaining green pepper and pimiento.
Pour this over the decorative layer. Chill until firm, about 3 hours.
Pull away from edges and quickly dip into hot water; invert on
platter.

Suggested garnishes. Small whole pickled beets, sweet gherkin
pickles, carrot curls, small mounds of chopped onion or tender
green-topped spring onions (scallions). Pass horseradish cream,
mayonnaise or vinaigrette sauce. Makes 12 to 14 servings.

Variations
You may prefer a more pronounced vinegar flavor; if so use
1 cup vinegar, only 5 cups broth.

If you find vinegar flavor too pronounced, use ½ cup white wine in place of vinegar.

Instead of green pepper and pimiento, use sliced or finely diced cooked beets and cooked carrot in the Sülze.

Aal in Gelee
(JELLIED EEL)

Bones and head of eel
4 cups water
1 onion
1 carrot, cubed
1 stalk celery with leaves
1 bay leaf
2 or 3 parsley sprigs
1 teaspoon salt
1 teaspoon mixed
  pickling spices

2 to 3 pounds eel, skinned
  and cleaned
1 cup cooked green peas
Thin slices of lemon
1 hard-cooked egg, sliced
Sliced stuffed olives
1 envelope unflavored
  gelatine
¼ cup cold water

To make stock, cook the bones and head of the eel in water with the onion, carrot, celery, bay leaf, parsley, salt and pickling spices; boil 20 minutes. Strain, saving carrot. Cook the eel in the strained stock until tender, another 20 to 25 minutes. Remove, saving stock.

Cut the cooked eel into cubes or slices. Arrange on a platter with the peas and carrots, lemon and egg slices and the sliced olives in a pattern.

Dissolve the gelatine by sprinkling first over cold water, then, when softened, add 2 cups of the hot stock, stir until clear. Chill until it becomes syrupy in appearance, then spoon one layer of gelatine over the eel and vegetables. Let this set, then add remaining gelatine. Chill overnight. Makes 4 to 6 servings.

Eier Canapés
(EGG CANAPÉS)

Place hard-cooked egg slices on toast circles. Top half of the slices with balls of cream cheese blended with salt and horseradish to taste; top remaining slices with strips of anchovy.

Ochsenmaulsalat
(TONGUE SALAD)

It is quite possible that Beethoven had been enjoying this typical Rhineland *Vorspeise* the night he ended up behind bars in a tiny jail on the south bank of the Rhine across from Bad Godesberg. It was in the composer's younger days when he was found completely inebriated one night on the river bank after an evening of carousing and was escorted to the jailhouse to sleep off his drunk. The building is no longer used as a jail and might even have been torn down long since except for its illustrious visitor who forever immortalized it.

Ochsenmaulsalat is a tart mixture which tastes just right with a glass of chilled Rhine wine, though some will say it's even better with beer.

3 cups cooked tongue, cut in thin slivers	6 tablespoons olive oil
	6 tablespoons vinegar
¼ cup minced onion	Sugar to taste
2 green peppers, seeded and chopped (optional)	Salt and pepper to taste
	½ teaspoon mustard

Combine all ingredients. Serve chilled. Makes 5 cups or enough for 6 to 8 hors d'oeuvre servings.

(The addition of green peppers is not typically German, but I found it made the mixture both more attractive in appearance and zestier in flavor.)

Kümmelstangen

(CARAWAY CRISPS)

2 cups sifted all-purpose
 flour
1 teaspoon baking powder
1 teaspoon salt
½ cup butter
2 tablespoons cream
 cheese (cold)

1 egg, beaten
1 egg white, unbeaten, or
 milk
Caraway seeds
Coarse salt or kosher salt

Combine flour, baking powder and salt. Chop in butter and cream cheese until fine. Add egg, work with fingers to a smooth dough. Chill ½ hour. Roll out between sheets of waxed paper or on a pastry cloth to ¼-inch thick. Cut into strips 1 × 3 inches. Brush each with egg white or milk. Sprinkle with caraway seeds and salt. Twist each, place on ungreased baking sheet. Bake in oven preheated to 400° F. until golden, about 15 minutes. Makes about 36.

Käsestangen

(CHEESE TWISTS)

2 cups sifted all-purpose
 flour
½ teaspoon salt
2 tablespoons vegetable
 shortening
½ pound (2 sticks or 1
 cup) cold firm butter

6 tablespoons ice water
1 to 1½ cups shredded
 or grated sharp Cheddar
 cheese or Cheshire
 cheese

Combine flour and salt, cut in vegetable shortening, work with fingers to blend well, then cut in 1 stick (½ cup) of the butter until in pieces the size of peas. Add the ice water 1 tablespoon at a time, blend to form firm dough. Roll out one-half at a time; dot each roll of pastry with butter in tiny pieces, and spread over each the cheese, dividing evenly. Fold over each in thirds, let stand 10 minutes, then roll out again. Again fold each in thirds, this time chill in the refrigerator for 10 minutes. Roll out a third time, this time between sheets of waxed paper to prevent sticking to the board. Pastry should be about ¼-inch thick—thicker than for pies. Cut into strips ½ × 2 inches, twist, then chill 15 minutes. Bake in oven preheated to 425° F. until crisp and golden, about 15 minutes. Makes about 60.

Kümmel Käsestangen. Add 2 tablespoons caraway seeds to the flour, proceed as in preceding recipe.

*   *   *

The following four salad recipes are based on *Vorspeisen* I tasted while in the city of Bremen. In a charming small shop, I was fascinated with the display of hors d'oeuvres for sale and asked to buy a selection so that I might taste these luscious-looking salads. My hostess, blond young Fraulein Brenning, asked the chef to come to the front of the shop and inquired whether he would give us his recipes. He shook his head. "I don't have any recipes, these are made with the tips of my fingers," he explained. We bought the four kinds nevertheless, I tasted each in turn and jotted down notes as to what they contained, and after reaching home tried to reconstruct them. If not exactly as the Bremen chef made them, all are delicious and typically German in flavor.

Escorial Salat

(ESCORIAL SALAD)

¼ pound boiled or leftover baked ham, minced fine

2 apples, cored, peeled and diced

2 2¾-ounce jars tiny Danish or California shrimp, drained

1 teaspoon prepared mustard

2 tablespoons mayonnaise

1 tablespoon sour cream

Seasonings to taste

Combine all ingredients. Chill. Serve as an hors d'oeuvre. Makes 2 to 2¼ cups.

Pfifferlingsalat
(PICKLED MUSHROOMS BREMEN STYLE)

1 4-ounce can small button
mushrooms, drained
1 can pfifferlinge
mushrooms, drained[1]
2 tablespoons chopped
green pepper
1 sweet gherkin, chopped
1 tablespoon minced or
grated onion

1 tomato, finely chopped
1 tablespoon minced
parsley
¼ cup vinegar
2 tablespoons oil
Seasonings to taste

Combine all ingredients. Marinate 24 hours. (For sharper taste, marinate only 1 hour.) Makes 2 cups.

Viking Salat
(VIKING SALAD)

1 8-ounce jar pickled
herring, drained
½ green pepper, seeded
and diced
1 pimiento, drained and
diced
1 large orange, diced

1 large tart apple, cored,
peeled and diced
1 teaspoon grated onion
2 tablespoons oil
1 tablespoon vinegar
Salt to taste

Combine all ingredients, marinate an hour in refrigerator, serve as an hors d'oeuvre. Makes about 2 cups, enough for 4 small servings.

---

[1] These little brown mushrooms are a great delicacy; available in cans from food specialty shops. If not available in your area, use twice the quantity of button mushrooms instead.

Fleischsalat auf Bremer Art
(MEAT SALAD BREMEN STYLE)

¼ pound boiled ham,
  cut into thin strips
2 frankfurters, minced, or
  ½ cup minced bologna
½ cup diced salami or
  other dry firm sausage

3 sweet gherkins, diced
¼ cup mayonnaise
1 tablespoon vinegar
Salt to taste
Freshly ground black
  pepper

Combine all ingredients. Serve as an hors d'oeuvre. Makes about 2 cups.

Gefüllte Tomaten
(STUFFED TOMATOES)

6 small tomatoes
Salt and pepper
4 ounces Swiss cheese,
  finely diced (1 cup)
1 cup diced cooked ham

1 teaspoon brandy or
  kirsch
½ cup whipped heavy
  cream

Scoop out center of tomatoes, leaving ¼-inch shell. Sprinkle salt and pepper in the tomato shells. Combine cheese and ham, blend in brandy-flavored whipped cream. Use this as a stuffing for tomatoes. Serve on lettuce as an hors d'oeuvre or buffet salad. Makes 6.

Note: These tiny stuffed tomatoes are sometimes glazed with aspic, which gives them a more elegant appearance and keeps them fresh-looking longer. Brush on several layers of Wine Aspic*, placing a sliced pimiento-stuffed olive over the top of each after first layer of aspic is partially set.

Käsetrüffel

(CHEESE TRUFFLES)

6 tablespoons butter,
softened
1 8-ounce package cream
cheese, softened
1 tablespoon cream

Pinch of salt
1 teaspoon sugar
1 cup grated dry
pumpernickel

Combine butter, cheese, cream, salt and sugar. Form into small balls. Grate the dry bread by rubbing over a fine grater or dry in slow oven, then break in pieces, crush in blender or with rolling pin. Roll the cheese balls in the crumbs until thoroughly coated. Chill on waxed paper until firm. Makes 10 to 12.

Variation. Instead of pumpernickel crumbs, crushed or ground almonds or walnuts may be used.

Gefüllte Eier

(STUFFED EGGS)

"Deviled eggs," the American picnic favorite, have some fancy German cousins. In Germany, stuffed hard-cooked eggs are a favorite *Vorspeisen,* which may appear elaborately garnished on the hors d'oeuvre plate, in simple form as an evening snack for beer, or may be served as a luncheon dish.

BASIC RECIPE

6 hard-cooked eggs
3 tablespoons mayonnaise
1 teaspoon prepared
mustard

1 teaspoon olive oil
(optional)
Salt and pepper

Cut eggs in half lengthwise; remove the yolks, mash lightly with fork. Add to the yolks the mayonnaise, mustard, oil, salt and pepper. Blend well. Pile mixture lightly in hollowed egg whites. Makes 12.

Garnishes. Frequently a ribbon of thick mayonnaise, or a mixture of cream cheese and a little anchovy paste, is pressed from a pastry tube over the top of each stuffed egg. Over this decorative ribbon red or black caviar may be sprinkled, or capers, or a sliver of tomato or pimiento.

Variations

To mashed yolks, add 1 tablespoon minced parsley or chives.

Omit mayonnaise and mustard, add 2 mashed anchovy fillets to the yolks. Garnish with pimiento.

Add ¼ cup finely minced celery and 1 teaspoon grated onion to the yolks; omit mustard. Garnish with tomato slivers.

Add ½ cup flaked cooked fish (halibut, haddock, salmon or eel) and 1 teaspoon grated onion; reduce mustard to ½ teaspoon. Garnish with caviar or capers.

Add ½ cup minced cooked seafood (shrimp, crab or lobster) to the yolks, omit mustard, add a pinch of curry powder. Garnish with pimiento.

Add ¼ cup liver pâté to yolks, omit mustard, use ½ cup sour cream in place of mayonnaise. Sprinkle each egg with minced parsley.

To the mashed egg yolks add 1 tablespoon black caviar and ¼ cup sour cream, omitting mayonnaise and mustard. Season with a few drops lemon juice. Garnish with additional caviar.

Handkäs mit Musik
(HAND CHEESE WITH CHOPPED ONION)

There are a number of country cheeses in Germany called *Handkäs* —made of whey, seasoned with cumin and molded by hand usually into "fingers" about 4 inches long. These farmers' cheeses are not noteworthy by themselves, but when topped with *Musik* make a delightful snack to serve with beer. Harzer cheese is one *Handkäs* sometimes available in cheese specialty shops in this country. Or try the *Musik* on thick slices of Neuchâtel, Tilsiter cheese or Limburger.

MUSIK

1 cup minced raw onion	**Dash of cayenne**
3 tablespoons salad oil	**⅓ teaspoon powdered**
2 tablespoons vinegar	**cumin**
Salt and pepper to taste	

Combine ingredients, let stand 15 to 20 minutes. Use as a topping for individual servings of cheese placed on pumpernickel bread. Makes 1 cup topping, enough for 8 to 10 snacks.

Käse Pfälzer Art
(PALATINATE CHEESE PLATE)

This is a make-your-own canapé plate. Arrange on a platter wedges of cream cheese (*Quark*), sprinkle the cheese generously with paprika. Next to the cheese arrange small piles of chopped onion, slices of tomato, sliced hard-cooked egg, and pimiento strips. Butter curls are also sometimes arranged on this plate, or serve butter separately. On another plate, arrange slices of rye and pumpernickel bread.

Each person first spreads bread with butter, then smears cheese over the butter, sprinkles the cheese with chopped onion, then adds egg or tomato slices and pimiento. This is eaten like an open-faced sandwich. Good with beer or white wine.

Camembert Canapés

On each plate, place a wedge of German Camembert (or domestic American Camembert), a mound of chopped raw onion, a smaller mound of minced anchovy, and some chopped pimiento or a mound of paprika (about 1 teaspoon). These are mixed by each person according to taste. Salt and pepper shakers and oil and vinegar cruets should be on the table, to be used for seasoning. The mixture is spread over thickly buttered rye or pumpernickel bread. Great with beer.

Gänseleberbutter
(GOOSE LIVER PÂTÉ)

1 goose liver	½ teaspoon dried basil
6 tablespoons butter	½ teaspoon dried
1 slice stale white bread	marjoram
½ cup Madeira	1 teaspoon Parmesan
½ teaspoon dried	cheese (optional)
thyme	Salt to taste

Cut the goose liver in half, sauté in 1 tablespoon of the butter until well browned. Mash with a fork to a paste. Soak the bread in the Madeira until very soft and soggy; squeeze out the wine, saving it. Blend softened bread with the mashed liver. Add the Madeira, the three herbs, the cheese and the rest of the butter. Season to taste with salt. Beat into a paste. Chill. Serve on rye bread with sprigs of watercress. Or make into canapés by spreading on toasted bread cut into squares. Makes ¾ cup pâté.

Hühnerleberbutter. Use ½ pound chicken livers instead of goose liver in the above recipe. Chicken fat may be used instead of butter, if preferred, but the butter will make the texture creamier and firmer.

Mit Zwiebel (With Onion). If desired, 1 small minced onion may be cooked with the liver (either goose liver or chicken livers).

Bratwurst im Schlafrock

(SAUSAGE IN JACKET)

12 bratwurst sausages or pork sausage links

PASTRY

2 cups sifted all-purpose flour	**6 tablespoons shortening**
½ teaspoon salt	**1 3-ounce package cream cheese**
1 teaspoon baking powder	**2 tablespoons milk**

Parboil the sausage links in water to cover for 5 minutes; drain off water, lightly brown in skillet. Drain on paper towels.

Combine flour, salt and baking powder for the pastry. Chop in shortening and cream cheese; work in milk to form a dough the consistency of pie crust. Chill thoroughly, then roll out between sheets of waxed paper. Cut into 12 squares or rectangles. Roll each around the sausage links so that the ends of sausages can just be seen. Bake in oven preheated to 400° F. until pastry is golden and flaky. These are quite rich. Makes 12. Serve as hot snacks with beer.

Frankfurters in Schlafrock. Use cocktail frankfurters. Wrap in the pastry and bake as above. Frankfurters need not be precooked before enclosing in pastry.

Schwäbische Schnecken

(SNAILS SWABIAN STYLE)

1 can snails with shells (24 snails)	**1 cup canned beef gravy**
1 tablespoon minced onion	**½ cup red wine**
½ teaspoon basil	**2 tablespoons minced parsley**
3 tablespoons butter, softened	

Drain the canned snails, place snails in shells. Add the onion and basil to the softened butter, blend until smooth. Place a dab of this butter in each shell over the snails. Combine the beef gravy with the wine; add the snails, heat to boiling, then lower heat and cook covered for 5 minutes. Add parsley. Serve as a first course, a hot hors d'oeuvre,[2] or a snack with beer or wine. Makes 24. As a first course, allow 3 per serving.

Schnecken in Brotteig
(SNAILS IN PASTRY)

1 recipe for pastry for 2-crust pie, or 1 package pie crust mix
1 can snails, thoroughly drained
Parsley Butter or Kräuterbutter*

Prepare pastry dough in usual manner, roll out dough, cut into 3-inch squares. Into each square of pastry place a snail and a small dab of Parsley Butter or *Kräuterbutter*. Roll over pastry and seal. Bake in oven preheated to 425° F. until crisply golden, 15 to 18 minutes. Serve hot as an hors d'oeuvre. Makes 24.

Parsley Butter. Crush 4 tablespoons minced parsley in a mortar with pestle; work in 1 or 2 tablespoons grated onion and 4 tablespoons softened butter. If garlic flavor is desired, crush a garlic clove with the parsley. Makes ¼ cup.

---

[2] As a hot hors d'oeuvre, serve on plates with tiny lobster forks.

Suppen

(SOUPS)

To a German, there's something wrong with a luncheon or dinner that does not start with soup. Whether it's clear broth or one in which dumplings float, a bread soup or a hearty soup of lentils and frankfurters, a meal worthy of the name should always include soup in some form. The German *Hausfrau* of today is almost as likely to use bouillon cubes, canned soups or dehydrated soup mixes as her American counterpart, but the really fragrant stick-to-your-ribs soups are those that simmer for hours and are filling enough to serve as a meal in themselves.

Fleischbrühe or *Kraftbrühe*, clear broth or bouillon made with soup bones and "soup herbs," is essential not only for soup-making, but for sauces, stews, any number of dishes in the German cuisine. There is nothing mysterious or difficult about making such a broth or stock. The bones are placed in a kettle, covered with water, and the vegetables which the Germans call "soup herbs" put in the pot with the bones. "Soup herbs" include onion, carrot, celery and parsley. Occasionally a pinch of marjoram or thyme may be added, and some cooks like a bay leaf, too. Such a broth should simmer an hour to two hours, with the scum that rises to the top being removed periodically. When cooled enough to handle easily, it is strained, then chilled so that the fat will rise to the top and can be scraped off. Such a broth can be stored in glass jars in the refrigerator and will keep two weeks. Or freeze in portions ready to use as needed.

Usually a clear soup is served with one enormous dumpling in each soup plate, or, if not a dumpling, Spätzle, noodles, pancakes or bread cubes. Bread soup is one of those family dishes which makes good use of leftovers, for its goodness depends on a little well-flavored leftover gravy stirred into the broth. Pork gravy is especially recommended.

Kraftbrühe
(CLEAR BROTH OR BOUILLON)

This is the basis for many German soups, with different garnishes added.

1 beef marrow bone	Several parsley sprigs
2 pounds beef soup meat, or 2 pounds chicken necks	2 quarts water
	1½ tablespoons salt
	½ teaspoon Kitchen
1 small white turnip, diced, or 1 parsnip	Bouquet, Maggi liquid seasoning or Gravy-
1 carrot, cubed	Master
2 celery-leaf sprigs	

Place marrow bone and meat or chicken necks in large pot with the vegetables, celery and parsley sprigs. Add water, salt, and Kitchen Bouquet. Bring to a boil, skim two or three times, lower heat, simmer uncovered 3 hours. Add cold water from time to time to replace that lost by evaporation. Cool. Strain. Chill so that all fat rises to top and can be skimmed. Should make 6 cups rich-flavored broth.

Note: If chicken necks are used, reduce salt to 1 teaspoon, and 1 tablespoon concentrated beef stock base or 3 beef bouillon cubes.

With Tomatoes. In addition to the other vegetables listed, 1 or 2 chopped fresh tomatoes or a cup of canned tomatoes may be added to above.

Eierstich
(CUSTARD CUBES FOR SOUP)

1 teaspoon soft butter	½ cup milk
1 whole egg	¼ teaspoon salt
1 egg yolk	Dash of nutmeg

Rub butter inside of upper part of double boiler, over bottom and part way up sides. Beat together whole egg, egg yolk, milk, salt and nutmeg. Pour into the buttered double boiler. Heat over hot (not boiling) water for 20 minutes until firm. Turn out, let cool, cut into small diamond shapes. Add 3 or 4 to each serving of clear soup. Makes enough for 4 to 6 servings. Will keep a week or longer in refrigerator.

Flädlesuppe
(PANCAKE SOUP)

This delicious soup was served to us at the fabulously luxurious Hotel Sommerberg in the Black Forest resort of Wildbad, a strikingly modern hotel perched on the very top of a mountain, with a glorious view of forests stretching away below.

6 cups clear beef broth (Kraftbrühe)*
Flädle
1 or 2 tablespoons minced parsley

The broth should be made from bones, as in a preceding recipe; broth made with bouillon cubes or powdered concentrate is not good enough. Prepare the *Flädle* in advance, cut into strips, add to the hot broth shortly before serving. Sprinkle parsley over each serving.

Flädle
(PANCAKES)

½ cup all-purpose flour   ¼ teaspoon salt
½ cup milk   Dash of nutmeg
1 egg

Beat together in blender or with electric mixer the flour, milk, egg
and seasonings until smooth. Let batter stand ½ hour. Pour out batter on hot greased griddle (an electric skillet set at 400° F. is fine),
tilt pan so batter will spread evenly. Turn as soon as lightly browned
on one side. While still warm, cut into thin slivers. Makes about
12 thin pancakes, enough for 6 servings of soup.

Bauernsuppe
(PEASANT SOUP)

1 pound stewing beef,   2 tablespoons vinegar
  cut into ½-inch pieces   2 quarts hot beef broth,
1 large onion, sliced   or 1 quart beef broth
2 tablespoons butter or   and 1 quart hot water
  drippings   3 medium potatoes, peeled
1 teaspoon salt   and diced
1 bay leaf   1 tablespoon minced dill
1 clove garlic, crushed   2 tablespoons grated
Dash of paprika   Parmesan (optional)
3 tablespoons flour

Sauté beef and onion in butter or drippings until well browned.
Add salt, bay leaf, garlic and paprika. Sprinkle with flour. Stir and
cook over low heat until flour is absorbed and browned. Sprinkle
with vinegar and stir thoroughly over low heat. Add hot broth and

simmer 45 minutes. Add potatoes, cook slowly another hour. Sprinkle with dill and cheese. Makes 6 to 8 servings.

(This is hearty enough to serve as a main course, preceded by herring or other hors d'oeuvres, and followed by salad or fruit. Makes 4 entree servings.)

Hamburger Aalsuppe
(EEL SOUP OF HAMBURG)

This curious soup is as much loved by the people of Hamburg as *bouillabaisse* is by Frenchmen. It is a strange combination of flavors, and takes a bit of getting used to, but is more delicious than it sounds.

2 pounds fresh eel, cut into 2-inch pieces
2 cups water
2 tablespoons vinegar
6 peppercorns
Salt to taste
1 leek or small onion, sliced or chopped
1 carrot, diced small
1 celery stalk, diced
3 cauliflower buds, thinly sliced
2 tablespoons minced parsley
1 cup shelled green peas
6 cups beef broth
1 cup white wine
1 small can pear halves in syrup or cooked prunes, pitted
2 tablespoons minced parsley

Cook the eel until tender in the water, add vinegar, with peppercorns and salt (about ¾ teaspoon salt, or to taste). Drain, set aside. In another pot, add the vegetables to the beef broth, cook just until tender. Add wine, the strained eel and the pears or prunes. Heat without allowing to boil. Serve in soup dishes with parsley scattered over the top. Serves 6.

Note: Usually small semolina dumplings are served in the soup, but these are not really necessary. Sometimes bits of meat, either lamb or beef, will also appear in the soup.

Käse Bouillon mit Ei

(CHEESE SOUP WITH EGG)

4 eggs, beaten
1 cup homogenized milk
   or dairy half-and-half
2 tablespoons grated
   cheese

2 tablespoons minced
   chives
4 cups hot beef bouillon

Beat eggs until fluffy, add milk, cheese and chives. Beat ¼ cup of the heated bouillon into egg mixture, then add mixture to remaining bouillon, beating constantly over low heat until smooth and slightly thickened. Serve at once. Makes 4 to 6 servings.

The following recipe for lentil soup was given me by Chef Herbert Burmeister of North German Lloyd's M.S. *Europa*. Germans would serve this as a first course, but for most of us it is hearty enough for an entree. Be sure to pass the vinegar cruet at table: a few drops of vinegar perks up the meaty flavor of the broth marvelously.

Linsensuppe

(LENTIL SOUP)

2 large onions, cubed
1 celery stalk, chopped
1 leek, sliced (optional)
1 medium potato, peeled
   and cubed
3 slices bacon, diced
1 tablespoon butter
½ pound (about 1 cup)
   lentils
1 carrot, finely diced

4 frankfurters, thickly
   sliced
Salt to taste (2 to 3
   teaspoons)
1 tablespoon tomato
   catsup
12 cups (3 quarts) water
1 turkey or large chicken
   leg (optional)
Vinegar in cruet

Place onions, celery, leek, potato, diced bacon and butter in large heavy pot; cook until soft but not browned. Wash lentils, drain, add to pot (pre-soaking is not necessary). Add carrot, sliced frank-furters, salt, catsup and water. If you have a cooked turkey leg (left over from roast turkey) or a chicken leg purchased from a chicken parts counter, add it for richer flavor. Bring the water to a boil, lower heat, simmer covered 3 hours or until lentils are soft. Add more water as needed; as lentils swell much of the water will be absorbed. Pass the vinegar cruet at table: a few dashes of vine-gar added to each serving will add important flavor. Makes 4 to 6 servings.

Kartoffelsuppe Schwäbische Art
(SWABIAN POTATO SOUP)

2 or 3 potatoes, peeled and thinly sliced	8 cups water or beef broth
1 small onion, chopped	Salt to taste
1 to 2 tablespoons butter	Leftover gravy (optional)
1 to 2 cups diced cooked beef	2 cups cooked Spätzle*

Cook potatoes and onion in butter until onion is yellow. Add cut-up meat and water or broth and any leftover gravy that may be around. Add salt as needed. Simmer until potatoes are very soft. Add *Spätzle*. Makes 8 servings.

Grüne Kartoffelsuppe
(GREEN POTATO SOUP)

3 medium potatoes, peeled and diced	½ teaspoon salt or to taste
1 cup diced yellow turnip (rutabaga)	1 tablespoon flour
	6 cups beef broth
2 large leeks, or 2 medium onions, chopped	2 tablespoons sour cream or heavy sweet cream
1 celery stalk with leaves, diced	1 or 2 tablespoons minced parsley
2 tablespoons butter	1 cup Pumpernickel Croutons
1 cup canned tomatoes	

Place the potatoes, turnip, leeks or onions, celery and chopped celery leaves in a large heavy pot with butter. (Leeks should be used to give this soup authentic flavor and color: chop the well-washed green tops as well as the white part of the leek.) Add the tomatoes, salt and flour; cook 1 to 2 minutes. Add beef broth, simmer covered until vegetables are very tender, about ½ hour. Stir in cream 5 minutes before removing from range. Serve garnished with parsley and Pumpernickel Croutons. Makes 6 servings.

Pumpernickel Croutons. Cut 2 slices pumpernickel bread into ½-inch cubes. Toast in moderate (350° F.) oven until dry and crisp. Toss with 1 tablespoon melted butter. Makes 1 cup.

Grüne Erbsensuppe mit Saurer Sahne
(GREEN PEA SOUP WITH SOUR CREAM)

2 cups shelled fresh peas
or 1 box (10 ounces)
frozen peas
2 cups water
½ teaspoon salt
2 cups beef or chicken
broth
2 tablespoons butter,
softened
2 tablespoons flour

1 egg yolk
½ cup sour cream
½ teaspoon sugar
1 tablespoon minced
parsley
½ cup croutons or ¼
cup slivered smoked
tongue, ham or
Mettwurst

Cook peas in water with salt until soft. Purée in blender or force through food mill or sieve. Add beef or chicken broth. Blend together butter, flour, egg yolk and sour cream, making a thin paste. Add this to the pea purée, heat slowly, stirring, until creamy smooth and slightly thickened. Stir in sugar and taste to see if it needs more salt. Serve topped with parsley and croutons or slivers of meat. Makes 4 servings.

Brotsuppe

(BREAD SOUP, FRANCONIAN STYLE)

6 slices slightly stale
pumpernickel or dark
rye bread
8 cups beef broth or
water, heated to boiling
1 medium onion, chopped

1 or 2 tablespoons meat
drippings
2 or 3 tablespoons
leftover gravy,
preferably pork gravy

Break bread into cubes, cover with boiling-hot broth or water. Let stand until soft. Separately sauté onion in meat drippings until soft and yellow. Add bread and broth, simmer ½ hour. (If water is used, add salt to taste.) Stir in gravy. Makes 6 to 8 servings.

Mit Rahm (With Cream). Instead of leftover gravy, add 2 tablespoons heavy cream.

Mit Apfeln (With Apples). Cook 2 or 3 chopped pared apples with the onion; add grated lemon peel to broth.

Prinz Orloff Suppe

(PRINCE ORLOFF SOUP)

This soup was served as the first course when I dined at the sumptuous Humplmayr Restaurant in Munich. The preceding night I had attended a magnificent production of *Die Fledermaus,* so I particularly enjoyed this exquisite soup, named after the prince in the Strauss opera.

1 recipe Kraftbrühe*
(clear beef broth)
1 tablespoon brandy
Thin slices of leek

1 tomato, chopped
Leberknödel, in tiny balls
Minced parsley

Heat together the strained clarified beef broth and brandy. Add leek and tomato pieces, cook 5 minutes. Separately prepare *Leberknödel;* add to simmering-hot broth 10 minutes before soup is to be served. Sprinkle parsley over each serving of soup. Makes 6 servings.

Leberknödel

¼ cup hot milk
5 slices stale white bread
½ pound steer liver, ground
2 tablespoons minced parsley
2 tablespoons softened butter

2 tablespoons flour, or
1 tablespoon cornstarch or arrowroot
2 eggs, separated
Grated rind of 1 lemon
Dash of nutmeg
⅛ teaspoon marjoram or thyme

Add hot milk to bread; soak until very soft, squeeze out any excess moisture. Add the ground liver, parsley, butter and flour or cornstarch to the bread, blend with fingers to a paste. Add egg yolks, lemon rind and seasonings, beat well. Beat egg whites until stiff, fold in. With a spoon, form a small ball, drop a test dumpling into hot broth. If dumpling does not hold together, work a little extra flour into the mixture, try another dumpling. Do not crowd pot with dumplings, cook just a few at a time. Remove with slotted spoon as they bob to top (after 5 to 6 minutes); keep warm. Serve 2 or 3 dumplings in each serving of soup. Makes 6 servings.

Krabbensuppe

(SHRIMP BISQUE)

1 pound small shrimp in
the shell
2 quarts (8 cups) water
1 to 2 teaspoons salt
1 teaspoon caraway seeds
½ teaspoon powdered
fennel
2 tablespoons chopped
onion

2 tablespoons butter
½ cup flour
3 or 4 egg yolks
1 tablespoon Madeira or
brandy
1 tablespoon minced fresh
dill

Cook the shrimp in salted water with caraway seeds, fennel and onion just until shells turn pink. Cool in the water. Take out shrimp, saving water, then remove shells; discard. Chop the shrimp, sauté in butter 2 minutes; stir in flour, cook 1 minute. Slowly stir in the shrimp stock, pouring into the pan through a fine strainer. Bring to a boil, lower heat, simmer until smooth. Add some of hot broth to egg yolks, then combine the two. Stir in Madeira or brandy. Serve topped with minced dill. Makes 8 servings.

* * *

A soup which is listed frequently on German menus is called Lady Curzon, after the Chicago-born wife of the British viceroy of India whose court at Delhi at the turn of the century was noted for its opulence and splendor. Whether or not the American-born viceroy's lady actually invented the soup, or whether it was merely one of the delicacies served at palace banquets, it's fun to think this delicious concoction so popular with the Germans of today has at least a faint American background. It makes a truly elegant first course.

Lady Curzon Suppe

4 cups (2 11-ounce cans)
    clear turtle soup[1]
2 tablespoons minced
    fresh or canned
    mushroom (optional)
1 egg yolk

2 tablespoons heavy cream
¼ teaspoon curry powder
1 tablespoon Madeira or
    brandy
2 tablespoons grated
    Parmesan cheese

Heat soup to boiling; if fresh mushroom is used, add to broth, simmer 5 minutes. Blend egg yolk with cream and curry powder. Add a little of hot soup to mixture, then combine the two. Heat, stirring constantly, until soup is consistency of cream. Stir in Madeira or brandy. Pour into heatproof individual casseroles, sprinkle cheese over top, place under broiler until top is lightly browned. Makes 4 servings.

Variation. Omit mushroom and cheese, prepare as above but just before serving, float a teaspoon of heavy cream over top of each serving, sprinkle with minced parsley.

*   *   *

In Germany, fruit soups are often served hot, topped with semolina dumplings as a luncheon or supper dish, but Americans will enjoy them more chilled as a refreshing summer appetizer or even as dessert. Fruit soups are sometimes made with berries, cherries, apples or peaches.

---

[1] If the canned turtle soups contain sherry, use ½ tablespoon brandy or Madeira—but do add additional spirit, the soup needs it.

Birnensuppe
(PEAR SOUP)

2 pounds Bartlett or
  Kieffer pears, peeled,
  cored and diced[2]
4 cups water
½ teaspoon aniseed or
  ⅛ teaspoon crushed
  anise

1 stick cinnamon
Sugar to taste (about
  ½ cup)
¼ cup raisins
¼ cup medium-sweet
  sherry, Madeira or
  brandy

Cook the pears in water with aniseed and cinnamon until very soft. Force through food mill or sieve. Add sugar to taste. Serve chilled topped with raisins that have been soaked in wine or brandy. Makes 4 servings.

Pflaumensuppe
(PLUM SOUP)

2 pounds red tart plums,
  pitted, or 2 1-pound
  14-ounce cans purple
  plums, pitted
4 to 6 cups water

Sugar to taste
1 tablespoon cornstarch or
  arrowroot
Croutons or dollops of
  sour cream for garnish

Place plums and water in saucepan, with 1 or 2 of the plum seeds. Bring to a boil, simmer until fruit is very soft. (If using canned plums, simmer for 5 minutes.) Force through food mill or sieve. Add sugar. Thin cornstarch or arrowroot with a little of the purée, add to soup, then heat until slightly thickened, the consistency of light cream. Cool, then chill. Serve cold, topped with crisp croutons or spoonfuls of sour cream. Makes 6 servings.

---

[2] This can also be made with canned Bartlett pears, omitting sugar, using the canned syrup for 2 cups of the water.

Fisch

(SEAFOOD)

Many of the supermarkets and fancier delicatessens in West Germany are equipped with tanks where live fish swish around suspiciously as if knowing they are about to be selected by discriminating *Hausfrauen* for the kettle. Frozen, canned and dressed fresh fish are available in the West German markets, too, but the live fish offer a special advantage—only when purchased alive can fish be successfully cooked "blue," the favorite German method. *Forelle Blau* ("blue trout"), *Lachs Blau* ("blue salmon") and *Karpfen Blau* ("blue carp") are words one sees frequently on restaurant menus. It means the fish have been marinated or cooked in a vinegar solution which turns the skin to a shimmery blue and blanches the flesh to snowy white. Trout often are tied in rings, the tail fastened to the head, before being placed in boiling broth, so that when removed from the water they retain this attractive ring shape. *Forellen in Gelee* (trout in aspic) is usually curled in such a ring so that in its gleaming jellied dress, artfully garnished, it looks like an improbable blue crown.

There is a substance just under the gills of the fish skin which turns blue when treated with vinegar, a substance which evaporates quickly once life has left the fish. But even discounting the bluish tinge, the flavor advantage of fresh-killed fish is enormous. I wonder why in our markets no one has ever thought of instituting this very efficient practice of keeping fish alive in tanks?

One day in Berlin, my hosts were discussing which had the better flavor, boiled or fried fish—and the majority present agreed vehemently that boiled fish was much better! I could only wonder how most Americans would react to such an opinion. Boiling, of course, is a misnomer. Technically the fish is not boiled at all, but poached gently in a flavored broth. Smaller fish are merely plunged into broth which has been brought to a boil, then the heat turned off. After 10 or 15 minutes in the broth, they are exactly right for eating. And I agree that when fish are truly fresh, the delicate sweet flavor can be better appreciated if they are so poached.

From lakes and rivers throughout West Germany, fresh-water fish are delivered daily to markets: carp, eel, trout, river and lake salmon, pike, perch and various others unique to the region. Shiploads of salt-water fish and shellfish arrive every day at the North Sea ports of Hamburg and Bremen: turbot, halibut, sole, cod, haddock, to say nothing of sweet-fleshed lobster and crayfish, shrimp and oysters which one can enjoy at restaurants overlooking the harbor—or at fine restaurants as far away as Munich or Berlin, where signs on the tables proclaim that their lobster is flown in daily from Hamburg.

Turbot is a member of the flounder family which is not available in the United States, but its cousin, the halibut, is much the same in flavor, and is abundantly available—fresh in our coastal markets, frozen elsewhere.

For their poached or "blue" fish, the Germans have a wide variety of sauces of uniquely Nordic flavor. Horseradish Cream (*Sahnemeerettich*) and melted butter are the two one encounters most often. The fish may be served bathed in melted butter, with fluffy white Horseradish Cream in a separate sauceboat. Mustard Sauce, Caper Sauce, Parsley and Dill Sauces, Tartar and Remoulade are a few other favorite fish sauces. It's the sharp, tart flavor that so effectively offsets the delicacy of the poached or "blue" fish.

Fried fish in Germany is not greatly different from fried fish anywhere else in the world. Some of the baked fish dishes resemble those of France, others, typical of north Germany, have a counterpart in Scotland or Denmark. But there are others, such as the *Fischpie* (or *Fischpastete*) and *Gefüllte Fischrouladen,* which are unique to Germany.

Smoked fish in fascinating variety are available in every market, but these are generally served as hors d'oeuvres (*Vorspeisen*) or snacks, rather than used in entrees.

Aal mit Dillsosse
(EEL WITH DILL SAUCE)

1 3-pound fresh eel,
skinned and cleaned,
cut in thick slices
Salted water

2 cups Dillsosse*
2 hard-cooked eggs,
chopped

Cook the eel in salted water until tender, about 20 minutes. Drain, saving stock. Use the stock in making sauce (for recipe see Index). To the sauce add chopped eggs, spoon this over the slices of eel to serve. Makes 4 to 6 servings.

Grüner Aal mit Gurkensalat
(FRESH EEL WITH CUCUMBERS)

1 2- or 3-pound eel,
skinned, cut into 2-inch
pieces
4 or 5 parsley sprigs
1 bay leaf, crumbled
Salted water
1 teaspoon lemon juice
2 tablespoons butter
2 tablespoons flour

1 tablespoon chopped
parsley
1 tablespoon chopped dill
or fennel
1 teaspoon chopped
chervil
½ cup sour cream
Cucumber salad

Place eel in pot with herbs, salted water to cover and lemon juice. Simmer gently until eel is tender, 15 to 20 minutes. Remove fish to platter. Boil down stock to 1 cup. Melt butter, stir in flour, then slowly add the stock through a sieve. Cook until slightly thickened. Add chopped herbs and sour cream, cook over lowest heat a few minutes longer. Serve the sauce over the fish; cucumber salad is always served with it. Makes 4 servings.

Karpfen
(CARP)

This is a favorite fish throughout Germany and in every fish market as well as the larger supermarkets, carp can be purchased alive, swimming in tanks, as can eel. Carp is always served on New Year's Eve (called Sylvester in Germany). In Hamburg, "blue carp" is served with melted butter and Horseradish Cream. In Bavaria, a caper sauce is preferred. In Silesia (now East Germany) parsley and brown butter are traditional.

Silvesterkarpfen
(CARP FOR NEW YEAR'S EVE)

1 3-pound carp, cleaned

STOCK

Carp head
2 or 3 onions, stuck with cloves
1 carrot, cubed
Parsley and celery sprigs

½ cup red wine or beer
3 cups water
4 or 5 peppercorns
1 teaspoon salt
1 tablespoon vinegar

SAUCE

½ cup ground gingerbread or gingersnaps
½ cup red wine or beer

Juice and grated rind of 1 lemon
Salt and sugar to taste

Combine ingredients for the stock, bring to a boil, cook 20 minutes. Strain, saving stock. Lay the carp in a kettle, cover with the stock, bring slowly to a boil, cook 15 minutes. Cool in the stock, then remove carefully.

For sauce, measure 2 cups of the stock, combine with remaining ingredients, simmer until thickened. Replace carp in this sauce. (The whole fish may be placed in sauce or it may be cut in portions as preferred.) When ready to serve, reheat just until fish is heated through. Serve garnished with small onion rings arranged over the top. Makes 6 servings.

Blauer Karpfen
(BLUE CARP)

2 pounds fresh carp	1 onion
½ cup tarragon vinegar	1 carrot, cubed
½ cup boiling water	Parsley and celery sprigs
1 quart cold water	1 bay leaf
2 teaspoons salt	½ lemon

Place the fish in a bowl. Add vinegar to boiling water, bring again to the boil, pour over the fish. Let stand uncovered in place exposed to the air 1 to 2 hours. Remove from vinegar, place fish on a rack or in cheesecloth. Combine remaining ingredients, bring water to the boil, cook 20 minutes; strain. Place fish on rack in kettle, cover with strained stock, simmer gently, covered, about 20 to 25 minutes. Turn off heat, let stand in liquid until cool enough to handle easily, then remove to platter, trim off skin and brush melted butter (about ¼ cup) over top. Serve garnished with parsley sprigs and lemon wedges, with *Sahnemeerettich* (Horseradish Cream)*, *Remouladensosse* (Remoulade Sauce)* or green mayonnaise. Makes 6 servings.

Note: "Blue trout" and "blue eel" are prepared in the same way, but small trout need only be plunged in rapidly boiling water, then lifted out again. The length of cooking time for eel depends on size. To test whether any fish so cooked is done, plunge a fork into the center of the back: if the flesh easily comes away from the bone, it is sufficiently cooked.

The following recipe is adapted from one given me by Oskar Behrmann, chef of the renowned Hotel Vier Jahreszeiten (Four Seasons) in Hamburg, which has three superb restaurants, all under Chef Behrmann's direction. The chef's recipe as given to me was for turbot, which is not available in American markets. Halibut, however, is very similar in flavor. The Hamburg chef used the entire turbot, removing the bones, then filling the boned fish with the stuffing so that it looked like a whole fish (even with head and tail). I have suggested here using the tail end of the halibut, stuffing it in the same way. Or the filling can be placed inside fillets of sole and the sole rolled up, like *rouladen*. (See *Gefülltes Seezungefilet*.)

Gefüllter Heilbutt

(STUFFED HALIBUT)

Tail end of halibut, weighing about 3 pounds
1 cup fish stock (made with halibut bones)
3 tablespoons butter
6 ounces already-shelled shrimp, cooked
½ cup cooked or canned crabmeat or lobster meat

3 tablespoons flour
¼ cup heavy cream
2 tablespoons brandy
1 3-ounce can mushroom bits and pieces
½ cup fine bread crumbs
Salt and pepper to taste
4 tablespoons melted butter

Ask your fishman or butcher to remove the center bone from the fish, saving the bone for you, and perhaps giving you a head or tail for making the stock. Make the stock by covering the bones and head with 2 cups water, adding "soup herbs" (cubed onion and carrot, sprigs of parsley and celery leaves) and salt; simmer ½ hour, reducing liquid to 1 cup. Strain.

Melt 3 tablespoons butter, add shrimp and crab or lobster, sauté briefly, just to blend with butter. Add flour, allow it to cook 30 seconds. Slowly stir in the fish stock, then the cream and brandy, and finally the mushrooms with their liquor and the bread crumbs.

Season to taste. Let cool so sauce will thicken, then spoon as much as possible into pocket of fish. Brush 2 tablespoons of melted butter over bottom of large shallow baking dish; add remainder of stuffing, place fish over the stuffing. Cover dish with foil; bake in oven preheated to 350° F. for 30 minutes; remove foil. Brush remaining melted butter over top, bake 10 minutes longer. Serve with curried rice and a green salad. Makes 6 servings.

Gefülltes Seezungefilet
(STUFFED FILLET OF SOLE)

Prepare the same stuffing as for *Gefüllter Heilbutt*. Use 6 fillets of sole. Place ⅙ of stuffing in each fillet, roll up, secure with toothpicks, place overlapped side down in buttered baking dish. Cover with foil, bake 20 minutes, remove cover, add melted butter over top, bake 10 minutes longer.

Seezungenfilets mit Bananen
(FILLETS OF SOLE WITH BANANA)

4 individual fillets of sole	8 to 10 blanched almonds
4 tablespoons butter	or ¼ cup slivered
Salt, powdered cumin or	blanched almonds
curry powder	Juice and grated rind of
4 large bananas, cut in	1 lemon
half lengthwise	Parsley sprigs

Cook fillets of sole in butter just until delicately browned on one side. Remove to platter; sprinkle with salt and cumin; keep warm.

Sauté the bananas in the same butter; remove to platter when lightly browned. Sauté the almonds until browned, sprinkle over fish. Pour the remaining butter over the fish. Sprinkle grated lemon rind and lemon juice over all. Garnish with parsley sprigs. Makes 4 servings.

Seezungen mit Curry Sahnensosse

(SOLE WITH CURRY CREAM SAUCE)

4 fillets of sole	Curry Sahnensosse
½ cup water	4 bananas, cut in half
½ cup white wine	lengthwise
½ teaspoon salt	1 tablespoon chopped
Butter	candied ginger

Roll up each of the fillets, fasten with toothpicks. Place overlapped side down in casserole or heavy pan so that they are close together. Add water, wine, salt and a tablespoon of butter. Cover casserole, bring slowly to simmering, poach over very low heat on top of stove for 10 to 15 minutes.

When sole is done, remove carefully to platter; keep warm. Use the liquid in which the fish cooked in making the *Curry Sahnensosse* (recipe follows). In another pan, sauté the banana slices in butter until lightly browned. Place banana slices around the fish. Sprinkle candied ginger over bananas and fish. Pour sauce over all. Serve with rice and broiled tomatoes. Makes 4 servings.

Curry Sahnensosse

(CURRY CREAM SAUCE)

2 tablespoons butter	1 cup fish stock
2 shallots or 1 small	¼ cup raisins or dried
onion, minced	currants
1 medium apple, peeled	¼ cup heavy sweet cream
and diced	or sour cream
2 tablespoons flour	1 teaspoon lemon juice
1 teaspoon curry powder	Grated lemon rind

Melt butter, add shallots or onion and apple, cook until soft. Add flour and curry powder, cook 1 minute. Slowly add fish stock, then the raisins or currants. Simmer until smooth and thickened. Turn off heat; add cream and lemon juice and the grated rind. (If sour cream is used, omit lemon juice.) Makes 1¼ cups.

Fischfrikadellen mit Spinat[1]
(FISH BALLS WITH SPINACH)

1 pound codfish or
   haddock, cooked
¼ cup minced onion
1 medium potato, cooked
   and mashed, or 2 slices
   bread, soaked in ¼
   cup milk

1 egg, beaten
Salt and pepper to taste
Fat for frying
Spinat*
Mostrichsosse* or
   Curry Mousselinesosse*

Put cooked codfish and onion through food grinder. Add potato or soaked bread, egg, salt and pepper, working to a paste with fingers. Wash hands, then form fish balls 1½ inches in diameter. Sauté in fat until well browned on all sides. Serve over a bed of creamed spinach, passing the sauce to serve with the fish. Makes about 12 fish balls or 4 servings. *For cocktail appetizers,* make smaller balls (¾ to 1 inch in diameter), serve hot or cold with *Curry Mousselinesosse.*

Schellfischpudding
(HADDOCK PUDDING)

2 pounds haddock
Salt
3 to 4 medium
   potatoes
1 medium onion, sliced
2 tablespoons butter

2 eggs, beaten
½ cup sour cream
½ cup milk
½ cup buttered bread
   crumbs

---

[1] These are also sometimes called *Fischbouletten* or *Fischklösse,* depending on which part of Germany you happen to live in.

Sprinkle haddock with salt, let stand 1 hour. Partially cook potatoes in jackets; peel and slice. Arrange haddock and sliced potatoes in layers in buttered casserole. Sauté onion in butter until soft; place over haddock. Combine eggs, cream and milk, pour over all. Spread buttered crumbs over top. Bake covered in oven preheated to 350° F. for 30 to 40 minutes. Makes 6 servings.

Note: Instead of fresh fish, smoked or kippered fish may be used in this recipe, which then becomes a first cousin to the baked Finnan Haddie of Scotland.

Gekochter Kabeljau
(POACHED COD)

2 pounds fresh codfish

STOCK

1 cup water	2 hard-cooked eggs,
1 cup dry white wine	sliced
1 onion, stuck with	¼ cup melted butter
cloves	Parsley sprigs
Parsley and celery sprigs	Sahnemeerettich*,
1 carrot, cubed	Mostrichsosse* or
1 teaspoon salt	Caper Sauce*
2 slices lemon	

Combine ingredients for stock, bring to a boil, cook 20 minutes. Strain; pour back into pan. Place codfish (in one piece or cut into steaks) in stock, cook covered 15 to 20 minutes. Remove from broth, arrange sliced eggs over top, spoon melted butter over eggs and fish. Garnish with parsley. Pass one of the suggested sauces. Makes 6 servings.

Gefüllte Fischrouladen

(FISH ROLL-UPS)

2 pounds fillets of sole
 or flounder
Salt
3 slices bacon, diced
1 small onion, minced
¼ pound mushrooms,
 chopped
¼ cup chopped
 gherkins or chopped
 celery

2 tablespoons minced
 parsley
1 tablespoon flour
3 or 4 tablespoons
 melted butter
¼ cup grated Parmesan
 cheese
1 teaspoon paprika
½ cup white wine

Cut fish into 6 rectangular servings. Sprinkle the fillets with salt, let stand 15 to 30 minutes. Cook bacon, onion and mushrooms together until bacon is crisp and onion soft; add gherkins or celery and parsley, blend well. Sprinkle with salt. Spread this mixture over the fillets, dividing among them. Roll up each fillet, fasten with toothpicks, then dredge with flour. Brush half the melted butter over bottom of baking dish, place fish roll-ups in it, dribble remaining butter over top. Sprinkle cheese and paprika over all. Pour wine in baking dish. Bake in oven preheated to 350° F. for 20 to 30 minutes. Serve with *Salzkartoffeln** and *Sauerkrautsalat**. Makes 6 servings.

Gebratener Moselhecht
(BAKED PIKE MOSEL STYLE)

1 2-pound pike, cleaned,
or 2 smaller pike
Salt
4 to 6 tablespoons butter
1 small onion or 2
shallots, minced
1 small carrot, very finely
diced
1 tablespoon minced
parsley

1 cup fish stock, chicken
or vegetable broth; or
half wine, half stock or
broth
½ cup sour cream
1 egg, beaten
½ cup grated Swiss cheese

The fish may be baked whole or cut in portions as preferred. Sprinkle with salt, let it stand ½ hour. Butter a shallow baking dish or casserole with half the butter, lay minced vegetables and parsley over bottom. Place the fish over the vegetables, dot with rest of the butter. Add stock; cover with foil. Bake in oven set at 350° F. for 10 minutes. Beat sour cream and egg together. Remove foil, spread cream-egg mixture over top of fish; then sprinkle with cheese. Return to oven, bake until fish is done, 10 to 15 minutes longer. Makes 4 to 6 servings.

Hamburger Fischpie oder Fischpastete
(SEAFOOD PIE HAMBURG STYLE)

2 pounds halibut
(preferably the tail cut)
1 1-pound sole or flounder
Soup herbs (carrot,
parsley, celery, 1 small
onion)
¾ pound (12 ounces)
shrimp, shelled

1 1-pound can white
asparagus, drained
3 tablespoons butter
3 tablespoons flour
¼ cup heavy cream
1 egg yolk
Butter Pastry

Poach the halibut and sole (or flounder) together in boiling salted water along with "soup herbs" 15 to 20 minutes. (Since the sole is smaller, it can be added to the water 5 minutes after the halibut.) Let cool in broth; remove fish from broth when it can be handled easily, then separate white flesh from bones and skin. Strain broth; add the shrimp, cook only until shrimp start to turn pink, about 3 minutes. Remove shrimp; save stock.

Place the boned meat of halibut and sole in 1½-quart buttered casserole. Arrange shrimp and chopped pieces of asparagus over top.

Make a sauce of butter, flour, and 2 cups of the strained fish stock. Cook until thickened and smooth. Beat cream with egg yolk; add some of hot broth, then combine the two. Taste for seasoning; add salt if needed. Pour this sauce over the ingredients in the casserole. Prepare pastry; spread over top. Bake in oven preheated to 375° F. until pastry is golden and crisp. Makes 6 to 8 servings.

BUTTER PASTRY

1 cup sifted all-purpose flour
½ teaspoon baking powder
Pinch of salt
1 teaspoon sugar or ½ teaspoon vanilla
6 tablespoons butter
1 small egg, beaten
1 teaspoon grated lemon peel

Combine flour, baking powder, salt, and sugar or vanilla. Chop butter into flour until particles are size of peas. Add the egg and lemon peel, blend, knead lightly to make a dough. Press out with heel of hand between sheets of waxed paper to fit top of casserole. Lay over seafood mixture. Bake until crisp and golden.

Hummer in Weissbier

(LOBSTER IN WHITE BEER)

2 1-pound lobsters, or ½ pound shelled cooked lobster meat
½ cup lobster stock or water
2 tablespoons butter
2 shallots, minced
2 tablespoons flour
¼ teaspoon salt
¼ teaspoon crushed fennel
2 or 3 caraway seeds
1 cup light beer or dry white wine[2]
1 egg yolk
Minced parsley

If live lobsters are used, cook in boiling salted water for 20 minutes. Remove meat from shells when cool enough to handle, cut in dice. Save ½ cup of the stock for sauce. If already-cooked lobster meat is used, use water in sauce.

Melt butter, cook shallots in butter until soft. Stir in flour, salt and fennel; cook until flour bubbles. Add caraway seeds, slowly stir in beer, then the stock or water. Simmer until well blended and slightly thickened. Add some of hot sauce to egg yolk then combine the two. Cook, stirring constantly with whisk, over hot water or very low heat until creamy-thick. Add diced lobster meat to the sauce. Sprinkle with parsley. Makes 3 or 4 servings.

Hummer mit Dillsosse

(LOBSTER IN DILL SAUCE)

2 1¼-pound Maine lobsters, or 4 small lobster tails (2 9-ounce packages frozen lobster tails)
½ teaspoon salt
Celery sprig
2 tablespoons butter
2 tablespoons flour
1 tablespoon minced fresh or frozen dill
4 to 6 tablespoons sour cream

---

[2] *Weissbier* is a tart beer very light in alcohol not obtainable in American markets. White wine is really more nearly like it than our domestic light beer.

If using Maine lobsters, put live lobsters in kettle, cover with water, add salt and celery sprig, boil 20 minutes or until shells turn bright red. Drain; cool; remove meat and dice. Save shells and 1½ cups of the stock.

If using lobster tails, remove undershell, place tail flesh side down on cutting board and slit down back of hard shell. Gently pull flesh partially away so that red side of flesh is loosened. Heat to boiling 2 cups water with ½ teaspoon salt and a celery sprig; add lobster tails, cook over moderate heat (simmer, don't boil) 7 or 8 minutes until shells are bright red and flesh pure white. Turn off heat; let lobster remain in stock until cooled, then remove from shells and dice or thickly slice the meat.

Make a sauce by melting butter in saucepan, stirring in flour, then slowly adding 1½ cups of the strained stock.[3] Add salt to taste if needed. Add dill, turn off heat, stir in sour cream. Add this sauce to the diced or sliced lobster meat, serve lobster in the cleaned shells. Makes 2 to 4 servings.

Hummer Ragout
(HAMBURG STYLE LOBSTER RAGOUT)

1 pound fresh lobster meat, cooked, diced

STOCK

1½ cups chicken broth	**1 small can white**
½ cup Rhine wine	**asparagus spears,**
Several parsley sprigs	**drained and chopped**
1 small onion, quartered	**1 4-ounce can small**
1 celery-leaf sprig	**button mushrooms**
1 sweetbread	**1 tablespoon capers**
2 teaspoons lemon juice	**2 tablespoons heavy cream**
2 tablespoons butter	**1 tablespoon minced dill**
2 tablespoons flour	**2 egg yolks**

---

[3] In most cases, the original 2 cups water will cook down to 1½ cups stock. If more than this is lost by evaporation, add water to make 1½ cups stock.

Combine the chicken broth and wine; add parsley, onion and celery; cook 5 minutes. Strain, reheat to boiling, add sweetbread and lemon juice, cook 20 minutes. Remove sweetbread, saving stock. When sweetbread is cool, remove membrane, cut in small dice.

Melt butter, stir in flour, cook until it bubbles. Slowly add the stock; cook until smooth and thickened. Add the asparagus, mushrooms and capers; cook 5 minutes. Add the cream, the dill and the diced lobster meat. Cook until lobster is thoroughly heated. Beat egg yolks, add a little of the hot sauce, combine the two. Cook over lowest heat, stirring until sauce is creamy-smooth. Serve the lobster over toast points. Makes 4 servings.

Scampis Rolandia is a curious name for a German dish. *Scampi* is the Italian name for shrimp, Roland was the protégé of Charlemagne who died defending the pass of Roncesvalles in northern Spain in 779.

The use of an Italian name for shrimp was merely the whim of the Bremen chef at the Ratstuben Deutsches Haus, a restaurant overlooking the enchanting market square of Bremen, where I tasted this delicious morsel. The name Rolandia is in honor of the statue of Roland which stands in the square, a beloved Bremer landmark.

Bremen is a city that loves legends, and the Roland legend is a top favorite, along with the Grimm Brothers' fairy tale of the "Four Musicians of Bremen." (The Four Musicians, for those whose memory of fairy tales is hazy, were a donkey, a dog, a cat and a rooster who with their "music" terrified robbers into fleeing from a house the creatures wanted for themselves.) Whether Roland ever was in Bremen is doubtful, but at least one minstrel tale credited him for having helped to conquer the pagan Saxon tribes for Charlemagne, thus bringing Christianity to this northern land. The statue in the square is of heroic proportions and Roland stands facing the cathedral with an enigmatic smile, presumably warning the power-hungry bishops that he was watching their machinations. At his feet lies a small cripple, whose tale is also a part of Bremer legend, but of much later date. In the eighteenth century, a baroness offered part of her park to the city, as much land as a man could cover by foot in a single day, as long as she could choose the man.

FISCH

Her choice was a pathetic little man with crooked legs, who proved his valor by running as fast as he could from dawn to dusk, covering many acres, but at the end of the exhausting day, he dropped dead. He lies immortalized on the market square, under Roland's protection.

*   *   *

The shrimp with the Italian-medieval name has a distinctly oriental flavor, and is served with a most delicious curry-flavored sauce. Altogether, it is just about as international as a dish can be. And wonderful! A most unusual offering.

Scampis Rolandia

(SHRIMP ROLANDIA)

1 pound medium shrimp
  in the shell
2 cups water
1 tablespoon lemon juice
¼ cup chili sauce or
  tomato catsup
1 tablespoon Worcestershire
  sauce

½ teaspoon salt
Curry Mousselinesosse*
¼ cup flour
¼ cup shredded coconut
3 to 4 tablespoons
  butter
Hot cooked rice

Shell the shrimp, using the shells to make shrimp stock: place shells in a saucepan, cover with 2 cups salted water, cook 20 minutes, reducing liquid to 1 cup. Marinate the shelled shrimp for 30 minutes in mixture of lemon juice, chili sauce or catsup, Worcestershire sauce and salt. While shrimp marinates, prepare the *Curry Mousselinesosse*.

Remove shrimp from marinade, place on 6 individual skewers (bamboo skewers or large poultry skewers). Combine flour and coconut, roll the skewered shrimp in the mixture. Sauté in butter until shrimp are bright pink and lightly browned. Serve over rice, topped with the sauce. Makes 6 servings.

Kaiser Krabben mit Dillsosse

(LARGE SHRIMP WITH DILL SAUCE)

1½ pounds shrimp in
shells
Celery sprig
2 tablespoons butter
2 tablespoons flour

1 tablespoon minced fresh
or frozen dill
4 to 6 tablespoons sour
cream

Cook shrimp in salted water to which a celery sprig has been added, just until shells turn pink, about 5 minutes. Water should merely simmer, not boil hard. Let shrimp cool in the broth, then remove, saving the broth, and shell the shrimp.

To make the sauce, melt butter in saucepan, stir in flour, let cook until flour bubbles. Add dill and stir in 1 cup of the shrimp broth slowly. When smooth and thickened, turn off heat, stir in sour cream. Add the shrimp. Makes 4 servings.

Austern Ragout

(OYSTER RAGOUT)

This is made exactly like *Hummer Ragout** except that 1 pint fresh or frozen shucked oysters are added to the sauce instead of lobster meat. Simmer oysters in the sauce until edges curl, no more than 5 minutes. Then add the egg yolk (as for the *Hummer Ragout*), cook, stirring, until creamy-smooth; serve over toast points.

Fleisch

(MEAT)

Since the days when Tacitus visited "Germania," the people of this northern land have always been hearty meat eaters. Pork is now as it has always been the most-used meat, and every bit of the *Schwein* is consumed in one way or another, from the trotters to the snout.

Next to pork, veal is most favored. In recent years, with the influx of Americans into West Germany, beef has become more popular, but the quality of German beef is inferior to ours, and those who visit Germany with a longing for tender rare steaks may be disappointed. The European veal, on the other hand, is far more tender and flavorful than ours, and the things German cooks do with veal cutlets are worth making a trip to West Germany to taste. Lamb is used very little, except in the north.

The most renowned of all German beef recipes is, of course, sauerbraten, and the number of recipes I collected for sauerbraten ran into the dozens. The old-fashioned way was to marinate the beef in a spiced vinegar mixture for at least three days in order to tenderize the tough meat of oxen which had grown old as farm beasts before they were butchered. Today, when tractors have replaced ox-drawn plows, and better quality beef is available, it is no longer necessary to marinate the meat this long, and wine may be used instead of vinegar, if preferred. One of the best versions of sauerbraten I tasted had been marinated in red Burgundy, not in vinegar at all. Instead of gingersnaps (as most American recipes for sauerbraten call for), Nuremberg *Lebkuchen* is frequently used, broken into bits to be added to the gravy, which produces a smooth, subtle, not too biting flavor.

In northern Germany, the meat for sauerbraten is often marinated in buttermilk rather than a vinegar mixture. This gives the pot roast a still different flavor, and the buttermilk makes the meat very tender, very juicy.

Marinating then pot-roasting is a method applied to other meats besides beef. Venison is marinated in a vinegar mixture or, even better, in buttermilk. Pork marinated in beer is quite delicious. The Germans seem to prefer pot roasts to oven roasts—and those cuts of meat that are oven-roasted are always cooked to the well-done stage.

It is the frequent use of fruit with meat that, above all, marks German meat cookery as distinctly different from that of other countries. Roast saddle of venison, for example, is usually accompanied by half a pear filled with lingonberry jam. The dish called "Silesian Heaven" consists of pork chops cooked with mixed dried fruit.

Generally speaking, herbs are used sparingly in flavoring meats. A pinch of marjoram, some minced parsley, a bay leaf added to the sauce for stews, these are the most-used herbs. Minced fresh dill is used for seafood, but seldom for meat. Juniper berries and caraway seeds are favorite spices, though curry powder is also used sometimes to spice meats.

A modern innovation is the frequent use of bottled tomato catsup—Heinz catsup, exactly like the kind we use. This is added to many meat sauces. So is cream, either heavy sweet cream or sour cream.

German cooks make much more use of "variety meats" than we do. Tongue is extremely popular. Brains, sweetbreads, heart, liver and kidneys are used in most interesting ways. And the thrift of the German *Hausfrau* is expressed in imaginative use of such parts as the neck bones, the knuckles, shins, feet and even the ears. Beef marrow is used not only to make dumplings, but is a favored ingredient in stews, and may be purchased by gram weight in German butcher shops.

Wild game appears on restaurant menus everywhere in West Germany and is offered for sale in butcher shops alongside the fresh tongue and the brisket of beef and the trimmed steaks of cutlets for *Rouladen* which are standard meat items. It was venison season when I visited the country last, and everywhere we went, *Rehblatt*, shoulder of young roebuck, was listed on restaurant menus. In a frozen food counter in Munich, I saw packaged frozen wild boar (alongside imported frozen chicken parts from Georgia!). Even bear meat is often served as a specialty in Black Forest restaurants.

But how can one mention the meats of Germany without growing enthusiastic about the wonderful sausages, the *Wurst* which hangs in garlands and festoons on the walls of every butcher shop. I am told that there are upwards of three hundred different kinds of sausages, from the plump links of *Bratwurst* to the long thin frankfurter called a *Polnische,* the bright red smoked *Mettwurst,* the small pale *Weisswurst* of Munich, the thick rolls of *Blutwurst* (blood sausage or pudding) and the astonishingly good *Zwiebel-wurst,* which is a form of liverwurst containing bits of fried onion. There is even a "curry wurst" especially for cooking in a tomato sauce spiced with curry. Besides the links and rolls of *Wurst* hanging from pegs on the walls, there are innumerable jellied meats and pâtés, including *Sülze,* traditionally made in Germany with calf's feet and veal neck bones, and *Leberkäs* (liver cheese) a delicious cold meat loaf which contains only a trace of liver and no cheese at all.

Bratwurst means sausage for frying, and the most famous are those of Nuremberg where one traditionally orders the small savory pork links in multiples of six. A dozen make a normal serving, but some people have been known to put away eighteen, or even twenty-four, at a single sitting. The sausages are cooked over open grills in the snack shops known as *Bratwurstglöckl,* with huge hoods above the grills to capture the smoke. The wonderful fragrance of the smoking meat is enough in itself to provoke a multiple order.

If "hot dog" is an American name for frankfurters in buns, the idea of eating sausage in this manner has been common in Germany for many, many years. I recall on my first visit to Germany, in the thirties, that whenever the train stopped at a station and the big train windows were rolled down, girls or women offered hot sausages from carts rolled right up to the train, handing them up in buns through the windows. The crisp German buns are delicious, with far more flavor than our soft rolls, and usually one has a choice of several kinds of sausage to go inside them, with a generous dab of *Senf* or Düsseldorf mustard to spice the meat. At a kiosk on the street in Bremen, I stopped to have a *Polnische Wurst* in a bun, a sausage which was a good ten inches in length, very spicy and peppery, encased in a comparably long crisp caraway-seeded roll.

Besides the sausages, there is Westphalian ham, slow-smoked, bright red, usually sliced paper-thin and often served on a board accompanied by pumpernickel or black bread, sweet butter and gherkins. The flavor of Westphalian ham is something like that of both Italian prosciutto and the Serrano ham of Spain. We have no native American product like it. Traditionally it is smoked in a Westphalian *Himmel* ("heaven"), the large open hearth of a farmhouse chimney. In Swabia and Stuttgart, ham is always accompanied by *Kirschwasser* and beer. In Westphalia, the spirit is more likely to be *Korn,* a *Schnaps* made from rye, with a beer chaser.

One evening in Stuttgart I had such a serving of ham, bread and butter in a diminutive eating place not far from the *Staatsoper.* In a single room, five or six tables were crowded, and there was no such thing as a private table. Whenever a chair became vacant, waiting customers politely came over to ask whether they might take the seat, and the answer was always yes. In minutes, complete strangers would be talking to one another, for in such an atmosphere, formality is impossible. I was told that it was because the room was so tiny and so *gemütlich* that people liked to come here. There are many such eating places in Germany; those who are alone and wish to find companionship need only go to such a tavern and friendliness will await them. It is an endearing custom, and the cold cuts and sausages consumed in such an atmosphere taste all the better because they are a part of the setting.

Rheinischer Sauerbraten
(RHINELAND STYLE SAUERBRATEN)

4 to 5 pounds bottom round or rump of beef

VINEGAR MARINADE

**2 cups red wine vinegar
and 4 cups water; or 4
cups dry red wine, 1
cup water and juice of
1 lemon**
**1 cup thinly sliced onion
(1 large)**

4 or 5 peppercorns
1 bay leaf
¼ teaspoon thyme
2 whole cloves
Pinch of ground nutmeg
Several parsley sprigs

SAUCE

¼ cup flour
**4 tablespoons butter or
shortening**
2 carrots, sliced
1 or 2 onions, quartered
**1 tablespoon tomato
catsup**
**½ to ⅔ cup grated
Lebkuchen, dry
gingerbread or crushed
gingersnaps**

**2 tablespoons sugar or
gravy coloring (such as
Kitchen Bouquet)**
½ cup red wine
1 cup currants or raisins
½ cup slivered almonds
**Lingonberry preserves or
cranberry-orange relish**

Place beef in bowl. Combine vinegar and water (or red wine, water
and lemon juice), onion, peppercorns, bay leaf, thyme, cloves and
nutmeg; bring to a boil. Pour over meat. Cool; add parsley sprigs.
Place meat in refrigerator, marinate 2 to 3 days, turning several
times.

Remove from marinade (strain marinade and save), wipe dry.

Dredge with flour. Sauté in butter or shortening in large heavy pot or Dutch oven until well browned on all sides. Add carrots, quartered onion, tomato catsup and 1 cup of the strained marinade. Cover tightly, simmer 2½ to 3 hours or until very tender. Remove meat to platter. Strain or purée sauce, skim off fat, measure liquid. There should be 2 cups. (Add some of reserved marinade to make 2 cups if necessary.) Add the *Lebkuchen,* gingerbread or gingersnaps to the strained broth, also sugar, wine and raisins. Bring to a boil until thickened. Add almonds, cook a few minutes longer. Serve the sauce over the sliced meat with lingonberry preserves or cranberry-orange relish. Should be accompanied by potato dumplings, *Spätzle* or egg noodles. Makes 10 to 12 servings.

Bayrischer Sauerbraten
(BAVARIAN STYLE SAUERBRATEN)

3½ to 4 pounds boned rump or shoulder of beef

MARINADE

4 cups beer	1 onion, sliced
2 cups water	2 whole cloves
1 lemon, quartered	1 tomato, chopped
1 bay leaf	4 or 5 peppercorns

SAUCE

3 tablespoons flour	Sugar to taste
3 tablespoons butter or drippings	Salt to taste
1 lemon, thinly sliced	½ cup sour cream

Cover meat in bowl with the marinade. Leave in refrigerator 2 to 3 days, turning several times. Remove from marinade (strain marinade and save), pat dry, dredge with flour. Brown in butter or drippings, add 1 cup strained marinade, lemon, sugar (about 1 tablespoon), and salt (about 1 teaspoon). Cook covered until meat is very tender, 2½ to 3 hours. Remove, strain sauce, skim off fat. Add the cream, blend well and reheat slowly. Serve the sauce over the sliced meat. Always accompanied by potato dumplings and red cabbage. Makes about 10 servings.

Sauerbraten auf Norddeutsche Art
(SAUERBRATEN NORTH GERMAN STYLE)

3½ to 4 pounds boned rump or shoulder of beef, or
    shoulder of pork, or fresh ham
1 quart buttermilk
Few drops lemon juice

SAUCE

2 cups red wine	3 tablespoons flour
2 cups water	½ cup Lebkuchen,
1 tablespoon salt	broken in bits, or stale
1 bay leaf	gingerbread, or crushed
4 or 5 peppercorns	gingersnaps
1 tablespoon vinegar	¼ cup raisins or currants
3 tablespoons butter	

Wash and dry the meat. Place in a deep bowl, cover with the buttermilk and lemon juice, marinate in refrigerator 2 days, turning several times. Remove; wash off the buttermilk. Place meat in a pot or kettle, add the red wine, water, salt, bay leaf, peppercorns and vinegar. Cook, covered, 2½ to 3 hours or until very tender. Remove meat. Strain the stock, measuring 3 cups. Melt the butter in saucepan, stir in flour, then slowly stir in the stock, simmer until slightly thickened. Add the *Lebkuchen,* gingerbread or gingersnaps and the raisins or currants, cook until sauce is thickened. Add sugar to taste, if desired. Makes about 10 servings.

Schwarzwälder Rehrücken
(SADDLE OF VENISON BLACK FOREST STYLE)

1 saddle of young roebuck, 6 to 8 pounds
Vinegar Marinade*, or 1 quart buttermilk or red wine
Fat pork for larding

SAUCE

1 cup red wine
Flour to thicken pan
    drippings
¼ pound mushrooms,
    chopped[1]
1 cup water or stock

1 tablespoon grated lemon
    rind
2 tablespoons brandy
Salt and pepper to taste
½ cup sour cream

Garnish. Pear halves filled with lingonberry preserves or currant jelly

The meat, if fresh-killed, should be hung in a cool place to age for 1 to 2 weeks; ask your butcher if he will do this for you. Before cooking, soak in a Vinegar Marinade or in buttermilk or red wine for 24 hours. Remove from marinade, dry well, insert thin strips of fat pork through the lean of the meat with a larding needle or by forcing the fat in with a long skewer. To sear the meat, draw out the fat from ½ cup diced fat pork; brown the meat on all sides. Place in an open roasting pan, roast at 325° F. until meat thermometer registers 150° for pink or 165° for medium. Baste occasionally with red wine. When meat is done, remove from pan to platter. Add 2 to 3 tablespoons flour to pan drippings, cook 2 minutes. Add mushrooms, water or stock and grated lemon rind. Simmer until gravy is smooth and thickened. Add brandy, adjust

[1] The little brown *Pfifferlinge* mushrooms should be used in this, if they can be found canned in food specialty stores. This dish is sometimes listed on restaurant menus as *Rehrücken Baden-Baden.*

seasonings, cook 1 minute. Turn off heat, stir in sour cream. Serve slices of the meat covered with sauce, with jelly-filled pears as garnish. Makes 6 servings.

A shoulder of lamb which has first been marinated in buttermilk, then basted with red wine as it roasts, will taste extraordinarily like saddle of venison.

Gedämpfes Rindfleisch
(BOILED BEEF)

4 pounds rump or brisket of beef	2 or 3 parsley sprigs
Beef marrow bones (optional)	1 bay leaf
	1 celery stalk
2 carrots	1 tablespoon salt
2 onions	4 peppercorns
	6 cups water

Place the meat, bones, vegetables, herbs, salt, peppercorns and water in a pot. Bring to a boil, lower heat, simmer 3 to 4 hours, or until tender. Remove meat from the broth. Strain broth, then chill so fat will rise to top and can be skimmed off. Let meat stand 15 minutes, then slice. Use the stock in making soup for a first course. Serve the sliced meat with chilled Horseradish Cream* and apple-sauce, or with hot Horseradish Sauce*. (Leftover boiled beef can be used to make *Zwiebelfleisch** or *Rindfleisch mit Apfeln**.) Makes 10 to 12 servings.

Rindfleisch mit Apfeln
(BEEF WITH APPLES)

4 to 6 tart apples, cored and sliced	Few drops lemon juice
	Pinch of cinnamon
3 or 4 tablespoons butter or bacon drippings	¼ cup raisins or dried currants
1 tablespoon sugar or to taste	4 large slices cooked beef (boiled or roasted)
1 cup beef gravy	

Sauté the apple slices in butter or bacon drippings until lightly browned. Add sugar, beef gravy, lemon juice and cinnamon. Simmer until apples are soft. Add the raisins or currants and the beef slices, cook just until meat is heated through. Makes 4 servings.

Zwiebelfleisch

(BEEF WITH ONIONS)

6 large slices cooked beef (boiled or roasted)	2 large onions, sliced
	Leftover beef gravy
2 tablespoons butter or drippings	Minced parsley
	6 fried eggs

The meat should be cut into thin slices, one slice per serving. Melt the butter or heat the drippings in a skillet, add the onions, cook until lightly browned. Add the meat, gravy and parsley, cook until heated through. Top each serving with a fried egg. Makes 6 servings.

Schweinefleisch in Bier

(POT ROAST OF PORK IN BEER)

4 pounds pork shoulder or fresh ham	1 tablespoon sugar
1 onion, stuck with 2 whole cloves	4 peppercorns or a sprinkling of freshly ground pepper
2 or 3 large carrots, cubed	1 12-ounce bottle or can of beer
1 cup diced white or yellow turnip (optional)	1 cup stale pumpernickel crumbs
1 celery stalk	1 tablespoon tomato catsup
1 bay leaf	
1 tablespoon salt	

The day before dish is to be served, trim excess fat from meat. Place in large pot, cover with cold water, bring to a boil, cook 5 minutes, then pour off water. Add 2 cups fresh water, place vegetables, seasonings and beer in pot. Cook covered 3 hours. Immediately remove meat from broth. Strain broth, saving carrots and turnip; chill broth overnight, then discard fat which will rise to top and congeal. Place meat in pan in oven, fat side up, and roast until top is crisp and brown, about 45 minutes. Add to the strained broth the pumpernickel and catsup, boil until thickened. Adjust seasonings. Mash the cooked carrots and turnip together, season to taste, reheat. Serve the sliced meat covered with the sauce, accompanied by the puréed carrot-turnip mixture and potato croquettes. Makes 8 to 10 servings of meat.

Variation. Vegetables may be browned in the roasting pan with the meat instead of being puréed, if preferred. Also, cooked or canned small whole onions may be glazed in the pan drippings.

Rinderschmorbraten in Bier. Use a 4-pound rump of beef instead of pork, but do not parboil. Instead, sear the meat in drippings, then add vegetables, seasonings and beer, cook tightly covered until meat is tender. Remove meat from broth, skim off fat, then add dark rye or pumpernickel crumbs and catsup, simmer until thickened. Grated lemon rind is sometimes added to the sauce; sometimes a few capers are added. Serve meat sliced, covered with the sauce or gravy.

*   *   *

We have no such cut of pork as *Rippchen* in our regular markets, though it may be available in pork stores in German or Hungarian neighborhoods. Smoked pork chops are frequently sold packaged in supermarkets, and these can be prepared the same way.

Kasseler Rippchen
(CURED PORK RIB)

1 **cured rib roast of pork, or 6 to 8 thick cured or smoked pork chops**	2 **cups boiling water**
	2 **tablespoons flour**
	1 **tablespoon butter**
	Salt to taste
1 **large onion, sliced**	½ **cup sour cream**
1 **tomato, chopped**	

Place the roast or the chops in a roasting pan over onion and tomato. Bake covered at 375° F. for ½ hour; uncover, add 1 cup boiling water. Continue adding water as needed. If meat is in one piece, roast 1½ to 2 hours; if in chops, roast 40 minutes or until nicely browned. Remove meat. Strain or purée the liquid in pan. To gelatinous bits in bottom of roasting pan add flour and butter to make a roux. Stir and cook over moderate heat until flour bubbles; slowly add strained or puréed broth, stirring until smooth. Taste for seasoning; add salt if needed. Turn off heat, add sour cream. Serve with sauerkraut and parsley potatoes or with mashed potatoes and kale. Makes 4 to 6 servings.

Schinken in Burgunder
(HAM IN BURGUNDY)

1 **6-pound butt end ready-to-eat ham, skinned; or 1 3- or 4-pound canned ham**	½ **cup sugar (brown or white)**
	Whole cloves (optional)
2 **cups dry red wine**	1 **cup canned beef gravy**
1 **tablespoon prepared mustard**	1 **tablespoon currant jelly**

Marinate the ham in the red wine 24 hours before cooking, turning several times. Remove from wine, rub mustard over top fat, then sprinkle sugar over the mustard. Stud fat with whole cloves, if desired. Bake ham in oven preheated to 350° F. for 1 hour, basting with 1 cup of the wine used for the marinade. Add remaining 1 cup of the wine with the beef gravy and currant jelly; cook until smooth, about 5 minutes, serve as sauce with the ham. Remove ham to platter. Serve with the sauce. A 6-pound ready-to-eat ham makes 14 to 18 servings; a canned boned 3-pound ham makes about 12 servings.

Sliced Ham in Burgundy Sauce. Heat slices of cold baked ham in the following sauce: 1 can beef gravy, 1 cup red wine, 1 teaspoon Düsseldorf mustard, 2 tablespoons currant jelly, 1 tablespoon minced parsley, 1 tablespoon butter.

Ochsenzunge
(TONGUE)

The Germans are very fond of tongue and use it in innumerable ways, pickled, smoked, in salads, in ragouts, with many different sauces. Boiling a tongue is quite easy, and while jars of tongue are available in most of our markets, the price is more than twice that of the tongue you cook yourself. Be sure to keep the broth in which it cooked; it is useful as stock in making many sauces.

1 beef tongue	1 large carrot, cubed
Salt to taste (1 tablespoon for 6 cups water)	2 or 3 celery stalks with leaves, chopped
1 or 2 onions, stuck with 2 whole cloves	2 or 3 parsley sprigs
	4 or 5 peppercorns

Place the tongue in kettle, add cold water to cover and salt. Bring to a boil, reduce heat and simmer 2½ to 3 hours, skimming now and then. After first ½ hour, add vegetables, parsley and peppercorns. When tongue is tender (skin pulls off easily), remove from broth, skin while warm. Strain broth; chill. Reheat sliced cooked tongue in one of the following ways.

Ochsenzunge mit Madeira Sosse
(TONGUE WITH MADEIRA SAUCE)

8 to 12 slices cooked beef tongue, trimmed	Madeira to taste (1 to 2 tablespoons)
1 can (1¼ cups) beef gravy	1 tablespoon butter
1 cup strained tongue stock (see preceding recipe)	1 teaspoon Kitchen Bouquet or Maggi seasoning

Cut the tongue in long slices; trim for more even appearance. Combine beef gravy, tongue stock, Madeira, butter and Kitchen Bouquet or Maggi; bring to a boil, lower heat. Add sliced tongue, cook until sauce is reduced and thickened. Makes 4 servings.

Kalbszunge mit Pilzen
(TONGUE WITH MUSHROOMS)

24 to 30 slices cooked calf's tongue, or 12 to 16 slices beef tongue	1 can (1¼ cups) beef gravy
½ pound mushrooms, sliced	1 teaspoon Kitchen Bouquet
2 tablespoons butter	1 tablespoon Madeira or brandy
1 tablespoon flour	
1 cup strained tongue stock	

Slice the tongue neatly; trim. Sauté the mushrooms in butter until lightly browned; stir in flour. Slowly stir in tongue stock, then beef gravy, Kitchen Bouquet and wine or brandy. Simmer until sauce is reduced and thickened, about 20 minutes. Makes 6 servings.

Ochsenzunge oder Kalbszunge
(BEEF TONGUE OR CALF'S TONGUE)

Mit Rosinensosse (With Raisin Sauce). Cook the tongue with vegetables and herbs; when done, remove from stock, skin and slice, saving the stock. Serve with following sauce:

2 tablespoons butter	Grated rind of ½ lemon
2 tablespoons flour	Few drops lemon juice
1½ cups strained	(optional)
tongue stock	Salt and sugar to taste
½ cup white wine	1 tablespoon Kitchen
⅓ cup raisins	Bouquet

Make a roux of butter and flour. Stir in the strained stock, wine, raisins and lemon rind. Simmer until smooth. Add lemon juice, salt, sugar and Kitchen Bouquet. Makes 2 cups sauce.

Mit Meerettichsosse (With Horseradish Sauce). Just before serving, cover the sliced cooked tongue with *Meerettichsosse**. Garnish with sieved egg yolk and capers.

* * *

Schnitzel means a cutlet from the tender part of the meat. Most of the time it is veal, cut from the leg, but it can be pork, and a *Schnitzel* of pork is quite delicious. A *Schnitzel* may or may not be breaded. *Schnitzel natur* means it has not been breaded, only sautéed in butter until lightly browned on each side.

Kalbsschnitzel Natur
(SIMPLE SAUTÉED VEAL CUTLET)

Flour
Salt
2 pounds veal cutlet,
    ½-inch thick
3 or 4 tablespoons butter

½ cup water or beef or
    veal stock
Few drops lemon juice
1 tablespoon minced
    parsley
Salt to taste

Sprinkle flour and salt over meat on one side only. Cut into 4 to 6 pieces. Pound meat with edge of plate to flatten out and break down tissues (which makes meat more tender). Make several short incisions around edges to prevent curling. Sauté in the butter until well browned on both sides. Remove meat to platter. Add water or stock to pan, boil up, stirring to reduce gelatinous browned bits in pan; cook until liquid is reduced to half. Add lemon juice and parsley and salt to taste. Pour this unthickened pan gravy over the meat. Makes 4 to 6 servings.

Rahmschnitzel oder Kaiserschnitzel
(CUTLET WITH CREAM SAUCE, OR KAISER CUTLET)

Prepare veal cutlet as for *Kalbsschnitzel natur,* but after removing from skillet, add first ½ cup beef or veal stock to pan, boil up, stirring, until gelatinous bits are dissolved and liquid reduced to half. Then add ½ cup heavy sweet or sour cream, keeping heat low and stirring until smooth. Pour this sauce over the browned cutlets. Garnish with lemon slices and minced parsley. (Sometimes capers are added instead of lemon.)

Schnitzel mit Ananas
(VEAL CUTLET WITH PINEAPPLE)

This differs from *Rahmschnitzel* only in the addition of canned pineapple wedges. Brown the pineapple in the butter after the meat has been removed from the skillet. Place the browned pineapple around the meat, then continue with the sauce as above, adding first beef or veal stock, then sweet or sour cream. Garnish with minced parsley.

Schnitzel à la Holstein
(VEAL CUTLET À LA HOLSTEIN)

Prepare veal cutlet as for *Kalbsschnitzel natur* but over each serving place a fried egg, cross 2 anchovy fillets over each egg, and garnish with capers. Serve with lemon wedges.

The name *Schnitzel à la Holstein* has nothing to do with the province, Schleswig-Holstein. Rather, the method of preparing the veal *Schnitzel* is named after Count Holstein, who served as Bismarck's foreign minister and later became prime minister of Germany. Both Bismarck and Holstein were eminent gastronomes whose ability to put away great quantities of food was almost legendary.

Bismarck's favorite *Schnitzel* recipe called for seagull's eggs atop breaded veal cutlet.

Another method of serving *Schnitzel* in north Germany is to cover the cooked veal cutlet with a mound of tiny shrimp sautéed in butter. A modern version calls for shrimp and pieces of avocado.

Wiener Schnitzel

(VEAL CUTLET VIENNA STYLE)

1½ pounds veal cutlet,
   ½-inch thick
1½ teaspoons salt
2 tablespoons flour
2 eggs, beaten
2 tablespoons water
1 cup crumbs grated from
   stale hard rolls or
   French bread

3 tablespoons butter
3 tablespoons vegetable
   shortening
4 slices lemon
4 curled anchovies or
   capers

Cut the meat into 4 serving portions. Sprinkle each with salt, pound each side with side of plate until ¼-inch thick. Rub flour into one side only. Dip in beaten eggs blended with the water; then coat with crumbs. Chill at least ½ hour before cooking. Heat butter and shortening together in skillet without allowing butter to burn. Cook breaded cutlet in the fat until crisp and brown on each side. Keep warm until all pieces are cooked. Serve with a slice of lemon over each *Schnitzel* and a curled anchovy or a caper in the center of each lemon slice. (Lemon should be squeezed over meat with the tines of a fork at table.) Makes 4 servings.

*   *   *

According to the Germans, it was a German chef in Dürkheim, the Palatinate wine center, who invented this extravagantly delicious method of preparing *Schnitzel,* with both ham and cheese sealed inside thin slices of veal. That he gave the dish a French name is not surprising; don't we frequently do the same thing?

Kalbsschnitzel Cordon Bleu
(VEAL CUTLET WITH HAM AND CHEESE)

8 individual veal cutlets	4 tablespoons flour
Salt and pepper	½ cup fine dry bread
4 slices Swiss or	or cracker crumbs
Gruyère cheese	3 tablespoons butter
4 thin slices ham	1 tablespoon oil
1 egg, beaten	

Pound veal with mallet or edge of plate to flatten, working in salt and pepper sprinkled from shakers; trim edges. Place 1 slice cheese and 1 slice ham over half the cutlets, so that neither cheese nor ham overlaps edges. Brush edges with beaten egg, top each with another cutlet, pound edges to seal. Roll each in flour, then dip in egg, then in crumbs. Sauté in mixture of butter and oil until well browned. Transfer to casserole or roasting pan, place in oven preheated to 375° F., complete in oven, baking for 20 to 35 minutes. Makes 4 servings.

Schweineschnitzel
(PORK CUTLETS BREADED)

4 pork chops, cut ½-inch thick, boned; or 1½ pounds pork steak cut from leg (fresh ham)	1 cup crumbs grated from hard rolls or French bread
2 eggs, beaten	6 tablespoons shortening, or 3 tablespoons each
2 tablespoons water	butter and vegetable
½ teaspoon salt	shortening

Pound the boned pork chops with side of plate until ⅛-inch thick. Blend eggs, water and salt. Dip meat in egg, then coat with crumbs. Fry in shortening until crisply browned on each side. Makes 4 servings. Serve with lemon wedges, sprinkle lemon juice over *Schnitzel* at table.

*   *   *

There are few places in West Germany which serve food to compare with that of the Eisenhut Hotel in Rothenburg. During my stay at this enchanting medieval hostelry, whose rooms are furnished with priceless antiques and decorated with insouciant gaiety by Frau Pirner, the owner, I found every dish put before me more delicious than the one that had gone before. The following recipe for veal chops is quite simple, yet utterly delicious.

Kalbskotelette à la Eisenhut

(VEAL CHOPS AS PREPARED AT EISENHUT HOTEL)

4 veal loin chops,
   trimmed
½ teaspoon salt
½ teaspoon paprika
2 to 3 tablespoons butter
4 pieces light toast
¼ pound mushrooms,
   sliced
1 tablespoon flour, or ½
   tablespoon cornstarch or
   arrowroot

¼ cup light cream
Few drops lemon juice
2 tablespoons Rhine wine
   or 1 tablespoon brandy
2 tablespoons minced
   parsley
4 slices Swiss cheese

Sprinkle veal chops on both sides with salt and paprika. Sauté in the butter on both sides until lightly browned. Place each chop on a piece of toast on a heatproof platter. Sauté mushrooms in the same skillet as the chops, adding more butter if necessary. When lightly browned, stir in flour or cornstarch or arrowroot, then the cream, lemon juice and wine or brandy. Simmer about 4 minutes. Add minced parsley, pour over chops. Place a slice of cheese cut to fit over each chop. Place in oven preheated to 400° F. until cheese is melted but not browned. Makes 4 servings.

(If preferred, chops may be boned and pounded before sautéing.)

Kalbshaxe
(VEAL SHANK)

1 tablespoon butter or fat
1 medium onion, sliced
1 carrot, sliced
1 celeriac (celery root), or 2 celery stalks, sliced
1 teaspoon paprika
2 veal shanks, about 3 pounds each
¼ teaspoon thyme

¼ teaspoon basil
1 tablespoon minced parsley
2 cups water with 2 teaspoons salt, or 2 cups bouillon
Flour
Salt and pepper
2 or 3 tablespoons melted butter or margarine

In bottom of deep heavy pot (2½- to 3-quart capacity), melt butter, place onion, carrot, celery and paprika. Place veal shanks over the vegetables and add herbs, water and salt or bouillon. Simmer covered 1½ to 2 hours or until meat is tender. (This can be done a day in advance, if desired.) Remove meat from broth. Dredge meat with flour which has been mixed with salt and pepper. Place in roasting pan, brush or spoon melted fat over outside. Bake in preheated 350° F. oven until browned on all sides, basting occasionally and turning at least once.

The broth may be strained or vegetables may be left in, as preferred. (I like it best with the vegetables in it.) Thin 2 tablespoons of flour with the cold broth, then add to the broth and simmer until thickened. Serve potato dumplings (either the raw or cooked type) or noodles with the meat. Makes 4 to 6 servings.

Gefüllte Kalbshaxe
(STUFFED VEAL SHANKS)

Buy boned shanks, but be sure to ask butcher for the bones. Fill the boned meat with 2 cups herb-seasoned bread dressing (using your own recipe or packaged stuffing prepared as directed); tie up with thread or cord. Place the stuffed meat over the vegetables and cook as in preceding recipe, but place the bones in the same pot. When meat is tender, remove and discard the bones. Dredge meat with flour and brown in oven in the same way as for regular *Kalbshaxe*. This will be easier to carve and serve and the stuffing makes it go a little further.

Gefüllte Schweinerippchen
(STUFFED PORK CHOPS)

4 double pork chops

STUFFING

2 slices stale white bread, in small cubes	**½ cup raisins**
1 cup chopped apple	**4 tablespoons butter**
1 slice onion, minced	**¼ teaspoon salt**
	¼ cup dark rum

Slit pork chops through center. Sauté the bread, apple, onion and raisins in butter, sprinkle with salt. Stuff the chops with this mixture. Sprinkle outside of chops with salt. Bake in roasting pan at 325° F., basting occasionally with rum after chops have started to brown. Serve with sauerkraut and steamed potatoes. Makes 4 servings.

Rouladen
(BEEF ROLLS)

2 pounds top round of
  beef, thinly sliced, or
  1 flank steak, sliced
  horizontally
4 slices bacon, diced
3 dill pickles, sliced
  lengthwise

1 teaspoon mustard
Pinch of marjoram
2 to 3 tablespoons flour
2 tablespoons fat
2 cups beef broth

The meat should be cut into 4 to 6 thinly sliced portions in rectangular shape. Pound each with mallet or edge of plate until quite thin and all tissues have been broken down. Place bacon, pickle slices and mustard over each. Sprinkle with marjoram. Roll up, dredging outside of each roll with a little of the flour. Secure rolls with toothpicks. Sauté in hot fat in a skillet until well browned on all sides. Transfer to casserole. Add remaining flour to the pan drippings, cook a few seconds, then slowly add the beef broth. Simmer until thickened. Pour over meat in casserole. Cover tightly, simmer 1½ hours or until tender. Excellent when cooked ahead and reheated in its gravy. Makes 4 to 6 servings.

With Sauerkraut. Sometimes the dill pickle is omitted and instead sauerkraut is piled inside each roulade. About 1 cup sauerkraut will be needed.

Schlemmerrolle
(GOURMET'S ROULADE)

8 thin beefsteaks cut
from the top round,
each 3 × 6 inches
1½ pounds meat loaf
mixture (beef, veal and
pork ground)
1 teaspoon salt
¼ teaspoon marjoram
2 tablespoons minced
parsley
Freshly ground black
pepper
1 teaspoon Düsseldorf
mustard

1 egg, beaten
½ cup crushed unsalted
cracker crumbs
8 slices lean bacon
1 cup beef broth
¼ cup red Burgundy
1 teaspoon Worcestershire
sauce
1 tablespoon tomato
catsup
1 teaspoon cornstarch or
arrowroot
2 tablespoons sour cream

The steaks should be pounded thin and should be trimmed to form fairly even rectangles. Combine the ground meat, salt, marjoram, parsley, pepper, mustard, egg and cracker crumbs. Blend well with fingers. Divide into 8 portions, placing one portion over each steak. Roll steaks around ground meat mixture. Wrap a slice of bacon around each roulade, fasten with toothpick. Sear the roulades in a heavy skillet, turning to cook on all sides. Remove to shallow casserole. Pour off bacon fat. Add beef broth, wine, Worcestershire, catsup and the cornstarch or arrowroot thinned with a little cold water. Bring to a boil, simmer just until well blended, pour over the *Rouladen.* Bake in oven preheated to 350° F. for 35 to 40 minutes. Serve with sour cream spooned over top, with buttered noodles or *Spätzle** and cucumber salad. Makes 4 servings (2 *Rouladen* to each person).

Filetgulasch mit Smetana Sosse
(MINUTE STEAK WITH SOUR CREAM TOPPING)

1 to 1¼ pounds round
    steak cut ½-inch thick
¼ cup flour
Salt and pepper
3 tablespoons fat

1 medium onion, chopped
1 green pepper, cut in
    slivers
1 pimiento, cut in slivers
Sour cream

Cut the steak into 4 portions. Pound the flour, salt and pepper into each, using the edge of a plate, until flattened to ¼-inch thick. Slash edges. Cook quickly in the fat until well browned on both sides. Remove to warm plates. Sauté the onion, green pepper and pimiento in the fat until tender and lightly browned. Mound the sautéed vegetables over each serving of steak. Top each with a dollop of sour cream. Add enough water or beef broth to the pan drippings to loosen gelatinous bits, boil up, stirring to dissolve, then pour this clear pan essence over the steaks. Makes 4 servings.

Schweinsfilets mit Saurer Sahne
(PORK CHOPS WITH SOUR CREAM SAUCE)

4 large pork chops
2 tablespoons butter
2 tablespoons flour
1 teaspoon salt
¼ cup chicken stock or
    water

½ cup sour cream
2 tablespoons tomato
    catsup
1 tablespoon chopped
    capers

Sauté the chops in butter in a heavy skillet until nicely browned on each side. Remove from pan, add flour and salt, stir until smooth. Slowly add stock or water, then the cream, catsup and capers. Replace chops in sauce, simmer uncovered over lowest heat 10 to 15 minutes longer.

(If cream curdles, it is because heat is too high; sauce must not reach boiling point.) Makes 4 servings.

Schweinsrouladen
(PORK BIRDS)

1½ pounds boneless
  pork steaks, cut from
  shoulder, or 6 boned
  pork chops
Salt and pepper
2 tablespoons flour
1 large onion, minced
4 slices bacon, diced

¼ cup minced parsley
½ cup chopped raisins
½ cup chopped or
  crushed pineapple or
  chopped sweet gherkins
2 tablespoons butter
1 cup white wine or beer

Cut the meat in 6 rectangular pieces. Pound thin with edge of plate, working in salt, pepper and flour. Cook the onion and bacon together until onion is soft and bacon crisp. Add parsley, raisins and pineapple or chopped gherkins. Roll up the meat, tie with string or fasten with skewers. Brown in the butter on all sides, then add wine or beer, braise, covered, until meat is tender, about 20 minutes. Makes 6 servings.

Bratwurst in Bier, Berliner Art
(PORK SAUSAGE LINKS IN BEER, BERLIN STYLE)

12 to 18 Bratwurst
  (or pork sausage links)
Boiling water
1 teaspoon butter
Freshly ground pepper

1 cup beer
½ tablespoon arrowroot
  or potato flour
Salt to taste

Place sausage links in skillet, cover with boiling water, cook 2 to 3 minutes, then drain. Add butter to pan, brown the sausages on all sides. Drain off fat and discard. Add pepper and beer, simmer 15 minutes. Thicken sauce with arrowroot or potato flour and add salt to taste. Serve with mashed potatoes or *Himmel und Erde**. Serve 2 or 3 to each person, depending on size of the sausages.

*   *   *

FLEISCH

Wandering through butcher shops and supermarkets in various German cities proved a fascinating experience, for many meats in Germany are now sold ready to cook. *Rouladen,* for example, are sold already stuffed and skewered, ready for the pan. Kebabs, called *Spiess* (a word that means skewer or spike—it has nothing to do with the English word spy), are sold already cut to size on skewers, ready for the grill.

Standing before a butcher-shop window in Cologne with notebook and pencil, I jotted down some of the *Spiessbraten* combinations on display, and the first two of the following three recipes are made according to those combinations, bearing the same names as the Cologne butcher gave them.

Schaschlik Spiess
(GERMAN STYLE KEBABS)

¾ pound tender beef
¾ pound lean veal
¾ pound lean pork or sausage such as Mettwurst
½ pound calf's liver
8 strips bacon

2 large onions, thickly sliced
2 cups red or white wine or Vinegar Marinade*
3 or 4 tablespoons oil or melted fat

The beef, veal and pork should all be cut into squares ½-inch thick. The liver and the bacon should be cut into squares of uniform size. The meat should be inserted on 4 skewers, so that bacon and onion slices are added between cubes of meat, with the pork on the end in each case. Marinate in wine or Vinegar Marinade for 24 hours in refrigerator. Remove from marinade, grill over direct heat or under broiler until well browned on all sides, basting occasionally with oil or melted fat. Makes 6 servings.

With Vegetables and Fruit. Vegetables and fruit may be used in place of part of the meat. Tomatoes, mushrooms, green pepper, bananas and pineapple cubes are likely German choices.

Zigeunerspiess
(GYPSY KEBABS)

Use a combination of cocktail-size frankfurters, canned whole onions, squares of pimiento or green pepper and cubes of sirloin or tenderized chuck steak. Marinate for 24 hours in wine or Vinegar Marinade* as for the *Schaschlik Spiess**, then grill or broil, turning several times until well browned.

Wecksnappspiess

This dish I enjoyed in a restaurant in Cologne in the shadow of the magnificent cathedral which everyone locally calls the Dom. I have not been able to find a translation for the name of this dish; perhaps it's the chef's own name which he attached to his creation, for it was the chef of the restaurant who described for me exactly how he had made the dish.

8 1-inch cubes of ham	1 large onion, thickly
8 squares thick-sliced	sliced
bacon	Olive oil
1 veal kidney, thickly	½ cup minced parsley
sliced	Curryreis (Curried Rice)*
2 firm tomatoes, thickly	Tomatosossen (Tomato
sliced	Sauce)*

Arrange the ham, bacon, kidney, tomatoes and onion alternately on 4 skewers. Brush with olive oil. Grill directly over an open grate or under a broiler until nicely browned on all sides. As soon as kebabs are removed from the fire, roll in minced parsley. Serve over Curried Rice, topped with Tomato Sauce. Makes 4 servings.

[1] *Cheese is the most noteworthy product of the Allgäu, the province bordering Switzerland. Of thirty-six varieties, Emmenthal, Romadur, Weisslacker, and Limburger are the best-known cheeses.*

[2] *Swabia is famous for its Spätzle, a kind of noodle, its onion cake (Zwiebelkuchen), and luscious pastries flavored with Kirschwasser, the Black Forest cherry brandy.*

[3] *At taverns in Sachsenhausen, just across the river from Frankfurt, one dines on sauerkraut with Kasseler Rippchen (smoked pork ribs) washed down with quantities of local apple wine.*

[4] *Westphalia is world-renowned for its pungent smoked ham and slow-baked black pumpernickel bread. Pfefferpotthast, a savory stew, and delicate white asparagus are also memorable local specialties.*

Kalbsfrikassee mit Spargel
(VEAL STEW WITH ASPARAGUS)

1½ pounds stewing veal,
    cut in cubes
3 tablespoons butter
1 small onion, chopped
2 cups water
1½ teaspoons salt
1 cup Rhine wine
¼ teaspoon thyme
¼ pound mushrooms,
    chopped

2 tablespoons flour
1 1-pound can white
    asparagus, drained and
    chopped (saving liquid)
2 egg yolks
¼ cup cream
Grated rind of ½ lemon
    (or thin slivers of lemon
    rind)

Sauté veal in 2 tablespoons of the butter until lightly browned. Add onion, cook until soft and yellow. Add water, salt, wine and thyme; simmer, covered, 2 to 3 hours until meat is very tender. Remove meat from broth, place in casserole or ovenproof serving dish; keep warm. Sauté mushrooms in 1 tablespoon butter; stir in flour, cook 1 minute. Strain veal broth, bring to a boil, reduce to 1½ cups liquid. To this add the asparagus liquid; slowly add broth to mushrooms. Add asparagus, chopped in small pieces; simmer 5 minutes. Beat egg yolks until thickened, blend with cream; add some of hot broth to egg yolks, then combine the two. Simmer sauce over low heat, stirring with whisk, until smooth and creamy. Pour over veal in casserole. Sprinkle grated lemon rind over top. Serve with *Spätzle* or noodles. Makes 6 servings.

Kalbsfrikassee in Dillsosse. Omit asparagus and white wine from preceding recipe, add 1 tablespoon minced fresh or frozen dill, increase cream to ½ cup. If desired, 1 cup cooked or canned green peas may be added with mushrooms.

Rindsgulasch
(BEEF GOULASH)

1 pound stewing beef, cubed
2 tablespoons fat
2 or 3 onions, sliced
½ teaspoon salt
1 tablespoon paprika

2 tablespoons flour
1 1-pound can tomatoes, sieved
1 cup beef broth
½ cup sour cream

Sauté the meat in fat until browned. Add the onions, salt and paprika. Cover tightly, simmer 1 hour over lowest heat. Stir in flour, brown lightly, then add the tomatoes and beef broth. Simmer uncovered 1 hour longer. Turn off heat, stir in sour cream. Serve with egg noodles. Makes 3 servings.

*   *   *

The Germans prepare meat balls and meat patties in dozens of ways, but hamburgers as we know them are not only unknown in the city of Hamburg, they aren't to be found anywhere in Germany. You may be told in Berlin that *Bouletten* are like American hamburgers, but they are not. *Bouletten* are meat patties, of the same size and shape as our hamburgers, but instead of being all meat, the meat is mixed with egg, usually seasoned with onion or parsley or some other herb, and instead of being broiled or grilled they are fried in fat ½-inch deep.

Deutsches Beefsteak is the name given to the meat patties of Hamburg, but these, too, are made by adding bread (or crumbs) and egg to the ground meat, and are as likely to be made of a mixture of beef, veal and pork as of beef alone. Usually, too, they are served with a topping of fried onions.

The "hamburgers" of Bremen (*Bremer Beefsteak*) are made by blending mashed potatoes with ground meat. Those made in Bavaria, called *Fleischpflanzel,* are blended with bread soaked in milk, usually seasoned with marjoram and basil, and are served topped with brown gravy.

Still another name given to fried meat patties or meat balls in northern Germany in *Klopse*. But *Königsberger Klopse,* a famous dish from the city of Königsberg (now inside the Soviet Union), are meat balls simmered in stock rather than fried, served with a caper sauce.

Then there is Beefsteak Tartare, which is ground raw meat seasoned to taste at table, said to have been adapted originally from the Tartar fashion of scraping meat from a fillet to eat raw—and according to aficionados of this delicacy, the most tender Beefsteak Tartare is made by scraping rather than grinding the beef. But even Beefsteak Tartare has raw egg added to it, along with minced onions, capers, parsley and plenty of black pepper. Plain ground meat balls or patties are simply unknown!

Deutsches Beefsteak, oder Bouletten, oder Klopse
(MEAT PATTIES)

1 cup crumbled stale white bread	1 egg, beaten
¼ cup milk	1 tablespoon minced parsley (optional)
1 pound ground beef or a mixture of ground beef, veal and pork	1 small onion, minced (optional)
¾ teaspoon salt	6 tablespoons fat

Soak the bread in milk until soft. Add the meat, salt, egg, parsley and onion. Blend with fingers; form into 4 thick patties. Fry in hot fat until well browned on each side. Makes 4 servings.

Beefsteak à la Mayer. Prepare *Deutsches Beefsteak,* serve each topped with a fried egg.

Beefsteak mit Zwiebelringen (with Onions). Prepare *Deutsches Beefsteak;* serve topped with onions which have been fried in butter.

Bremer Beefsteak. Omit bread and milk, use ½ cup leftover mashed potato instead, add 2 tablespoons thick sweet or sour cream.

Fleischpflanzel. Prepare like *Deutsches Beefsteak,* but season with ½ teaspoon each basil and marjoram rather than parsley.

Beefsteaks mit Mostrichsosse (with Mustard Sauce). Prepare *Deutsches Beefsteak.* Remove patties to a platter. Pour off all but 2 tablespoons of the drippings, blend in 2 tablespoons flour and 1 tablespoon Düsseldorf mustard; simmer until mixture bubbles. Add 1 cup beef broth or water and salt to taste. When sauce is smooth and thickened, turn off heat, blend in 2 tablespoons sour cream. Serve this gravy over the patties.

Königsberger Klopse
(MEAT BALLS KÖNIGSBERG STYLE)

2 cups slightly stale large bread crumbs from hard rolls

2 pounds ground lean beef

1 pound ground pork

2 minced shallots or 1 small white onion, minced

½ teaspoon grated lemon rind

1 teaspoon lemon juice

1 tablespoon juice from jar of capers

2 anchovies, minced, plus 1 teaspoon salt (or omit anchovies and use 2 teaspoons salt)

White pepper

2 eggs, beaten

1 egg white

6 cups beef or veal stock

CAPER SAUCE

4 tablespoons butter

1 shallot, minced

4 tablespoons flour

½ cup white wine

1 egg yolk

1 tablespoon capers

Few drops lemon juice

Salt and pepper to taste

Pour water over the crumbs; when thoroughly soaked, squeeze out the water. Add soaked bread to the ground beef and pork, work with fingers to a paste. Add minced shallots or onion, lemon rind, lemon and caper juice, the minced anchovies, salt and pepper, then the beaten eggs and the egg white; work until smooth, form into 2-inch meat balls. Bring broth to a boil. While boiling rapidly, add the meat balls, taking care not to crowd the kettle or pot. Cook for 12 to 15 minutes, until meat balls come to top. Remove from broth with slotted spoon. Strain broth and save.

Keep meat balls warm while preparing the sauce. Melt butter in skillet or saucepan, add minced shallot, cook until shallot is soft. Stir in flour, cook until it bubbles. Slowly stir in 2½ to 3 cups strained broth and wine, simmer until smooth and thickened. Beat the egg yolk until thick, add some of the broth, then combine the two, cook, stirring constantly, until consistency of thick cream. Add capers and lemon juice. Taste for seasoning, add more salt if it needs it and pepper to taste. If sauce is too thick, add more broth. Add the meatballs to the sauce, keep them warm in the sauce until time to serve. Serve with *Salzkartoffeln** and *Bohnensalat**. Makes 12 servings.

Beefsteak Tartare
(RAW BEEF FILLET)

1 pound top sirloin of beef, scraped with sharp knife or ground twice
2 egg yolks
¼ cup finely minced onion
1 or 2 tablespoons capers

1 anchovy fillet, minced
¾ to 1 teaspoon salt
Freshly ground pepper
Mustard
Tabasco sauce (optional)
1 to 2 teaspoons olive oil (optional)

The most tender tartare steak is made by scraping the meat with a very sharp knife. Much easier, of course, is to have the butcher grind it for you, but it must be put through the grinder at least twice. The best quality meat must be used, and it must be served within a few hours after it is ground.

The tartare is always mixed at table. The meat is shaped in a ring with the egg yolk in the center. Around the edge of the meat are the selected seasonings: a mound of chopped onions, one of capers, another of anchovies. The pepper grinder is at the side, along with the mustard jar, the Tabasco and a cruet of olive oil. Seasonings are added according to taste. For those who are particularly fond of tartare, one pound is enough only for 2 servings.

The above recipe was given me by North German Lloyd, for this is a specialty of the line, always served with a flourish by the Chief Table Steward himself.

Geschmorte Rindsleber

(BRAISED LIVER)

1 pound beef liver, sliced ½-inch thick	1 onion, chopped
1 cup milk	2 cups beef broth
3 tablespoons flour	2 tablespoons lemon juice
½ teaspoon salt	1 to 2 tablespoons sugar
4 tablespoons oil or drippings	¼ cup sour cream

Cut the liver into strips 1-inch wide. Soak in the milk for 1 hour. Remove from milk, dredge with flour blended with salt. Sauté in the hot oil or fat until browned on all sides. Remove. Add chopped onion, cook until lightly browned; spoon these over liver. Add the beef broth, lemon juice and sugar to pan, replace liver and onions, simmer 5 to 10 minutes. Thicken if preferred with a little cornstarch (make a paste of 1 tablespoon cornstarch with a little water, then add to the sauce, simmer until clear and smooth). Turn off heat, stir in sour cream. Serve with parsley potatoes and dilled carrots. Makes 4 servings.

Geflügel und Wildgeflügel

(POULTRY AND GAME BIRDS)

Banks of chickens turning on roasting spits in public places are as common a sight in West Germany as in most other highly developed countries of the world today and at the Oktoberfest in Munich, spit-roasted chickens are consumed in the same enormous quantities as *Weisswurst* and beer. Yet, surprisingly, the Germans have very few noteworthy chicken recipes. When chicken is served, it is usually prepared in the simplest manner, roasted, or sautéed in butter, or boiled (when the broth made from it becomes as important as the chicken itself).

There are three famous German chicken recipes. One is *Küken-ragout,* which both Bremen and Berlin claim as their own, a sauced mixture of chicken, tongue, shrimp and other surprise ingredients. The other is *Backhähnchen,* chicken pieces rolled in an egg-crumb-Parmesan cheese mixture, browned in fat then baked until the outside is crisp and golden—a way of preparing chicken which one also finds in northern Italy. *Königinpastetchen* or "queen's pastries" are patty shells filled with a mixture of chicken, tongue and mushrooms in a wine sauce, not totally unlike the *Kükenragout* of northern Germany.

The *Vierländer Poularde* of Hamburg is also renowned, but it is nothing more than a very young, very tender battery-raised chicken sautéed gently in butter. I dined on one of these infant chickens in the Ratskeller of Hamburg, a dignified oak-paneled room dominated by a huge ship's model hanging from the ceiling. The atmosphere was hushed, formal and very elegant. The waiters, deftly placing food on the white-clothed tables with something of the same grace as tennis players, seemed to move across the polished dark floors with scarcely a sound. Our wine was a Moselle, a 1958 Reiler Goldlay-Gräfinstück, truly a poem captured in a bottle, golden-smooth, scintillating, beautiful, and the sommelier who poured it clearly appreciated the worth of the bottle he held in his hands. As one might expect, each dish was perfection. There was first a clear soup—always soup first in Germany, then as an entree, tongue with mushrooms in a smooth brown sauce, and following this, the chicken, with dessert to follow, a *Kirsch*-flavored compote of greengage plums, cherries, grapes and almonds.

Perhaps I had expected too much of the chicken. I tasted the sauce analytically, to guess its seasonings, and could only detect the delicacy of chicken essence and browned butter. And that is it. The chicken itself is the *Vierländer Poularde,* famed for its tenderness and flavor, raised in a region near Hamburg which specializes in battery-raised chickens, as well as top-quality ducks and geese. Yet, quite honestly, I found the flavor no better than our own top-quality broilers, all of which these days are battery-raised.

The Hamburg Ratskeller, a dining room reserved during the day for the use of senators and town fathers, fiercely guards its ancient traditions. The ship's model which hangs above the tables is a replica of the ship which belonged to the sixteenth-century pirate Störtebecker who so terrorized the coast of north Germany in his day that all the Hanseatic towns were forced to join together in defense, forming what became known as the Hanseatic League. Störtebecker finally was captured and beheaded, and my dinner companion told me that according to legend, the pirate marched headless past the twelve chained members of his crew before he collapsed and died.

Whether the poultry of Vierlande was as famous in the sixteenth century as today I do not know, but one feels, sitting in that august room, that the town fathers who over the centuries have been patronizing this "cellar" were men of superior tastes in food and wine, who would settle for nothing less than the best.

If chicken receives less attention from the Germans than from us, other birds are used more. Duck is prepared in many interesting ways, both wild and domesticated duck; goose is popular, not only at Christmastime, but throughout the year; pheasant and partridge appear frequently on German tables. One of my top favorites is Pheasant with Sauerkraut, an astonishingly delicious combination. (The recipe for this will be found in the Sauerkraut chapter.)

I have included a recipe for *Hasenpfeffer* in this chapter even though technically neither hare nor rabbit qualifies as *Wildgeflügel,* but because the meat of young rabbit is something like that of dark chicken meat, this seemed the logical place for the renowned German recipe.

Bremer Kükenragout
(BREMEN STYLE CHICKEN RAGOUT)

1 3- to 4-pound plump stewing chicken	½ pound fresh mushrooms
1 pound boned veal or lean pork, cubed, or ½ cup diced cooked tongue[1]	4 tablespoons butter
	1 tablespoon flour
	1 cup cooked green peas
	3 egg yolks
1 calf's brain or sweetbread	½ cup cream
	Toasted almonds
1 pound small shrimp, shelled and cooked	Parsley sprigs

Cook the chicken and veal or pork in salted water about 2 hours until tender (or, in a pressure cooker, 30 minutes). Remove chicken and meat; when cool, bone and dice the meat. Strain broth, chill. (This can be done ahead.)

Blanch the brain or sweetbread by cooking in acidulated water (1 tablespoon vinegar or ¼ cup white wine in 4 cups water) about 20 minutes. Cool; remove membrane, dice. Sauté the mushrooms in 2 tablespoons of the butter until lightly browned. Remove mushrooms, add flour to the butter, cook until flour bubbles. Measure 1½ cups strained chicken broth, skim off congealed chicken fat. Add broth slowly to the butter-flour mixture, beating with whisk. Separately beat egg yolks until thick; add some of the hot broth, combine the two, keeping heat as low as possible (or place over hot water). Add remaining butter 1 tablespoon at a time, beating constantly until thickened. Remove from heat; add cream. To this sauce add the chicken, veal, pork or tongue, diced brain or sweetbread, shrimp, mushrooms and peas. The classic German way is to garnish with half-moons of puff paste but toasted almonds and parsley sprigs are just as attractive for garnish and much easier. Serve with buttered rice. Makes 8 to 10 servings.

---

[1] Tongue is the traditional German ingredient in this recipe, but for American tastes, veal or pork may be preferable. If tongue is used, it should be cooked separately and added sparingly, or the tongue flavor will overpower the delicacy of the chicken and sweetbread.

Königinpastetchen

(QUEEN'S PASTRIES)

8 patty shells
3 tablespoons butter
3 tablespoons flour
1 cup chicken broth
¼ cup white wine
Salt and pepper as needed
2 egg yolks

½ teaspoon lemon juice
1½ cups diced cooked chicken or turkey
¼ to ½ cup diced cooked tongue
1 4-ounce can button mushrooms, drained

Prepare patty shells from a standard puff paste recipe, or use frozen patty shells, or buy them already made from bakery. To make filling, melt butter, stir in flour, slowly add chicken broth, then wine. Add salt and pepper as needed. Cook, stirring, until slightly thickened. Beat egg yolks, adding a little of the hot broth, then combine the two. Beat with whisk while cooking over very low heat or hot water. Remove from heat, add lemon juice then the chicken, tongue and drained mushrooms. Fill patty shells. Makes 8 servings.

Backhähnchen nach Süddeutscher Art

(YOUNG COCKERELS OR BROILERS SOUTH GERMAN STYLE)

2 small broilers, quartered
Salt
2 eggs, beaten
1 cup fine crumbs[2]
½ cup grated Parmesan cheese
¼ teaspoon powdered ginger (optional)

¾ cup lard for frying, or ½ cup vegetable shortening and ¼ cup butter
Lemon wedges or slices

---

[2] For best results, grate outside crust of hard rolls or French or Italian bread for the crumbs. This will give a much better crust than commercial crumbs.

Rub the chicken pieces with salt. Dip in eggs, then in mixture of crumbs, cheese and ginger. Chill. Heat lard or mixture of shortening and butter to 370° F. in deep heavy skillet; brown chicken pieces on all sides. (Fat may be strained and used again for frying.) Transfer chicken to roasting pan, complete baking in oven previously heated to 400° F. for 20 to 25 minutes. Serve with lemon wedges or arrange overlapped lemon slices above chicken. The lemon juice should be pressed over the chicken at table. Makes 8 servings.

Junges Huhn Nach Jäger Art
(YOUNG HEN HUNTER'S STYLE)

1 2½-pound broiler-fryer, cut up	6 shallots or scallions, minced
Salt	Lemon juice
2 tablespoons olive oil	1 tablespoon tomato paste or catsup
1 tablespoon butter	½ cup Rhine wine
¼ pound button mushrooms or Pfifferlinge	2 tablespoons brandy

Dust the cut-up chicken pieces with salt. Heat olive oil and butter in skillet until butter is melted and fat starts to sizzle. Add chicken pieces, brown quickly until crisp on all sides, about 20 minutes. Remove to platter; keep warm.

Add the mushrooms and shallots to the pan; sauté a few minutes, then add the remaining ingredients which have been blended together. Boil up, stirring to dissolve all gelatinous bits in the pan. Pour the sauce over the chicken. Serve immediately with noodles which have been tossed with butter and poppy seeds. Makes 4 servings.

Kapaun mit Champignons

(CAPON WITH MUSHROOMS)

1 young capon, 6 to 7
pounds dressed weight
Salt and pepper
½ lemon
Parsley sprigs
2 tablespoons butter,
softened

½ pound mushrooms,
sliced
1 slice bacon, diced
1 teaspoon tomato paste
or 1 tablespoon tomato
catsup
½ cup white wine

Sprinkle capon inside and out with salt and pepper. Rub skin of capon with cut side of lemon; place lemon and parsley sprigs in the cavity. Place capon breast-side-up in shallow roasting pan. Rub breast and legs with softened butter. Preheat oven to 375° F. Roast until butter melts into bottom of pan, about 15 minutes, then add sliced mushrooms and bacon to pan, continue roasting. Blend tomato paste or catsup with wine. When capon has been in oven 1 hour, start basting with wine, using a kitchen syringe. Roast until meat thermometer in leg registers 175° F., about 2 hours. Makes 6 servings.

Gebratene Gans

(ROAST GOOSE)

Roast goose is the great holiday dish throughout Germany and for most Germans, it wouldn't be Christmas without it. For those Americans of German or mid-European background (including Bohemians, Austrians and others whose ancestral roots go back to that region), there may be similar nostalgia toward goose. For most Americans, it has never taken, and I suspect it never will, for two reasons. First, there is the formidable amount of fat which exudes from the goose as it roasts, and second, even when the results are triumphant, the pickings are slim. A ten-pound goose costs considerably more than a ten-pound turkey but it makes only four good servings.

I have been told that roasting a goose is quite easy, but my own experience belies this. In fact, my first attempt to roast a goose ended in such dismal failure, the bird went into the garbage pail. The flesh was tough and dry, the gravy swam with grease. It was a long time before I dared try again.

Frozen geese are now available in many of our markets, eviscerated and nicely dressed, and at Christmastime, it is possible to get a fresh-killed goose from specialty markets on order. The labels invariably say "young goose," but even those who buy geese several times a year have told me that finding a tender, fine-textured bird is always a gamble. Unfortunately it seems that because goose is not widely popular with Americans, less care is taken in selective breeding.

If the goose is frozen when purchased, it must be completely defrosted, then every bit of the yellow fat pulled off. It should be placed breast-side-down on a rack in a deep roasting pan with 1 cup of water in the bottom of the pan. As it roasts, it should be basted from time to time with *boiling water*. This helps to keep the flesh moist and reduces the amount of grease spattering on the oven wall. A tent of aluminum foil may be placed loosely above the bird for the same purpose.

It is also important to remove fat from the pan from time to time, using a deep ladle, and having a large can handy for holding the hot grease. A three-pound Crisco or Spry can is ideal. While the fat is still warm it should be strained through a paper filter to make nice clear *Schmalz*. You will have enough to last a long time.

Preparing the goose for roasting. The bird will probably already be eviscerated and all pin feathers removed. In this respect, at least, the American goose industry is superior. Prick the skin in many places, especially around the throat and wings, so that the fat will run out. Rub lemon juice, salt and pepper over the skin and sprinkle the cavities with salt. Wings and feet should be tied close to the body, using butcher's cord.

Stuffing. Germans insert a stuffing only to flavor the goose flesh. The herb mugwort is considered very important, combined with fruit, such as apples, or a mixture of fresh or dried apples, prunes and other dried fruit.

Those Americans who feel it is not a holiday meal without bread stuffing will probably want to stuff the bird with a seasoned bread mixture. One way is to add chopped apples and chopped cooked chestnuts to seasoned bread stuffing, allowing 1 cup stuffing for each pound dressed weight, or 12 cups bread stuffing for a 12-pound goose, plus 1 cup each chopped apples and chestnuts.

Roasting. Set the oven at 325° F., allow 2½ to 3 hours roasting time for a 12-pound bird, an extra 15 to 20 minutes for each additional pound. Use a meat thermometer set at 175° F. to be sure of results; insert the thermometer in the meaty part of the leg. After the goose has been turned breast-side-up it should brown quickly. If not, raise the temperature to 400° F. during the last 15 to 20 minutes of roasting—but scoop out fat from the pan first. After removing from oven, let the goose cool on a platter for 15 to 20 minutes for easier carving.

Making the gravy. The most important thing is to get rid of all excess fat, and this is not easy. Pour out *all* pan drippings, even the brown part. Let it stand until the fat has risen to the top, then skim off as much fat as possible. Put the remaining brown part in the refrigerator or freezer so that again the fat will rise to the top. After this fat has been skimmed off, add a few ice cubes to the brown essence—the ice will gather more fat to itself. Discard the ice cubes. Use only the clarified brown essence in making the gravy.

Stock made with the goose neck and giblets can be simmered on top of the stove while the goose is roasting in the oven. Add "soup herbs" (carrot, onion and parsley). Simmer about 1 hour; strain, let cool so fat will rise to top of broth, so that this can be skimmed off. Thicken the brown essence from the pan drippings with a little flour, slowly add the strained stock, simmer until smooth. Chopped cooked giblets may be added to the gravy if desired.

Accompaniments. Some Germans insist that red cabbage and boiled potatoes are always served with roast goose. Others consider sauerkraut and potato dumplings the only proper "go-withs." Again it depends on what region of Germany you come from. Often the goose is ringed with small baked apples when served.

Gänsefett oder Schmalz
(GOOSE FAT)

Place yellow solid fat pulled from inside the goose along with clear fat accumulated during roasting in a heavy saucepan or skillet. Add any pieces of *uncooked* skin. Heat until solid fat is liquefied, but keep heat low. When fat is entirely liquefied, add a quartered onion and 1 small apple (unpeeled). Cook until onion is soft but not brown. Remove apple before it becomes mushy. Strain fat through a fine sieve.

When solid again, the *Schmalz* may be spread on dark bread just as we use butter. Sometimes *Quark* (cream cheese or solid cottage cheese, like our "farmer's cheese") is spread over the *Schmalz*. Or the goose fat may be used instead of butter with potatoes boiled in their jackets. It is also used in cooking, both for stews and as the fat in making pastries.

(Another cherished use for goose fat in German households is as a remedy for chest colds. The chest is rubbed with a generous layer of *Schmalz*, then covered with flannel. 'Tis said to be a very effective remedy.)

Vierländer Ente
(DUCK VIERLANDE STYLE)

1 small (4-pound) duck	4 tablespoons (¼ cup)
3 medium apples, chopped	fine crumbs
¼ pound (½ cup) lean	Salt and pepper
ham, chopped	Lemon juice
1 shallot, minced, or 2	1 cup chicken broth or
tablespoons minced	clear bouillon
onion	¼ cup sour cream
3 tablespoons butter	

Remove all obvious fat from cavity and under skin of duck. Prick skin around neck and over breast so remaining fat will run out.

Sauté the apples, ham, and shallot or onion in butter briefly. Combine with crumbs, add salt and pepper to taste; stuff the breast cavity with this mixture. Truss in the usual way. Brush outside of duck with mixture of salt, pepper and lemon juice. Roast on rack in oven set at 350° F., or on rotisserie spit. After duck has started to brown, baste with some of the chicken broth. When duck is tender (leg will move easily), remove from oven or rotisserie. Pour off pan drippings. Discard all fat, using only the brown essence. Combine this with remaining broth or bouillon and sour cream, heat slowly until well blended without allowing mixture to boil. Serve as unthickened sauce over the duck. Makes 2 to 4 servings.

Ente Potrafka

(DUCK POLISH STYLE)

1 4-pound duck	1 duck liver, ground or
4 cups salted water or	minced
chicken broth	1 egg, beaten
1 onion	½ cup fine crumbs
2 ounces dried imported	1 tablespoon butter
mushrooms (Steinpilze)	2 tablespoons flour
½ pound ground lean	or 1 tablespoon
pork	cornstarch
	1 cup sour cream

Parboil duck in water or broth with onion until tender, about 1 hour. (Defrost frozen duck before cooking.) When cool, remove skin and fat, cut up duck meat. Strain the broth, chill, remove all fat. (This can be done preceding day.)

Soak the dried mushrooms in the strained broth overnight, then heat to boiling, cook 10 minutes or until tender. Remove with slotted spoon; dice 2 of them. Save broth.

Make meat balls of the pork, duck liver, diced mushrooms, egg and bread crumbs. Fry in butter until browned on all sides. Set aside.

Blend flour or cornstarch with cream, stir in 2 cups of the strained broth. Add the diced duck meat, the remaining mushrooms and the meat balls. Heat slowly. Do not allow to boil. Serve in a *Nudeln mit Kümmelkäse* (Caraway Cheese Noodle Ring)*. Makes 4 to 6 servings.

Gebratene Rebhühner
(ROAST PARTRIDGE)

2 aged partridges, dressed	1 teaspoon currant jelly
Salt	1 teaspoon arrowroot or
2 strips bacon	cornstarch (optional)
6 tablespoons butter	Grated rind of 1 lemon
¾ cup beef broth	
½ cup heavy sweet cream or sour cream	

Sprinkle the birds with salt inside and out. Wrap each with a strip of bacon. Brown butter in a heavy casserole, add the birds, place in 350° F. oven uncovered. Baste twice with the butter, using a kitchen syringe. After ½ hour, add the beef broth blended with the cream, and the jelly. Continue baking until birds are tender, about 20 minutes longer. If a thickened sauce is preferred, blend in arrowroot or cornstarch 5 minutes before removing from oven. Sprinkle grated lemon rind over top. Makes 2 servings.

Note: Cornish hens may be prepared the same way.

Hasenpfeffer has always been one of those dishes I regarded with awe, and so when I was in Germany, I looked forward to enjoying this delicacy. I had made it myself, from recipes in American books, and remembered it as a lovely dish. But tasting real hare in Germany was a shock. Hare is not the same as rabbit; it is game meat, and the dish I had was very gamy, indeed. Rabbit, especially rabbit raised domestically, is as delicate in flavor as chicken. Therefore I personally recommend domestic rabbit as the best to use in the following recipe—unless you really like the distinctly gamy taste of hare.

Hasenpfeffer

(HARE OR RABBIT IN PEPPER SAUCE)

1 hare or rabbit, cut up	1 tablespoon butter
1½ cups red wine	1 small onion, chopped
1 tablespoon lemon juice	¼ teaspoon thyme
1 medium onion, sliced	¼ teaspoon marjoram
3 tablespoons flour	1 celery stalk, minced
1 teaspoon salt	8 to 10 peppercorns
3 or 4 slices bacon, diced	Grated lemon rind

Place the hare or rabbit in a bowl, add red wine, lemon juice and onion. Marinate 24 hours. Remove pieces of hare or rabbit, saving marinade; pat pieces dry, dust with flour and salt. Place bacon and butter in heavy pot or top-of-stove casserole, sauté bacon until crisp, remove. Brown the pieces of rabbit or hare in the fat until crisp. Add the chopped onion after the pieces have been turned once. Add herbs, celery, peppercorns and the strained marinade. Cover tightly, simmer until meat is tender. If a thickened sauce is preferred, blend together 1 tablespoon butter and 1 tablespoon flour, form a small ball of it and add to liquid, simmer until thickened. Serve from the casserole with *Spätzle** or noodles. Makes 4 servings.

Spezialitäten

(REGIONAL SPECIALTIES)

There are certain uniquely German dishes which are difficult to classify. Silesian Heaven, for example, is a stew in the narrowest sense, yet so unusual a stew it belongs by itself. *Himmel und Erde* might be classed as a vegetable dish, yet if served as a vegetable, most Americans wouldn't know what to make of it. The same is true of *Birnen, Bohnen und Speck,* the north German dish in which pears, green beans and bacon are cooked together.

Onion Pie (*Zwiebelkuchen*), *Sauerkrautkuchen,* and the *Beeren-pie* of Schleswig-Holstein are also astonishingly different (and astonishingly good) snack foods, neither sweet pastries as we know them, nor entrees, nor appetizers.

Labskaus is usually described as the "sailor's hash" of Hamburg. It is a dish, quite frankly, that few Americans will take to. A strange combination of pickled pork, anchovies and dill pickles or pickled beets, it might be described as a very distant cousin of New England's corned beef hash.

The basic recipe for *Spätzle* might have been given in the chapter on Vegetables, Salads and Other Accompaniments, or in the Soups chapter, but after much deliberation I decided to include it here because it is paste quite different from egg noodles or the Italian pastas.

Birnen, Bohnen und Speck
(PEARS, BEANS AND BACON)

6 ripe pears, peeled and sliced	1 teaspoon salt
½ cup water	6 slices bacon
Thin sliver of lemon peel	¼ cup sugar
1 pound green beans, broken	2 tablespoons vinegar
	1 teaspoon lemon juice

Place the pear slices in a saucepan with water and lemon peel, bring to a boil, lower heat, simmer 15 minutes. Add the beans and salt, continue cooking while frying bacon in a skillet. When bacon is crisp, remove to paper towel to drain. Add sugar, vinegar and lemon juice to the bacon fat. Cook 3 minutes. Pour this sauce over pears and beans, continue cooking until tender. Add crumbled bacon to the beans. Makes 6 servings.

This specialty of Westphalia is much like the *Birnen, Bohnen und Speck* of Schleswig-Holstein, a mixture of vegetables, fruit and bacon in a sweet-sour sauce.

Blindes Huhn
("BLIND HEN")

4 large carrots, scraped and cubed	2 or 3 apples, peeled and sliced
½ pound green beans, broken in pieces	1 tablespoon sugar
3 tablespoons bacon	2 tablespoons vinegar
1 or 2 onions, sliced	Salt to taste

Cook the carrots and the beans in salted water until almost tender. Drain. Sauté the bacon until crisp; remove from pan. Cook the onions in the bacon fat until soft but not brown; add the apples, the sugar and vinegar, and the partially cooked carrots and beans. Replace crumbled drained bacon and salt to taste. Cook covered until vegetables are tender. Makes 6 servings.

Schlesisches Himmelreich
(SILESIAN HEAVEN)

1 **pound mixed dried fruit (pitted prunes, apples and pears)**	2 **tablespoons butter**
	2 **tablespoons cornstarch or arrowroot**
2 **cups water**	**Pinch of cloves**
1 **pound diced pork from shoulder, or 4 thick pork chops**	**Sugar to taste**
	Gekochte Kartoffelklösse
Salt	**(Cooked Potato Dumplings)***

Soak the dried fruit in water as directed on package; or simmer gently in water without previous soaking until soft. Dust the pork with salt; sauté the pork in the butter until lightly browned on all sides; remove to casserole. Drain fruit, saving liquid. Place fruit around meat. Add cornstarch or arrowroot to the butter, then stir in liquid from the fruit, cook until thickened. Season with cloves, sugar to taste and a pinch of salt. Pour sauce over meat and fruit. Cook tightly covered on top of stove at lowest heat for 20 minutes. Serve with *Gekochte Kartoffelklösse*. Makes 4 servings.

Himmel und Erde
("HEAVEN AND EARTH," A RHINELAND SPECIALTY)

4 **large potatoes, peeled and cubed**	**Salt and sugar to taste**
	Butter
3 **tart apples, peeled, cored and quartered**	**Blood sausage (optional)**

Cook the potatoes in salted water for 15 minutes; drain off most of water, add apples; cook until tender. Mash, season with salt, sugar and butter. The blood sausage is sliced, fried in a little fat and served over the potato-apple mixture. Makes 4 servings.

Note: Leftover *Himmel und Erde* can be made into delicious potato cakes. Form into patties with a spoon, shape between palms of hands, fry in butter.

With Onions. Omit blood sausage, fry onions separately in butter or *Schmalz,* serve as a topping for the potato-apple purée.

With Bacon. Fry bacon until crisp; serve *Himmel und Erde* topped with crisp bacon and a little of the bacon drippings.

*   *   *

Pichelsteiner is both a dish and a festival, a kind of community picnic where every family contributes something to the big kettle of stew. The custom goes back to the eighteenth century when the citizens of the village of Schönberg decided it was a fine day for an outing, and to celebrate St. Benno's Day, June 16, they made a procession up to the top of Buchelstein Hill. (The original name of the stew was Buchelsteiner, but Pichelsteiner is what it became.) Because there was no inn nearby, they brought along a big black pot in which to cook their food, and the participants all added whatever they had: chickens, pork, veal, potatoes, turnips, onions, parsley and so on. The resulting stew was so delicious, the outing became a regular event, held each year in June.

In the centuries since, many different versions of Pichelsteiner have turned up, and now many Bavarian restaurants serve their own "authentic" versions. Sometimes heavy cream is poured over the stew just before serving, to give the sauce special richness.

Pichelsteiner

(BAVARIAN PICNIC STEW)

Beef marrow
(about 1 cup)

2 pounds meat (beef,
pork, lamb or a
combination), cut in
large pieces

1 small head savoy
cabbage, cut in wedges
(about 3 cups)

1 pound white turnips,
peeled and diced

½ pound green beans,
cut

1 celeriac (celery root),
sliced

2 potatoes, peeled and
diced

1 large onion, chopped

1 or 2 tablespoons
parsley, chopped

Salt

Pepper

Paprika

2 tablespoons butter

2 cups beef broth or
water

Buy beef marrow bones, extract marrow from center of bones. Cover bottom of heavy pot or Dutch oven with beef marrow. Over this place alternate layers of meat and vegetables, sprinkling each layer with salt, pepper and paprika. Place marrow over the top. Dot with butter. Add broth or water. Cover tightly, cook over lowest heat 2 hours or until meat is very tender. Shake pan occasionally to prevent meat sticking to bottom. Makes 6 to 8 servings.

Note: Other vegetables sometimes added to a *Pichelsteiner* include cauliflower, carrots and Brussels sprouts. But when possible always use celeriac (celery root) rather than celery stalks.

Sachsenhäuser Topf
(STEW OF SACHSENHAUSEN)

1 pound stewing beef, cubed

½ pound lean pork, cubed

½ pound stewing veal, cubed

2 tablespoons fat

1 onion, chopped

1 clove garlic, chopped (optional)

1 tomato, chopped

3 potatoes, peeled and diced

3 cups water or dry white wine or cider

2 teaspoons salt

1 4-ounce can mushroom bits and pieces

1 cup fresh or frozen peas or green beans

2 tablespoons flour

1 teaspoon gravy coloring

2 tablespoons minced parsley

Brown the meat in the fat; transfer to casserole or Dutch oven, add onion and garlic to fat, cook until soft. Add tomato and potatoes, cook 1 minute. Add water, wine or cider (if cider is used, add 1 teaspoon lemon juice), and salt. Pour this over meat, cover tightly. Cook at low heat until meat is tender, 2½ to 3 hours. Add mushrooms and peas or beans during last ½ hour. Make a thin paste of flour and broth from the stew, add gravy coloring to this, stir into the stew and simmer 5 minutes. Add minced parsley just before serving. Makes 6 servings.

Note: This can also be made with leftover meat, using any combination in the refrigerator. Canned beef gravy may be used for part of the liquid, adding only 1½ cups water. Cook 1 hour instead of 3.

Gaisburger Marsch
(SPECIAL STEW OF STUTTGART)

1 pound stewing beef,
    cut in slivers
2 tablespoons fat
3 or 4 potatoes, peeled,
    cut in small pieces
2 cups beef stock

1 bay leaf
1 teaspoon vinegar
1 recipe Spätzle*
2 large onions, fried
    separately in pork fat

Sauté the beef in fat until well browned. Add the potatoes, cook 5 minutes, turning often. Add the stock, bay leaf and vinegar. Reduce heat, simmer covered ½ hour or until meat and potatoes are tender. Adjust seasonings, add salt and pepper if needed. Add cooked *Spätzle* during last 5 minutes. Serve topped with fried onions. Makes 6 servings.

* * *

In the city of Münster there is a restaurant-tavern so renowned that people travel from all over West Germany to visit it. Pinkus Müller, the owner, was a well-known popular singer before he decided to retire from the stage and open his own tavern, a warm, friendly gathering place where the original thick beams of the centuries-old building still line the ceiling and some of the booths are fashioned from old intricately carved peasant bedsteads. Münster is a university city, and students throng to Pinkus Müller's, many of them keeping their own beer mugs on the ledges between visits. As the evenings progress, someone is certain to start singing—sometimes the genial cherubic-faced proprietor himself. Pinkus Müller prepares many of the restaurant dishes, and his wife prepares others, for both are enthusiastic cooks. The following recipe for *Pfefferpotthast,* a Westphalian specialty, is one he gave me.

Pfefferpotthast
(PEPPERPOT STEW)

2 pounds short ribs of beef
2 tablespoons pork fat
4 to 6 onions, sliced
1 or 2 bay leaves
4 or 5 whole cloves
½ cup stale rye or pumpernickel bread crumbs

4 to 6 cups water
Salt
Pinch of cayenne
Freshly ground black pepper (lots of it)
Thin slivers of lemon peel
1 tablespoon capers
1 tablespoon flour thinned in 3 tablespoons water

The thing that distinguishes this Westphalian beef stew is the large amount of pepper used. The sauce should be very hot—inducing a thirst for the local *Schnaps* (*Korn*) and Dortmund beer.

Have the ribs cut in 2-inch lengths by the butcher. Sauté in pork fat until nicely browned. Add onions, cook until yellow and soft. Add remaining ingredients. Simmer covered 2 hours. Add flour during last 10 minutes. Serve accompanied by mashed potatoes, pickled beets, dill pickles and pearl onions. Makes 4 servings.

Berliner Eintopf
(BERLIN STEW)

2 to 3 cups cooked leftover meat (beef, veal or pork, or a combination), cut in cubes
2 tablespoons butter or fat
1 large onion, sliced
3 cups bouillon
3 or 4 potatoes, finely diced
½ pound green beans, broken in pieces

1 carrot, diced
3 or 4 wedges of cabbage
1 tablespoon tomato catsup
Salt and pepper to taste
1 teaspoon Düsseldorf mustard
1 slice stale (white or pumpernickel) bread, grated
Minced parsley

Place meat in pot, brown lightly in butter or fat. Add onion, cook until lightly browned. Add bouillon, vegetables, catsup, seasonings and mustard. Cover, simmer until vegetables are cooked, 30 to 45 minutes. Add bread crumbs during last 10 minutes, cook until sauce is thickened. Serve topped with parsley. Makes 6 servings.

Kalbsbrägen
(BREADED CALF'S BRAINS)

2 calf's brains	Fat for frying
3 cups water	Parsley sprigs
2 tablespoons lemon juice	Lemon slices
Salt	Remouladensosse* or tartar
¼ cup all-purpose flour	sauce (optional)
1 egg, beaten	
1 cup crushed cracker crumbs	

Soak the brains for 1 hour in cold water to which a tablespoon of lemon juice has been added. (If brains are frozen when purchased, defrost completely before using.) Remove from water, drain, place in fresh water with more lemon juice and 1 teaspoon salt. Bring to a boil, lower heat, cook at gentle simmer for 20 minutes. Turn off heat, leave brains in water until cool, then with sharp knife cut each brain in 3 slices. Dip each slice in flour blended with a little salt, then in egg, then in crumbs. Fry in hot fat ½-inch deep until golden on each side. Add parsley sprigs to fat, fry until crisp (about 15 seconds). Garnish each serving with the fried parsley and lemon slices. Pass *Remouladensosse* or tartar sauce if desired. Makes 2 servings.

Nieren Europa Art
(KIDNEYS AS PREPARED ON M.S. *Europa*)

2 veal kidneys, sliced	Salt and pepper to taste
4 tablespoons butter	¼ pound mushrooms,
1 tablespoon flour	sliced
½ cup beef broth or stock	Pineapple wedges
¼ cup medium sherry	Hot cooked rice
¼ cup sour or heavy	
sweet cream	

Sauté the sliced kidney in 2 tablespoons of the butter over moderate heat just until delicately browned, about 5 minutes. Stir in flour, cook a few seconds, then add the beef broth or stock and sherry. Cook 1 minute, add the cream. Season to taste with salt and pepper. Meantime in remaining 2 tablespoons butter, sauté the mushrooms and pineapple until lightly browned. Serve the kidneys in the sauce over rice with the sautéed mushrooms and pineapple as garnish. Makes 4 servings.

Labskaus

This sailor's hash of Hamburg is faintly like our corned beef hash —with an egg on top, too.

1½ pounds pickled pork,	2 anchovy fillets, minced
or 1 10-ounce can of	(optional)
corned beef	1 small jar or can pickled
6 medium potatoes	beets, or 1 large dill
4 tablespoons fat from fat	pickle, chopped (optional)
pork	4 to 6 fried eggs
1 large onion, chopped	
1 large herring, boned and	
chopped, or 1 jar	
pickled herring, drained	
and chopped	

Pickled or salted lean pork is the authentic meat for this hash, but if not available, corned beef may be used instead. The pickled pork should be cooked in water to cover until tender, cooled, then chopped and put through the food grinder. If canned corned beef is used, chop fine with knife. Boil potatoes in their jackets in *unsalted* water until tender; drain, peel, mash. Chop up fat pork, draw out fat in skillet, sauté the onion in this fat until yellow. Combine onion with the chopped or ground meat, the mashed potato, chopped herring, anchovy and ½ cup of the beets or pickles chopped. Mix together in a fine hash. Return mixture to pan in which onions were sautéed, cook until heated through. Top each serving with fried egg. Makes 4 to 6 servings of hash.

Note: Instead of adding chopped dill pickle or pickled beets to the hash, both may be served on the side as garnish. Most Americans would prefer it this way.

While this is called a breakfast dish, in reality the German first breakfast is the traditional continental one of coffee, rolls and jam, and the following hearty omelet is filling enough to be served as a supper dish.

Bauernfrühstück
(FARMER'S BREAKFAST)

6 slices bacon	6 eggs, beaten
1 tablespoon butter	½ teaspoon salt
1 medium onion, thinly	Pepper
sliced or chopped	2 to 3 tablespoons milk
4 medium potatoes, cooked	
and finely diced	

Cook bacon until crisp in a 10-inch heavy skillet. Remove, drain on paper; when cool crumble into bits. Pour off most of bacon fat from skillet, add butter, cook the sliced or chopped onion until soft. Add the potatoes, brown lightly.

Beat the eggs just until blended, add salt, pepper, milk and the crumbled bacon. Pour this over onion-potato mixture. Lift up and turn over eggs with spatula until eggs are firm. Serve at once with buttered pumpernickel and a cucumber or green bean salad. Makes 4 servings.

Linsen auf Schwäbische Art
(LENTILS SWABIAN STYLE)

3 medium onions, sliced	4 cups water
3 slices bacon, diced	Salt to taste
1 pound lentils	4 frankfurters, thickly
2 carrots, peeled and finely	sliced
diced	2 cups cooked Spätzle*
1 cup diced ham	(½ recipe)
2 cups cooked leftover	1 tablespoon minced
pork, venison, duck or	parsley
beef, cut in pieces	Vinegar, passed in cruet

Sauté the onions and bacon until onions are soft. Add the washed lentils, carrots, ham and cooked leftover meat. Cover with water and 2 teaspoons salt. Cook covered 1½ hours, adding more water as needed. When lentils are tender, adjust seasoning, adding more salt if needed, add frankfurters and *Spätzle*. Simmer 5 minutes longer. Serve sprinkled with parsley. Pass the vinegar; a dash of vinegar should be added to each serving. Makes 6 to 8 servings.

Zwiebelkuchen
(ONION PIE)

PASTRY

2 cups sifted all-purpose	1 medium egg, beaten
flour	1 tablespoon cream
1 teaspoon baking powder	(optional)
½ teaspoon salt	1 unbeaten egg white
¾ cup butter	

FILLING

2 cups chopped onions (4 large)	1 teaspoon caraway seeds
2 slices bacon, diced	½ tablespoon flour
2 tablespoons butter	½ cup heavy cream
¼ teaspoon salt	2 medium eggs, beaten

Pastry. Combine flour, baking powder and salt. Chop in the butter and work with fingers until mealy. Add the egg, blend until consistency of pie dough. Add cream if dough is not sufficiently moist. Work lightly, pat into bottom and sides of 9-inch round layer-cake pan. Brush egg white over bottom crust (this prevents crust becoming soggy).

Filling. Cook the onions and bacon in butter until very soft. Add salt and caraway seeds. Stir in flour, then slowly add cream. Remove from heat. Add a little of mixture to beaten eggs, then combine the two. Spoon into pastry-lined cake pan. Bake in oven preheated to 375° F. until pastry is crisp and golden and filling is firm. Serve as a snack with white wine. Serve hot from the oven. Makes 8 to 10 servings.

Note: In some regions, *Zwiebelkuchen* is made with a yeast-raised dough, but in Stuttgart and the Palatinate it is more often prepared in a pastry crust. Traditionally it is always served with new wine (and the Palatinate is one of the chief wine-producing districts).

Sometimes bacon is omitted and a mixture of ¼ cup sour cream and 1 beaten egg is poured over the sliced onions before baking, which forms a kind of custard.

Sauerkrautpastete oder Sauerkrautkuchen
(SAUERKRAUT PIE)

Same pastry as for Onion
Pie*
½ pound bacon, diced, or
8 frankfurters, sliced
1 small onion, chopped
1½ pounds well-drained
sauerkraut

1 cup light cream or milk
3 tablespoons tomato catsup
1 teaspoon paprika
Pinch of salt

Line a 9-inch round baking dish or cake pan with two-thirds of the dough pressed to fit. Cook bacon until it begins to brown, add onion, cook until soft, then add well-drained sauerkraut, simmer covered 20 minutes. (If frankfurters are used, sauté onion in 1 tablespoon fat, then add sliced frankfurters.) Place mixture in the pastry. Combine cream, catsup, paprika and salt; pour over sauerkraut. Roll out remaining dough, cut in strips, lay over top. Bake in oven preheated to 400° F. until crust is golden and flaky, about 40 minutes. Makes 6 servings.

Note: Like *Zwiebelkuchen,* this is sometimes made with a yeast dough (similar to pizza dough) instead of pastry. In this case the sauerkraut is placed over the dough but the cream mixture is not added until halfway through the baking period.

* * *

I was surprised to learn that in Hamburg and the nearby province of Schleswig-Holstein, the word "pie" is frequently used, spelled and pronounced exactly the same as in English. A German friend proofreading my manuscript insisted on changing the spelling of the following recipe name to *Beerenpastete,* yet the woman from Holstein who gave me the recipe while I was in Hamburg was equally insistent that the spelling of the last syllable should be "pie."

Fischpie is also sometimes used as the name of the delectable mixture of halibut, sole and shrimp under pastry which is a Hamburg specialty, though I have also seen this spelled *Fischpastete*.

Hamburg is just across the North Sea from Scotland and over the centuries there has been continuous intercourse between the two countries except for the interruption of wars. I suppose it's not really odd that certain English words have crept into local German usage.

Yet I'm sure there's no pie in Scotland to match the one that follows. When it was first described to me, I thought the combination sounded impossible. Instead, it proved to be a delicious surprise.

Beerenpie
(HOLSTEIN PASTRY OF BACON AND FRUIT)

PASTRY

2 cups sifted all-purpose flour	¾ cup butter
½ teaspoon baking powder	1 egg, beaten
1 tablespoon sugar	2 tablespoons milk or cream
½ teaspoon salt	
1 teaspoon grated lemon rind	

Combine flour, baking powder, sugar, salt and lemon rind, mix well. Chop in the butter to very fine particles. Add egg and milk or cream, blend to a dough. Divide into 2 parts, one part twice as large as the other. Press out the largest portion to fit into 9-inch round baking dish or cake pan. Roll out remaining portion and cut into lattice strips to lay over top.

FILLING

¼ pound Canadian style
bacon, or ½ pound
sliced regular bacon,
partially cooked

3 cups mixed fresh fruit,
such as berries, pears,
apples or stoned blue
plums[1]

Sugar to taste
1 teaspoon lemon juice

Place the partially cooked bacon in layers with the fruit. If dried
fruit is used, soak or cook in advance according to package directions, spoon with part of liquid over bacon in crust. Sprinkle a
little sugar over the fruit, 4 tablespoons altogether, and lemon juice.
If fresh fruit is used, peel, core or pit and slice. Use ½ cup sugar if
desired. When all of filling has been added, lay top crust over pie.
Bake in oven preheated to 400° F. for 40 minutes until crust is
golden and crisp. Serve as a luncheon or supper entree. Makes 4 to
6 servings.

Kohlrouladen[2]
(STUFFED CABBAGE)

8 large cabbage leaves
1 cup stale white bread
crumbs, soaked
1 pound meat loaf mixture
1 small onion, minced
1 tablespoon minced
parsley
¾ teaspoon salt

½ teaspoon marjoram
(optional)
Butter
1 cup beef stock or
seasoned tomato juice
¼ cup sour cream
(optional)

Cook the cabbage leaves 3 minutes in rapidly boiling salted water;
drain. (They should be limp enough to roll but not cooked through.)
Cover the crumbs with water, squeeze out water. Mix crumbs with

---

[1] This was tested with pears and blueberries and was quite delicious.
[2] This is also called *Gefüllter Krautkopf*.

the meat, onion, parsley, salt and marjoram, blending well. Divide into 8 portions, place one portion in each cabbage leaf. Roll up the leaves, folding over edges. Place with overlapped side down in buttered 8 × 8-inch baking pan or dish. Place dots of butter over top. Add half the stock or tomato juice. Bake in oven set at 350° F. for 1 hour. After first half hour, add remaining stock or tomato juice blended with sour cream. Makes 8 cabbage rolls, enough for 4 servings.

Spätzle

(SWABIAN NOODLES)

These are called "noodles" for want of a better name, but actually they are more like Italian pastas in consistency, of about the same thickness as macaroni dough, and should be "al dente." The same dough can be cut into many shapes or sizes. Sometimes it is made thinner and forced through the holes of a colander directly into boiling water.

2½ cups sifted all-purpose flour	2 eggs, beaten
½ teaspoon salt	½ cup water (more or less)

Combine flour and salt in mixing bowl, make a well in the center, add eggs and ¼ cup water, beat until a stiff dough forms, adding a little more water at a time until of the right consistency—thick, firm, coming away easily from the sides of the bowl. Knead until smooth. Let stand in bowl 30 minutes. Dampen pastry board with water, place dough on it, flour the rolling pin slightly and roll out to ⅛-inch thickness or a little thinner. Heat a kettle of salted water to boiling. With a sharp knife, cut off very thin slivers of the dough, transfer to a plate as it is cut, and push directly into rapidly boiling water. Do not crowd kettle. *Spätzle* will rise to surface when cooked, in about 5 minutes. Remove with slotted spoon, drain in colander. Add more slivers of dough to the boiling water, continuing until all is cooked. Recipe makes 4 cups, enough for 4 servings as a vegetable, 12 servings if added to soup.

Spätzle mit Spinat (with Spinach). When making *Spätzle* dough, reduce amount of water to ¼ cup, add 1 cup chopped raw spinach to the dough. Continue as in basic recipe.

Allgäuer Schinkenspätzle (Ham Spätzle in style of the Allgäu). Work into basic *Spätzle* dough 1 cup minced cooked ham, prepare as in basic recipe, but roll out as thin as possible. When cooked, toss with butter and shredded Swiss cheese.

Stuttgarter Spätzle. Prepare *Spätzle* as in basic recipe; when cooked, toss with 2 tablespoons butter and 1 beaten egg until well blended. A little minced parsley may be added, too, if desired.

Spätzle mit Kraut. Combine quantities hot *Spätzle* and cooked Swabian style sauerkraut or *Weinkraut.*

Pilz-Spätzle (Mushroom Spätzle). Toss cooked *Spätzle* with mushrooms cooked in butter. The little brown mushrooms called Pfifferlinge (available imported from Germany in certain food specialty markets) are especially delicious. These grow in the Black Forest.

Käsespätzle (Cheese Spätzle). Sauté sliced onion in butter until soft and golden. Arrange layers of *Spätzle,* onion and shredded Swiss cheese in a buttered casserole, dotting each cheese layer with bits of butter. Bake in a moderate-to-hot oven until cheese is melted (about 30 minutes at 375° F.).

Maultaschen

(SWABIAN RAVIOLI)

1 recipe Spätzle dough*

Prepare *Spätzle* dough, let stand 30 minutes while preparing filling. Roll out on dampened board as thin as possible, then cut into 6-inch squares.

FILLING

¾ **pound lean pork, ground**	2 **slices stale white bread, soaked in water**
1 **tablespoon butter**	1 **egg**
2 **to 3 tablespoons grated onion**	1 **teaspoon salt**
1 **pound fresh raw spinach, cooked and chopped, or**	**Dash of pepper**
½ **package frozen chopped cooked spinach**	**Dash of nutmeg**

Sauté the pork in butter until it loses pink color; add grated onion. Add this to the cooked spinach. Squeeze out water from bread; add soft bread to pork-spinach mixture. Work in egg, salt, pepper and nutmeg. Blend well.

Place a heaping teaspoonful of the filling in each pastry square; fold over, sealing the edges. Drop 5 or 6 at a time into a kettle of rapidly boiling salted water. Cook until they rise to the top, about 10 minutes. Remove with slotted spoon; drain. Makes about 12, enough for 4 servings.

Maultaschensuppe. Prepare *Maultaschen* as in basic recipe, but cut 4-inch squares of dough; serve in clear beef or chicken broth. Makes enough for 8 servings of soup.

Maultaschen mit Tomatensosse. Prepare *Maultaschen* as in basic recipe, serve as an entree with tomato sauce. This makes them very much like Italian ravioli.

Maultaschenomelett. Add already cooked or leftover soup *Maultaschen* to beaten eggs for an omelet. This makes a very filling luncheon or supper dish.

Maultaschen mit Zwiebelsosse. Sauté sliced onions in butter until lightly browned; add already cooked or leftover *Maultaschen*, continue cooking until *Maultaschen* are heated through.

Spätzle mit Schinken
(SWABIAN NOODLES WITH HAM)

1 recipe Spätzle*	1 medium onion, sliced
6 to 8 thin slices	4 tablespoons butter
Westphalian ham[3]	Bread crumbs moistened
½ pound mushrooms	with butter

Arrange the *Spätzle* in layers with the ham slices and the mushrooms and onion sautéed in butter. Spread crumbs over top; place under broiler or in hot oven until crumbs are nicely browned. Makes 4 servings.

---

[3] Prosciutto ham slices may be used instead of Westphalian—the two are somewhat similar. Even better than regular mushrooms for this dish are the little brown *Pfifferlinge* mushrooms.

Sauerkraut und
Sauerkraut Töpfe

(SAUERKRAUT AND SAUERKRAUT ENTREES)

After my recent gastronomic tour of West Germany, I concluded that one cannot dismiss sauerkraut simply as a vegetable. It is part of the German way of life.

Yet until the Mongol (or Tartar) hordes swept into Eastern Europe in the thirteenth century, sauerkraut was unknown in Germany. According to legend, at least, it was the Chinese who invented the dish, during the building of the Great Wall when the coolies were fed from barrels of cabbage preserved in sour rice wine. Salt was too precious to use then; wine (or vinegar) was cheaper. The Mongols learned about the sour cabbage when they conquered China, and brought it with them to Hungary. From Hungary it traveled to Austria, and from Austria to Germany. Which just goes to show how history plays strange tricks on people's food habits.

The ways of preparing sauerkraut in Germany are many. There are not only regional differences, but differences in personal preference, too. Some like it cooked long and slowly until very soft; others like it quite sour and crunchy. The liquid in which it simmers may be wine, beer, pineapple juice, beef bouillon—or just plain water. Caraway seeds or juniper berries are popular seasonings. Some insist a little grated raw potato should be added to thicken the liquid slightly; others prefer it thickened with flour, still others never thicken it at all.

Every region has at least one favorite sauerkraut dish. Frankfurt has two: *Kasseler Rippchen* (smoked pork ribs), and the *Frankfurterplatte* which includes not only the sausage which bears the city's name, but a selection of other pork products, too. In Berlin it's *Eisbein*—the pickled shin of pork, glistening with white fat, accompanied by *Erbsenpüree* (yellow split peas) and mashed potatoes as well as sauerkraut. Westphalia rates *Eisbein* as a top favorite, too, in fact a stained glass window in a Westphalian church pictures Christ and his disciples dining on *Eisbein,* sauerkraut and *Erbsenpüree* at the Last Supper.

I've never tasted *Snuten und Poten,* and I have an uneasy feeling that if it were served to me I would not be wildly enthusiastic, but to the people of north Germany, this selection of pig's snout and trotters with sauerkraut is a dish to arouse nostalgic memories. Sauerkraut has been known to go into pastry (see *Sauerkrautkuchen*), it is popular raw as a salad to serve with fish, and it sometimes becomes a stuffing for goose, along with chopped apples. Strangely, I have not found any German recipe for sauerkraut soup, which surprised me because the Poles make a delectable soup with sauerkraut. Perhaps one needs to look for this in the regions of East Germany bordering Poland.

My three favorites among the German sauerkraut dishes are *Ananaskraut* (made with crushed pineapple and pineapple juice), the Swabian style of cooking sauerkraut with apples, onion and white wine, and pheasant with *Weinkraut* (or *Champagnerkraut* as it is sometimes listed on menus), a most surprisingly wonderful dish.

I learned an important cooking secret from one German cook; always first rinse the sauerkraut with warm water, drain it well, then place the drained kraut with butter (or other fat) in a tightly covered heavy saucepan or casserole and simmer it gently for half an hour before adding liquid. This gives the sauerkraut a delicacy of flavor and makes it an entirely different dish from plain boiled kraut.

"Kraut," as I have already observed, does not mean sauerkraut, it means cabbage and the visitor to West Germany should always remember this. But then sometimes it *does* mean sauerkraut, as in *Weinkraut,* which is sauerkraut cooked in white wine; on the other hand, *Champagnerkraut* may mean either white cabbage cooked in wine, or sauerkraut cooked in wine, and how is one to know which? It's a good question!

It is not difficult to make your own sauerkraut, if you have a stone crock of suitable size and a cool (but not freezing) back porch or cellar where the cabbage can be left to ferment for three weeks. I made sauerkraut myself one year while living on a farm in Virginia; in fact, I made sauerkraut both from red cabbage and white cabbage, a bit of enterprise which as far as I know the Germans have not gone in for. My red cabbage sauerkraut had one great disadvantage: when it was cooked it turned to a funereal grayish-purple color! But the red sauerkraut *juice* remained a vivid scarlet red and proved to be a most wonderful antidote for hangovers.

In those days I knew only half a dozen ways to prepare sauerkraut, mostly dishes of the Austro-Hungarian school. Had I then had the know-how of German cooks at my command, we might have had sauerkraut a different way every night for a month.

Unfortunately many of the sauerkraut dishes which one runs into in Germany cannot be duplicated here because the meats are not available. *Pökelfleisch* is the cut of pork we call picnic butt but it has been pickled to give it bright red color and a flavor decidedly different from any meat in our markets. These and other cuts are often cooked right with the sauerkraut and naturally give the kraut their own distinct flavor.

Sauerkraut
(HOW TO MAKE YOUR OWN)

Shred cabbage very thin. Place in layers in a stone crock, sprinkling coarse salt (such as kosher salt or sea salt) thickly over each layer. On top place a plate which exactly fits the *inside* of the stone crock and place a heavy stone on the plate to weight it down. For the sake of hygiene, cover the crock loosely with a clean towel. After a while the cabbage begins to ferment, due to certain bacteria which cling to the cabbage leaves. After three weeks, the sauerkraut is ready to use. Always wash it well before using, so as to remove the bacteria which caused the fermentation (or the fermentation may continue in your own insides).

Gekochtes Sauerkraut

(COOKED SAUERKRAUT, BASIC RECIPE)

2 pounds prepared fresh
sauerkraut or 1 large
1-pound 12-ounce can
sauerkraut
2 tablespoons butter

Seasonings as desired
2 cups liquid (water, wine,
beer, juices, any meat
broth or bouillon)

Rinse sauerkraut with warm water in colander, drain well. Place in heavy saucepan or pot with the butter and seasonings (salt, pepper, caraway seeds, juniper berries, onion, apple, whatever you like). Cover pan tightly, simmer over lowest heat 15 to 30 minutes. Add liquid (omit salt if bouillon is the liquid), cook 30 minutes to 1½ hours longer, according to your taste. Makes 6 servings.

In Swabia they have a saying that sauerkraut is better the second time round than the first, and the third time round than the second—meaning that the longer it cooks, the better it tastes. The Swabian way of preparing sauerkraut is my favorite. I much prefer it to the Berlin, Bavarian, or Hamburg styles of cooking kraut.

Schwäbisches Sauerkraut

(SWABIAN STYLE KRAUT)

2 pounds fresh sauerkraut
2 or 3 apples, peeled and
sliced
1 large onion, sliced
2 tablespoons butter or
drawn-out pork fat
½ teaspoon crushed
juniper berries or
caraway seeds

1 teaspoon sugar
1 raw potato, grated
2 cups water or white
wine
½ teaspoon salt or to
taste

Rinse sauerkraut with warm water, drain well. Sauté the apples and onion in butter or pork fat until soft. Add juniper or caraway, sugar and the rinsed kraut. Simmer covered ½ hour. Add potato, water or wine and salt. Continue cooking until sauerkraut is tender to your taste (about 1 hour longer). Makes 6 servings.

Variation. Instead of grated raw potato, 2 tablespoons flour may be stirred into the kraut just before liquid is added. This creates a thickened sauce.

Sauerkraut mit Spätzle. Prepare as for *Schwäbisches Sauerkraut* but omit potato. Add 1 recipe cooked *Spätzle** during last 15 minutes.

Sauerkraut auf Bayrische Art
(BAVARIAN STYLE SAUERKRAUT)

2 pounds sauerkraut	1 tablespoon caraway seeds
1 or 2 onions, sliced	1 tablespoon sugar
2 slices bacon, diced	1 cup beef bouillon
2 tablespoons butter	½ cup white wine or beer

Rinse sauerkraut with warm water, drain well. Cook onion and bacon in butter until onion is soft. Add the drained kraut, caraway seeds and sugar. Cover tightly. Cook ½ hour. Add bouillon and wine. Simmer ½ hour longer or until kraut is cooked to your taste. Serve as a vegetable with sauerbraten or *Kalbshaxe**, or top with a selection of pork products such as boiled thick slabs of bacon, pig's feet, *Bratwurst,* frankfurters, blood sausage, or Regensburg sausage. On such a plate, *Erbsenpüree** and mashed potatoes are always served. Makes 4 to 6 servings.

Sauerkraut mit Leberknödel. In Munich, sauerkraut is often served with one large *Leberknödel** (liver dumpling) with each serving. In this case, the *Leberknödel* would be made in large balls, 2 or 3 inches in diameter.

Sauerkraut auf Hamburger Art
(SAUERKRAUT HAMBURG STYLE)

1 pound fresh or canned
sauerkraut
2 tablespoons butter or
drawn-out pork fat
1 carrot, sliced
1 small onion, stuck with
cloves

2 or 3 juniper berries
2 or 3 tablespoons chopped
parsley or celery leaves
1 cup bouillon
1 ham bone or smoked
pork chop

Rinse kraut with warm water, drain, place in a heavy pot with the butter, carrot, onion, juniper berries and parsley or celery leaves, simmer, tightly covered, over lowest heat for ½ hour. Add bouillon and ham bone or pork chop. Continue cooking ½ to 1 hour longer or until done to your taste. Very good with wild game. Makes 3 or 4 servings (double for 6 to 8 servings).

Ananaskraut
(SAUERKRAUT COOKED IN PINEAPPLE JUICE)

1 pound prepared fresh or
canned sauerkraut
2 tablespoons butter
1 cup pineapple juice

¼ cup crushed or diced
canned pineapple
(optional)
1 tablespoon minced parsley

Rinse sauerkraut in warm water; drain. Place in pot with butter, simmer tightly covered ½ hour. Add pineapple juice and crushed or diced pineapple. Cover, cook ½ hour longer or until done to taste. Add minced parsley just before serving and a pinch of salt if you think it needs it. This is especially good with baked spareribs, baked ham or roast pork. Makes 3 or 4 servings (double for 6 to 8 servings).

Weinkraut

(SAUERKRAUT COOKED IN WINE)

2 pounds prepared fresh sauerkraut	1 cup bouillon or water (plus salt to taste)
2 tablespoons butter	⅓ cup dry white wine

Rinse kraut in warm water, drain well. Cook with butter in heavy, tightly covered pot over lowest heat ½ hour. Add bouillon or water and wine, continue cooking covered ½ to 1 hour longer. Makes 6 to 8 servings.

Champagnerkraut. As observed before, this name sometimes means white cabbage cooked in white wine (or leftover champagne), or it could mean sauerkraut cooked in champagne or white wine, exactly like *Weinkraut.*

Garniertes Sauerkraut

(GARNISHED SAUERKRAUT)

1 pound sauerkraut	½ cup beef or chicken broth
1 tablespoon pork fat	
1 carrot, diced	4 frankfurters
1 large onion, sliced	4 slices roast ham
1 teaspoon minced parsley	½ pound pickled pork (or 1 tin corned beef)
3 or 4 juniper berries	
½ cup white wine	Salt and pepper to taste

The sauerkraut should be rinsed and drained as usual. In a heavy pot, melt the pork fat (*Schmalz*), sauté the carrot and onion until lightly colored. Add the sauerkraut, parsley, juniper berries, wine and broth. Simmer covered 45 minutes to 1 hour. Add the frankfurters, ham, pickled pork or corned beef (corned beef would never be used in Germany, but since pickled pork is so hard to find in our markets, the corned beef serves as a substitute). Continue cooking 15 to 20 minutes longer. Add salt and pepper if needed. Serve with boiled potatoes or *Salzkartoffeln**. Makes 4 very hearty servings, a one-dish meal.

Eisbein mit Sauerkraut
(PICKLED PORK SHIN OR HOCK WITH SAUERKRAUT)

It is the meat that makes this dish, and unless you know of a pork store that carries German specialties, you will have a hard time finding an *Eisbein*. It is not just the cut, but the way the pork is pickled that gives the meat its unique flavor. Also, you must be fond of pure white boiled pork fat, to be eaten by the forkful, for it is the glistening white fat that is considered by Germans to be the real prize in this dish. After you have swallowed a bite of the fat, and smacked your lips over this, you dig inside for the bright red meat clinging to the bone. Then you begin to offset the bites of meat with helpings of sauerkraut, *Erbsenpüree* and mashed or boiled potatoes. Mustard is served on the side.

In Westphalia I was told you always start the meal with a shot of *Korn,* which is a pure white *Schnaps* made of rye, and that this will help you to digest the Eisbein. Quantities of beer are also required to wash down this dish which a Westphalian artist would lead us to believe was served to the disciples at the Last Supper.

(For myself, Eisbein makes a last supper. I can do without it.)

Here is a recipe for *Eisbein mit Sauerkraut* as it appears in Mary Hahn's *Praktisches Kochbuch.*

1½ pounds pickled pork shin (Eisbein) for each serving	Sauerkraut (cooked as desired)
2 onions, sliced	Erbsenpüree (mashed split peas)*
Mixed pickling spices	Boiled potatoes
½ bay leaf	

Cook the pork with onions, spices and bay leaf in water to cover until tender, about 2 hours. Drain. Serve with it the sauerkraut (cooked with any desired seasonings), purée of split peas and potatoes.

Schweinsknöchel mit Sauerkraut
(PIG'S KNUCKLES WITH SAUERKRAUT)

6 pig's knuckles	2 bay leaves
1 celery stalk	Salt and pepper
1 large onion, quartered	Boiling water
2 tablespoons salt	Sauerkraut auf Hamburger
6 to 8 peppercorns	Art*

Place all ingredients but sauerkraut in pot with water 3 inches above the knuckles. Simmer 2 hours or until meat is very tender. Remove knuckles from broth, serve over a mound of sauerkraut along with ham and mixed sausages. Mashed potatoes and *Erbsenpüree** should be served on the side. Serve 1 pig's knuckle to each person. Makes 6 servings.

The following is a favorite dish in the apple wine taverns of Sachsenhausen, a Frankfurt suburb, though the night I was in Sachsenhausen the sauerkraut we were served was of the plain, boiled variety. After several glasses of apple wine, gay songs and a linking of arms with everyone at your table, the sauerkraut-flavoring becomes of secondary importance. But for home cooking, the following recipe is better.

Kasseler Rippchen mit Kraut
(SMOKED PORK RIBS WITH KRAUT)

2 slices bacon, diced	2 or 3 crushed juniper
2 apples, peeled and	berries
chopped	⅓ cup dry white wine
1 onion, chopped	½ cup water
1 pound prepared fresh	1 pound smoked pork
or canned sauerkraut	chops
¼ teaspoon crushed cumin	

Cook bacon, apples and onion together until onion is soft. Add sauerkraut, spices, wine and water. Cook uncovered for 10 minutes. Add the chops, cover, simmer 1 hour. Serve with *Salzkartoffeln**. Makes 3 or 4 servings.

Snuten und Poten
(PICKLED PORK AND SAUERKRAUT)

To be authentic, this should be made with pig's snout—which gives the dish its name. But since pig's snout is not readily available in our markets, the following recipe calls only for pig's knuckles—and properly, *pickled* pig's knuckles should be used.

6 to 8 pickled pig's knuckles	¼ teaspoon thyme
3 slices bacon, diced	2 carrots, cubed
2 onions, chopped	1 celery stalk, diced
2 pounds sauerkraut, rinsed and drained	3 large potatoes, peeled and diced
	Salt to taste

Place the pig's knuckles in water to cover; cook until tender when pierced with fork. Drain, saving 2 cups of the liquid. Cook the bacon and onions together until onions are soft. Add sauerkraut, stir in thyme; add carrots, celery, potatoes and the knuckles, pushing down into kraut. Add the reserved 2 cups of broth. Cover, simmer 1 to 1½ hours. Add salt if needed. Makes 6 to 8 servings.

Ungarisches Kraut
(HUNGARIAN STYLE SAUERKRAUT)

1 pound prepared fresh or canned sauerkraut	1 teaspoon paprika
1 onion, chopped	1 teaspoon caraway seeds
1 tablespoon drawn-out pork fat	1 tablespoon flour
	1 cup tomato juice
	½ cup sour cream

Rinse kraut with warm water; drain. Cook the onion in fat until soft; add paprika and caraway seeds, then the kraut. Cook tightly covered over low heat ½ hour, sprinkle with flour, then stir in tomato juice, cook ½ to 1 hour longer. Turn off heat, stir in sour cream. Makes 3 or 4 servings.

Note: This is even better if diced lean pork is sautéed with the onion. For 1 pound sauerkraut, use ½ pound lean pork.

Überbackenes Sauerkraut
(SAUERKRAUT-POTATO CASSEROLE)

6 large potatoes, cooked in jackets	1 pound sauerkraut
3 or 4 tablespoons milk	1 small onion, sliced
5 tablespoons butter	2 tablespoons grated Swiss
Salt and pepper	cheese

Slip the skins off the potatoes while warm, mash with milk, add 2 tablespoons butter, salt and pepper, and beat until fluffy. Divide in half. Place half the potatoes in the bottom of a buttered 1½-quart casserole.

Rinse the sauerkraut with warm water, drain well. Sauté the sliced onion in 1 tablespoon of butter until soft; add the sauerkraut, simmer covered 10 minutes. Spoon this over the layer of potatoes. Add remaining potatoes. Spread grated cheese and 2 more tablespoons of butter over the top. Bake covered in 350° F. oven for about 35 minutes, uncovering during the last 10 minutes. Makes 6 to 8 servings.

Sauerkrautsalat
(SAUERKRAUT SALAD)

1 pound sauerkraut
1 apple, peeled and diced
½ cucumber, thinly sliced
(optional)
2 tablespoons minced
onion

1 tablespoon oil
Dash of vinegar
Minced dill or parsley
Salt if needed

Wash the sauerkraut with warm water, drain well. Add remaining ingredients; toss to blend. Serve chilled as an accompaniment to fish. Makes 6 servings of salad.

Combining sauerkraut with poultry will not surprise the people of Baltimore, Maryland, where it is traditional to serve sauerkraut with turkey for Thanksgiving dinner. Far better than turkey with sauerkraut is pheasant, and Fasan mit Weinkraut, a specialty on North German Lloyd ships, is truly superb, a gastronomic delight.

Fasan mit Weinkraut
(PHEASANT WITH SAUERKRAUT COOKED IN WINE)

1 large pheasant, or a
brace of young
pheasants, cleaned,
aged, ready for roasting
Salt and pepper
2 slices bacon

3 onions, chopped
5 tablespoons butter
2 pounds sauerkraut
1 cup canned beef gravy
½ cup white wine
1 raw potato

Sprinkle the pheasant (or pheasants) inside and out with salt and pepper. Wrap a strip of bacon around each bird. Place in a large shallow casserole, preheat oven to 400° F., brown the birds in the hot oven for 15 minutes; remove.

Meantime, sauté the onions in butter until soft. Rinse the sauerkraut with warm water, add to the onions, cover tightly, simmer over low heat 15 minutes. When pheasant has been taken from the oven, remove the bird from the casserole, add the beef gravy to the pan juices, simmer until well blended. Add half of this to the sauerkraut along with the wine and the raw potato grated into the kraut. Place the sauerkraut in the bottom of the casserole with the pheasant over it. Return to the oven with heat reduced to 350° F. for another 30 minutes for young pheasants, 1 hour for a large, more mature bird. Add the remaining canned gravy to the pan juices, simmer 5 minutes, serve as gravy. Makes 4 servings.

Note: Wild duck, partridges, grouse, or other game birds may be prepared the same way. This can also be done with Cornish hens or smaller whole broilers but the flavor will be different. It is the gamy flavor of the wild birds blended with the tartness of the sauerkraut that makes this dish so superb.

Ente mit Sauerkraut auf Nürnberger Art
(DUCK WITH SAUERKRAUT NUREMBERG STYLE)

The following dish is a specialty of the Schiess Haus, a hunting lodge near Nuremberg. There it is prepared with wild duck, which is more flavorful and less fatty than our domestic ducklings, but since wild duck is hard to come by in our markets, the domestic duck may be used—just be careful to remove excess fat from the pan as it cooks.

1 4- to 5-pound duckling	½ cup white wine or
Salt and pepper	light beer
½ lemon	½ cup Tokay grapes,
1 small whole onion,	seeded
peeled	2 tablespoons flour
2 pounds sauerkraut	1½ cups water
2 apples, peeled and	Mashed potatoes
chopped	

If duck is frozen, defrost completely. Remove all visible fat. Sprinkle with salt and pepper; truss for roasting. Rub skin with the cut side of the lemon. Place the peeled whole onion in the cavity and put duck on a rack in a roasting pan. Roast in 350° F. oven until a meat thermometer in the leg registers 170° F., about 1 to 1½ hours. Remove excess fat from pan periodically.

As duck is roasting, combine sauerkraut, apples and wine or beer; simmer covered ½ hour.

When duck is more than half done (130° F.), remove from rack, pour off remaining pan drippings into bowl and when this has cooled to room temperature, chill in freezing compartment so that fat will rise to top and can be easily removed.

Arrange the sauerkraut in a casserole, place the duck above it; if preferred, cut the duck into quarters. Arrange seeded grapes over the top of the sauerkraut, around the edge of the duck. Return casserole to oven, bake ½ hour longer.

When pan drippings have cooled, remove fat. To the brown essence, add 2 tablespoons flour, stir to blend; to this add 1½ cups water and salt to taste. Simmer to make a gravy. When duck is done, remove to platter. Add half the gravy to the sauerkraut. Pass the rest. Serve accompanied by mashed potatoes. Makes 2 to 4 servings.

Gemüse, Salate und Beilagen

(VEGETABLES, SALADS AND OTHER ACCOMPANIMENTS)

It is not true that the only vegetables to appear on the German table are sauerkraut, red cabbage and potatoes.

But at times you begin to wonder.

It is true that the Germans do more things with potatoes than any other people. And their tricks with sauerkraut are so numerous, I have devoted an entire chapter to the subject. But the Germans also do quite interesting things with asparagus (one Black Forest restaurant boasts of having more asparagus dishes on its menu than Howard Johnson's has ice cream flavors), green beans, kohlrabi, carrots, celeriac and spinach. There are also the dried legumes, of which yellow split peas (*Erbsen*) are a leading favorite. *Erbsenpüree* is as important on the Berliner's beloved *Eisbein* plate as the sauerkraut and the mashed potatoes.

Uniquely German are the dishes in which fruit and vegetables are cooked together: pears with green beans, apples with potatoes, apples with carrots, green beans and onions. Until I tasted these combinations, I was decidedly skeptical. Happily, I can report them to be delightful, though perhaps not the kind of thing one would serve night after night. (Recipes for these combinations are found with *Spezialitäten*—see Index.)

Many vegetables are stuffed with a bread crumb mixture or a meat-and-bread mixture—tomatoes, onions, cabbage, even cucumbers are so stuffed. I have not included recipes for these for they are done exactly as we do them, with almost identical stuffings.

As one might expect in a northern climate, root vegetables have always been widely used by the Germans as these can be stored in a root cellar through the winter months. Parsnips, salsify (oyster

plant), carrots, beets, turnips and celeriac (which Americans sometimes call celery root or celery knobs) are as common on the
German table as green beans and peas are with us. All members of
the cabbage family are well represented, too: cauliflower (*Blumen-
kohl*), kale (*Krauskohl*), kohlrabi, and Brussels sprouts (*Rosen-
kohl*). To save every bit of the water in which vegetables are
cooked, a sauce is often made of the liquid, the vegetables served
in the sauce.

Salads appear on the German table much more frequently than
I would have guessed, but they are quite different from the salads
of the Mediterranean. For one thing, the dressing is more tart,
usually made of equal parts oil and vinegar, sometimes with a
pinch of sugar added to offset the vinegar. For another, the salad
is usually served on the same plate with the meat and hot vegetables.
For this reason, I have given salad recipes along with vegetable
recipes instead of putting them in a separate section.

There are some salads made with meat, seafood or chicken
which are really entrees in themselves. These have been included
in this chapter for want of a better place, though perhaps they are
closer to the minced salads served as hors d'oeuvres to be found in
the *Vorspeisen* chapter. Because the German meal pattern is so
different from ours, it is sometimes hard to know just where to
present certain recipes.

Beilagen include potatoes, rice, noodles and dumplings of all
sorts. Certain of these, like *Spätzle,* are often called *Mehlspeisen,*
meaning "flour foods," and may appear as the main dish on the
German table on those days when there isn't enough of a meat
food to satisfy hearty German appetites. *Spätzle* becomes such a
dish when topped with fried onions and cheese. Plum dumplings
may appear as the star on the plate, dribbled with melted butter,
or may be served as an accompaniment to meat instead of potatoes.

There are a number of quick German tricks with vegetables
which are noteworthy. A topping of bacon and fried onion over
tender green beans is superb. Hazelnut butter on broccoli is worth
writing home about. The cucumber salad which is a staple in the
German menu is prepared with consummate skill, simple as it is.
And the little trick of shaking boiled potatoes over low heat to dry
them thoroughly and make them mealy gives potatoes an altogether
different taste.

Green cabbage is prepared in almost as many ways as sauerkraut, though again, nomenclature becomes difficult, as the word for cabbage may be *Kraut* or *Kohl* depending on the region. Our American cole slaw was originally *Kohlsalat*. Red cabbage is *Rotkohl* in some regions, *Blaukraut* in others. It is called "blue" because the color when cooked is sometimes a purplish blue rather than red. It needn't be this way; if vinegar is used from the start in cooking and the sauce thickened with cornstarch, the attractive deep red color can be preserved.

In all German recipes calling for asparagus, white asparagus is meant, though for those who prefer green asparagus, the same sauces may be used. To Germans, and to most other Europeans as well, the white is considered a far greater delicacy. While fresh white asparagus is rarely seen in our markets, our canned white asparagus is comparable to that served in Germany.

Salzkartoffeln
(SALTED POTATOES)

These are so much better than ordinary boiled potatoes, the two cannot even be classed together. The secret is in steaming away all remaining water so that the starch particles puff to mealiness. Peel and quarter potatoes in the usual way, boil them in salted water, covered, until fork-tender, about 20 minutes. Drain thoroughly. Return to saucepan. Sprinkle with salt. Hold *uncovered* over low heat, shaking the pan, until not a drop of moisture is left, then add a big lump of butter and, if you like, some parsley. Cover the saucepan, place in a warm place on the stove, or over the lowest possible heat, to keep warm. (I find I can achieve the same results by covering the saucepan after the water has been drained off, but I use a heavy Magnalite saucepan. When using regular aluminum, the above method is best.) These are also sometimes called *Schwenkkartoffeln*.

* * *

Schnoor is the name of an ancient narrow street in Bremen whose charming buildings are a good three hundred years old, a street studded with art galleries and antique shops. At one end of the street is a delightful small restaurant whose name is simply Schnoor 2, a place no more than twelve feet wide but with a succession of intimate small rooms on each floor. It is a place as full of customers at midnight as at six P.M., where one dines by candlelight surrounded by priceless antiques, under low-beamed ceilings. The following recipe was given to me by the chef of Schnoor 2, Hans Moeller, who modestly acknowledged that it was his own creation.

Mandelbällchen
(ALMOND-STUDDED POTATO CROQUETTES)

4 cups light fluffy mashed potatoes	2 egg whites, beaten until soft peaks form
2 egg yolks, beaten until light	½ to ¾ cup crushed almonds
2 to 3 tablespoons flour	Fat for deep frying

Make your own mashed potatoes, with butter, milk and seasonings to taste (it will take 4 large potatoes); or use instant mashed potato mix. Beat in the egg yolks. Chill until potatoes can be handled easily, then form into 2-inch croquettes, roll each in flour. Dip in the egg white, then the crushed almonds, until well coated with almonds. (Easiest way to crush almonds is in an electric blender.) Fry in deep fat preheated to 375° F. until golden on all sides. Makes 8 croquettes, enough for 4 servings.

Prinzesskartoffeln
(PRINCESS POTATOES)

5 or 6 medium potatoes, cooked	2 tablespoons butter
2 slices Canadian style bacon, diced	1 tablespoon flour
2 tablespoons onion, chopped	1½ cups milk
	Salt and pepper

While potatoes are cooking, in a separate pan cook bacon and onion in butter until onion is soft. Stir in flour, slowly add milk, cook over low heat until sauce is thickened and smooth. Cut cooked potatoes into ½-inch dice, add to sauce. Season to taste with salt and pepper. Makes 6 servings.

Meerettichkartoffeln
(POTATOES MASHED WITH HORSERADISH CREAM)

4 or 6 potatoes	½ cup dairy sour cream
Boiling salted water	1 tablespoon horseradish
Salt	Minced parsley
1 tablespoon butter	Melted butter
Freshly ground pepper	

Cook potatoes in boiling salted water until tender; drain. Sprinkle with salt, cover pan, shake until potatoes are mealy. Mash, adding butter and freshly ground pepper, then add dairy sour cream, horseradish, and a little minced parsley. Whip as for mashed potatoes. Serve with melted butter over top. Very good with pot roast.

Kümmelkartoffeln
(CARAWAY POTATOES)

2 pounds small new potatoes
2 or 3 tablespoons melted butter
2 tablespoons caraway seeds

Scrub potatoes, scraping off only part of the peel. Place 1 tablespoon melted butter in shallow baking dish. Cut each potato in half, promptly placing cut side down in the butter. Sprinkle remaining butter and caraway seeds over the top. Bake in 400° F. oven 30 minutes or until fork-tender, or in 350° F. oven 45 to 50 minutes. Excellent with steak or grilled chops. Makes 6 to 8 servings.

Bratkartoffeln

(SKILLET-FRIED POTATOES)

Peel and thinly slice raw potatoes.[1] Cook in fat in heavy skillet with cover, using enough fat to cover bottom of skillet ¼-inch deep. Fat should be sizzling-hot when potatoes are added. Sprinkle with salt and paprika. Cover tightly, cook over low heat, turning over potatoes with spatula once or twice as they brown, until tender, about 15 to 20 minutes. They should be gold-yellow in color, some slices crisply brown. (If sliced onion is cooked with the potatoes they become what the French call *Pommes Lyonnaise*.)

Speckkartoffeln. Like *Bratkartoffeln* except that first bacon is fried in the skillet, then when bacon has been removed, the potatoes are fried, covered, in the bacon fat. Onions may be added or not as you like.

* * *

Potato pancakes are one of the dishes for which the Germans are famed throughout the world. Sometimes these are eaten with apple sauce, in which case the potatoes are sprinkled with sugar. Sometimes they are sprinkled with salt, instead, and served as an accompaniment to meat. In Bavaria, they are often topped with crisp bacon slices, accompanied by sauerkraut. And in the Rhineland, frequently they are served with lingonberry preserves (much like whole fruit cranberry sauce).

There are even more ways of making potato pancakes than there are German names for the specialty. *Kartoffelpuffer* are not generally puffed up at all, but are flat and sometimes (when not properly cooked) a bit on the greasy side. Yet one of the many recipes I came across called for yeast to be added to the batter, which would make them deserve the name "puffer." *Reibekuchen*

---

[1] Cooked potatoes may also be sliced and fried this way, but in this case, do not cover pan.

or *Reiberdatschi*, other names, refer to the way the raw potato is grated. Sometimes the raw potato is grated directly into milk, sometimes into water which contains a little lemon juice. I like the water and lemon juice method because it keeps the grated potato white; otherwise, the potato when grated turns blackish almost immediately, giving the finished pancakes a purplish-brown tinge. It is important, of course, to squeeze out every bit of the water before adding the potato to the flour batter.

Adding chopped onion, chopped apple or minced parsley to the batter is another possibility. It is, as you can see, an adaptable dish and finding an "authentic" recipe for making the batter is a hit-or-miss process. Choose your own!

Kartoffelpuffer
(POTATO PANCAKES)

2 large potatoes, grated
  on medium grater
  (2½ cups)
Water with lemon juice
1 boiled potato, mashed

2 tablespoons milk
1 egg, beaten
½ to ¾ teaspoon salt
Fat for frying (about 6
  tablespoons)

Grate potatoes into water in which a little lemon juice has been squeezed. Drain, squeezing out liquid. Pour off liquid but collect starch left in bottom of bowl, add this to drained grated raw potato and the boiled potato. Beat with milk, egg and salt to form a batter. Drop batter for 3 or 4 pancakes at a time into hot fat in skillet, using 2 tablespoons fat for each batch of pancakes. When firm on bottom, loosen with spatula, turn to brown on other side. Continue until all batter is used. Serve immediately. Sprinkle with salt if to be served with meat; sprinkle with sugar if to be served with apple sauce. Makes 8 to 10 pancakes, enough for 2 or 3 persons.

Reibekuchen

(POTATO PANCAKES RHINELAND STYLE)

4 potatoes, grated medium-
fine
½ cup milk
1 medium onion, chopped
fine

1 large or 2 small eggs
6 tablespoons flour
½ teaspoon salt
Freshly ground pepper
Fat for frying

Grate potatoes into milk. Drain, add to chopped onion with eggs, flour, salt and pepper. Drop batter into hot fat, using 2 tablespoons fat for every batch of pancakes. Turn when brown on one side, cook until well browned on the other side. Drain on paper towel. Sprinkle with salt or sugar. Serve hot with apple sauce or cranberry sauce and black coffee. Makes about 16, enough for 4 persons.

Mit Apfeln (With Apple). Use only 1 small onion, add 1 chopped peeled apple.

Mit Petersilie (With Parsley). Add 1 or 2 tablespoons minced parsley to batter before frying.

Rohe Kartoffelklösse

(RAW POTATO DUMPLINGS)

1 cooked mashed potato
6 medium raw potatoes
(2 pounds)
Water with lemon juice
½ to ¾ cup flour (or
more as needed)
1 egg, beaten

1 teaspoon salt
1 cup slightly stale white
bread crumbs sautéed
in 2 tablespoons butter,
goose fat or chicken fat
Boiling water

The cooked potato should be freshly cooked, mashed by forcing through a fine sieve or ricer, or beaten in an electric mixer. Have everything else ready before the raw potatoes are peeled. Then grate the peeled potatoes on a medium-fine blade directly into a bowl of water blended with lemon juice. This keeps the potatoes white (otherwise they turn black as soon as grated). When all potatoes are grated, put into a cheesecloth bag and press hard to expel every bit of liquid. Then mix with the cooked potato, flour, egg and salt. Now comes the really difficult part. The dough should be kneaded with the fingers until it can be easily shaped into large balls, 2 to 3 inches in diameter. Then into center of each ball, a little fried bread is forced, with the ball sealed up around it. Make one test dumpling first, drop into rapidly boiling water. If this falls apart, add a little more flour to the dough before making any more dumplings. Cook the dumplings until they rise to the top, about 10 minutes. Serve with meat and gravy. Makes 8 to 12 dumplings, depending on size.

Gekochte Kartoffelklösse
(COOKED POTATO DUMPLINGS)

6 medium potatoes (2 pounds), cooked in their jackets
1 cup all-purpose flour
2 eggs, beaten
1 teaspoon salt

1 cup slightly stale bread crumbs fried in butter, goose fat or chicken fat
6 to 8 cups boiling beef or chicken broth
Melted butter

Peel the jackets from potatoes while warm, mash at once (do not add butter or milk). Work in flour, eggs and salt to a dough stiff enough to be kneaded with fingers. Shape into balls 2 or 3 inches in diameter. Force a few fried bread crumbs into the center of each, then seal over. Try one test dumpling first; if it falls short, add more flour to the dough before shaping others. Makes 8 to 12 dumplings, depending on size. Spoon melted butter over top, sprinkle with fried bread crumbs. May be served with meat, or they may be served as an entree, bathed in melted butter, topped with fried crumbs, accompanied by fruit compote.

An American woman of German background who frequently serves potato dumplings to her family tells me that the potato dumpling mix imported from West Germany, available in most of our supermarkets, works fine. "I used to grate potatoes for dumplings," she said, "but after I discovered the mix, I figured, why go to all that bother?"

Warmer Kartoffelsalat

(HOT POTATO SALAD)

6 medium white potatoes, or 15 to 20 new potatoes
6 slices bacon, diced
½ cup diced onion
1 teaspoon flour
2 teaspoons sugar
2 teaspoons salt or to taste

Freshly ground black pepper
3 to 4 tablespoons vinegar
½ cup water
Minced parsley

Cook potatoes in their jackets in salted water; when fork-tender, drain, peel, dice. Meantime, fry bacon until crisp; remove from pan, add onion, cook until tender. Drain off all but 1 tablespoon of the bacon fat. Add flour, sugar, salt and pepper to skillet; cook and stir until flour is lightly browned. Stir in vinegar and water, cook until slightly thickened. Replace bacon. Pour this hot dressing over the potatoes, stir to blend gently. Potatoes should look creamy. Sprinkle minced parsley over top. Makes 4 to 6 servings.

Kalter Kartoffelsalat

(COLD POTATO SALAD)

6 medium to large
potatoes, peeled and
quartered
Boiling salted water
1 small onion, minced
3 tablespoons oil
3 tablespoons vinegar

½ teaspoon prepared
mustard or freshly
ground pepper
2 to 4 tablespoons minced
parsley or dill (optional)
¼ to ½ teaspoon sugar
(optional)

Cook potatoes until tender; drain, saving ¾ cup of the liquid. Dice potatoes. Add minced onion and oil; toss. Bring the reserved ¾ cup cooking liquid[2] to a boil, pour over the potatoes and onion. Let stand several hours at room temperature but do not chill. Stir in vinegar, mustard or pepper, parsley or dill and sugar, if desired. This makes a creamy potato salad. Serve with sausages, fried fish, or veal or pork *Schnitzel*. Makes 6 servings.

Meerettichkartoffelsalat

(HORSERADISH-FLAVORED POTATO SALAD)

6 or 7 medium potatoes
(2 pounds) cooked in
jackets
8 tablespoons (½ cup)
olive oil
½ teaspoon salt
1 small onion, grated
3 tablespoons lemon juice

½ cup sour cream or
mayonnaise
½ teaspoon sugar (optional)
1 tablespoon minced
parsley or minced dill
1 teaspoon grated
horseradish

Slip off skins of cooked potatoes as soon as cool enough to handle. Dice. Add olive oil and salt, blend well. Add grated onion, lemon

---

[2] Many recipes specify using beef broth instead of the potato liquid, but when I tried this, the potatoes became brown in color. I personally prefer the above method.

THE ART OF GERMAN COOKING

juice, sour cream or mayonnaise, sugar, parsley or dill and horse-radish. Stir gently to blend. Serve cold but do not chill. Makes 6 servings.

Weisskohl in Saurer Sahne
(WHITE CABBAGE IN SOUR CREAM SAUCE)

½ firm white cabbage (about 4 cups shredded)

1 small onion, thinly sliced

1 cup beef bouillon or stock

1 tablespoon cornstarch or arrowroot

1 tablespoon butter

½ cup dairy sour cream

Shred the cabbage, place with onion in large saucepan, add the bouillon, simmer covered until cabbage is tender, 12 to 15 minutes. With slotted spoon remove cabbage to serving dish. Thicken the bouillon with the cornstarch or arrowroot (add a little of the liquid to the cornstarch to thin, then combine the two), add butter, simmer until smooth and thickened. Turn off heat, beat in sour cream until smooth and well blended. Pour sauce over the cabbage. This is a delicious sauce for cabbage, but should be served as soon after it is cooked as possible. Makes 4 to 6 delectable servings.

Champagnerkraut
(CABBAGE COOKED IN WHITE WINE)

3 tablespoons butter

2 medium onions, thinly sliced

2 tart apples, peeled and sliced

1 medium head cabbage (3 pounds), thinly sliced

1 teaspoon lemon juice

Grated rind of ½ lemon

½ cup hot water

¾ to 1 teaspoon salt

1 teaspoon sugar

1 small potato, grated (optional)

½ cup white wine or champagne

Melt butter in large heavy pot or top-of-stove casserole; sauté onions until yellow and soft; add apples, sauté briefly. Add cabbage, lemon juice and lemon rind, hot water, salt, sugar and grated potato. Cook, tightly covered, over low heat, for 15 to 20 minutes. Uncover, add wine, cook 5 minutes longer or until cabbage is tender. Makes 8 servings.

Krautsalat oder Kohlsalat

(CABBAGE SALAD OR COLE SLAW)

½ head cabbage, thinly
    sliced (about 3 cups)
Boiling water
3 tablespoons oil
¼ cup vinegar

¼ cup water
½ teaspoon salt
1 teaspoon sugar
Caraway seeds

Cover shredded cabbage with boiling water, let stand 3 or 4 minutes, then drain. Combine oil, vinegar, water, salt and sugar; bring to a boil, stir to dissolve. When cool, add to cabbage, toss, along with caraway seeds. Serve cold but not chilled. Makes 4 or 5 servings.

Rotkrautsalat

(RED CABBAGE SALAD)

½ head red cabbage,
    sliced
4 slices bacon, cooked
1 teaspoon sugar
2 tablespoons vinegar

¼ cup red or white wine
2 tablespoons olive oil
Salt and pepper to taste
Caraway seeds

Shred cabbage as we would do for cole slaw.[3] Cook bacon until crisp; remove bacon to paper towel to drain. Add sugar, vinegar

---

[3] The Germans usually soften the cabbage slightly by covering with boiling water, letting it stand in water 3 or 4 minutes, then draining. I prefer it more crisp, as it is in its natural state.

and wine to bacon fat, cook until sugar is dissolved. Pour this hot mixture over cabbage. Add oil, salt and pepper and about a teaspoon of caraway seeds. Sprinkle crumbled cooked bacon over top. Serve cold but do not chill. Makes 4 to 6 salad servings.

Mit Apfeln (With Apple). Add 1 peeled sliced apple to the bacon fat along with sugar, etc.

Rotkohl
(RED CABBAGE)

2 tablespoons butter
1 apple, peeled and
   sliced
1 small onion, sliced
   (optional)
4 cups (about) shredded
   red cabbage
¼ cup vinegar

2 to 4 tablespoons sugar
   or apple jelly
1 or 2 whole cloves or
   a pinch of powdered
   cloves
½ cup red wine
1 tablespoon flour or ½
   tablespoon cornstarch

Melt butter, add apple and onion, cook until soft. Add cabbage, stir to blend. Add vinegar, sugar or jelly, cloves and wine. Cook, covered, until cabbage is tender, about 12 minutes. Thicken the sauce with flour or cornstarch, first adding a little of the liquid with flour. Simmer until sauce is smooth. Makes 4 servings.

Blaukraut. Instead of using butter, 2 slices diced bacon are partially cooked, then the onion and apple added. Water is used rather than red wine and the sauce is not thickened. The color will be more of a purple than red, explaining the name.

Erbsenpüree
(YELLOW SPLIT PEA PURÉE)

1 pound (2 cups) dried yellow split peas	Pinch each of dried thyme and marjoram
6 cups water or stock	Salt as needed
1 whole onion	1 small onion, minced
1 carrot	2 tablespoons butter
1 turnip or parsnip	2 tablespoons flour

Check package directions to see whether peas require previous soaking; quick-cooking type do not. If pre-soaked, drain well. Add water or stock, whole onion, carrot, turnip, herbs and 1 teaspoon salt for 4 cups water (less salt if stock is used). Cook until peas are tender, 1 to 2 hours. Drain. Mash peas in blender or force through sieve. Sauté minced onion in butter until lightly browned; stir in flour, then stir into the drained mashed peas. Beat until fluffy, of same consistency as mashed potatoes. Makes 6 to 8 servings.

Grüne Bohnen mit Zwiebel und Speck
(GREEN BEANS WITH ONION AND BACON SAUCE)

1 pound green beans, cut	1 tablespoon flour
1 cup boiling salted water	Salt and pepper to taste
4 to 6 slices bacon, diced	1 to 1½ tablespoons
1 small onion, chopped	vinegar

Cook beans in boiling salted water until tender; drain, saving liquid. Sauté bacon until partially cooked; add onion, cook until soft. Pour off all but 1 tablespoon bacon fat, stir in flour, cook until lightly browned. Slowly add 1 cup of the bean cooking water; cook until smooth, seasoning as needed. Add vinegar to taste. Serve sauce over the beans. Makes 6 servings.

Quick Version. If preferred, a simple topping of diced bacon and onion cooked together may be sprinkled over the beans, with a dash of vinegar.

Bohnensalat

(GREEN BEAN SALAD)

1 pound green beans,
sliced lengthwise
Boiling salted water
3 tablespoons olive oil
3 tablespoons vinegar
3 tablespoons vegetable
stock or beef broth

½ cup thinly sliced onion
1 tablespoon minced fresh
or frozen dill, or ½
teaspoon dried dill weed
1 teaspoon sugar, if
desired

Cook beans until tender-crisp; drain, saving a little of the cooking water (unless you prefer flavor of beef broth). Make a sauce of the oil, vinegar, the reserved cooking water or beef broth, the onion and dill and sugar if desired. Pour this over beans, marinate several hours. Makes 4 to 6 servings.

Kohlrabi

4 kohlrabi, trimmed
Boiling salted water
2 tablespoons butter
2 tablespoons flour

¼ cup sweet or sour
cream
Seasonings to taste

Remove kohlrabi leaves, chop and set aside. Trim roots, slice, dice or cut in sticks. Cook roots in boiling salted water until tender, 20 to 25 minutes. Add leaves during last 5 minutes when roots are almost done. Drain, saving the liquid. Make a roux of butter and flour, slowly stir in the cooking water. When sauce is thickened and smooth, turn off heat, add cream. Add seasonings to taste: minced parsley, salt, pepper, a pinch of sugar if liked, or a dash of nutmeg. Makes 4 servings.

Spinat[4]

(CREAMED SPINACH)

2 pounds fresh spinach	Salt and pepper
3 tablespoons butter	¼ teaspoon dry mustard
2 tablespoons flour	Pinch of nutmeg
1 cup milk, or ½ cup milk and ½ cup light cream	

Wash spinach through several waters, then cook covered in the moisture clinging to leaves until limp, about 3 minutes. Drain, sprinkle with salt from shaker, purée in blender or chop fine. Make a sauce of the butter, flour and milk, seasoning sauce to taste. Stir puréed spinach into sauce. Makes 6 to 8 servings.

Sellerieknollen

(CELERY ROOT OR CELERIAC)

The big knob or root of celery is far more popular in Germany than the celery stalks we use. It is served both as a hot vegetable and cold as a salad. In our markets, celeriac is most available during winter months. If you don't see it, ask for it! It's worth learning about.

4 celery roots (1 per serving)	¼ cup cream
3 tablespoons butter	1 egg yolk, beaten (optional)
2 tablespoons flour	Seasonings to taste (salt, pepper, minced parsley)
1 cup chicken or beef broth	

---

[4] This is the way spinach is normally served in Germany, so it is not called "creamed spinach," only "spinach." Occasionally 1 or 2 egg yolks are beaten into the hot sauce and the stiffly beaten egg whites folded in, then the mixture is baked in the oven, when it becomes *Spinatpudding*.

THE ART OF GERMAN COOKING

Peel and trim celery roots. Slice crosswise or dice. Place in heavy pot with butter, cover tightly, cook over low heat 10 minutes. Stir in flour, then broth. Cook covered until celery is tender, about 15 minutes longer. Remove from heat. Blend cream and beaten egg yolk, stir into sauce, beating constantly until thickened. Add seasonings as needed. Makes 4 servings.

Selleriesalat

(CELERIAC OR CELERY ROOT SALAD)

2 large celery roots,
    trimmed and sliced
Boiling salted water
2 tablespoons olive oil
2 tablespoons vinegar

¼ cup beef broth or
    vegetable stock
1 teaspoon sugar
Seasonings to taste

Cook the sliced celery roots in boiling salted water until tender; drain, reserving ¼ cup of the broth for the dressing. Add oil and vinegar to the cooked celery plus the broth, sugar and any other desired seasoning. Makes 4 salad servings.

Teltower Rübchen

(GLAZED TURNIPS)

2 pounds small white
    turnips, peeled
2 tablespoons butter
1 tablespoon sugar

1 cup clear beef broth
¼ cup flour
3 tablespoons softened
    butter

Use very small turnips, or dice larger turnips. Melt butter, add sugar, cook until sugar is dissolved, add the turnips and cook over low heat, tightly covered, shaking pan occasionally, for 5 minutes. Add broth, simmer until turnips are fork-tender, about 25 minutes longer. Blend the flour and butter together, form marble-sized balls, and drop these into the broth during last 5 minutes of cooking. They will dissolve, thickening broth. Makes 6 servings.

Stangenspargel

(ASPARAGUS SPEARS)

2 pounds asparagus	½ cup slightly stale
Boiling salted water	bread crumbs
4 tablespoons butter	Grated rind of ½ lemon

Break off tough ends of asparagus, scrub spears. Place in skillet, add boiling water to cover, and for 2 cups water ½ teaspoon of salt. Partially cover skillet (cover should be a little loose so steam may escape), cook until asparagus is barely tender, 6 to 8 minutes. Drain, saving liquid for soup or sauces. Melt butter in skillet, add crumbs, sauté crumbs, stirring occasionally until lightly browned. Spoon over asparagus. Sprinkle grated lemon rind over top. Makes 6 to 8 servings.

Brechspargel

(BROKEN ASPARAGUS IN SAUCE)

2 pounds asparagus, white	2 tablespoons flour
or green, or 1 large	1¼ cups asparagus broth
can white asparagus	½ to 1 teaspoon prepared
Boiling salted water (if	mustard
fresh asparagus is used)	1 egg yolk
2 tablespoons butter	Minced parsley or chives

Break off tough ends of fresh asparagus, cut tender section into diagonal pieces 2 inches in length. Cook in boiling salted water just until tender; drain, saving liquid. (If canned asparagus is used, drain, saving the liquid, break spears into 2-inch lengths.)

Melt the butter, add flour, cook until flour is lightly browned. Stir in asparagus broth, cooking until smooth. Add mustard to egg yolk, beat in some of hot sauce, then stir egg yolk into the sauce, cook and stir a few seconds longer. Place asparagus in the sauce to serve. Serve topped with minced parsley or chives. Makes 6 to 8 servings.

The following recipe is for just one of twenty-six dishes listed on the *Spargel Karte* (asparagus menu) in the dining room of the Hotel Tettnang in the Black Forest.

Spargel Freiburg
(ASPARAGUS FREIBURG)

2 pounds fresh asparagus, green or white	**4 tablespoons butter**
	2 tablespoons grated Parmesan
Boiling salted water	**1 hard-cooked egg**

Break off tough ends of asparagus (or peel the hard outer part). Cook in boiling salted water until just tender, 7 to 8 minutes. Drain; save liquid for soup. Melt butter in saucepan, let it cook until lightly browned. Add cheese; spoon over cooked asparagus. Sieve the egg yolk; mince the egg white. Sprinkle both over top of butter-cheese sauce. Makes 6 to 8 servings.

Malteser Spargel
(ASPARAGUS MALTESE STYLE)

Over hot cooked asparagus, pour a sauce of equal parts melted butter and orange juice.

Spargel mit Haselnussbutter
(ASPARAGUS WITH HAZELNUT BUTTER)

Cook asparagus spears just until tender. Cover with a sauce of chopped hazelnuts (or walnuts may be used) sautéed in a generous amount of butter.

(On the M.S. *Europa,* we had broccoli served with hazelnut butter which was a toothsome combination. Broccoli is called *Spargelkohl* in Germany, but it is not often found in German markets.)

Leipziger Allerlei
(LEIPZIG VEGETABLE PLATTER)

2 cups (about) cauliflower
buds
2 large carrots, cubed
½ pound green beans, cut
1 pound green peas,
shelled, or 1 10-ounce
package frozen peas

¼ pound button
mushrooms
4 tablespoons (½ stick)
butter
Minced parsley

Cook cauliflower, carrots, beans and peas in separate saucepans, taking care not to overcook any of them. Drain well, saving ½ cup of liquid vegetables cooked in. Arrange on a platter. Sauté the mushrooms in butter until lightly browned. Add these to the platter. Dribble butter over the vegetables. Pour the reserved vegetable liquid over the vegetables. Sprinkle minced parsley over top. Makes 6 to 8 servings.

Rote-Rübensalat
(RED BEET SALAD)

2 bunches red beets
4 tablespoons vinegar
4 tablespoons water
1 teaspoon sugar
2 teaspoons caraway seeds
2 tablespoons grated onion

¼ teaspoon powdered
cloves
1 teaspoon horseradish
Salt and pepper
4 tablespoons olive oil

Cook beets without peeling in salted water until tender. Peel; dice or slice. Make a dressing with remaining ingredients, pour over beets, let marinate several hours before serving. Makes 6 servings.

Gurkensalat
(CUCUMBER SALAD)

1 large cucumber
½ teaspoon salt
1 tablespoon sugar
1 tablespoon cider vinegar

1 tablespoon minced
parsley
¼ cup sour cream
(optional)

Peel the cucumber so that a little of the green rind remains. Slice paper-thin. Sprinkle slices with salt, sugar and vinegar. Serve this way, topped with minced parsley; or marinate in salt and sugar 15 minutes, drain off liquid that has accumulated, toss with sour cream, *then* sprinkle with parsley. Makes 4 servings as a relish.

Kopfsalat[5] mit Buttermilchsosse
(LETTUCE SALAD WITH BUTTERMILK DRESSING)

½ cup buttermilk
1 tablespoon sugar
½ teaspoon salt
Few drops lemon juice
2 tablespoons cooked
bacon

2 tablespoons bacon fat
6 cups mixed lettuce and
watercress or other salad
greens

Combine buttermilk, sugar, salt and lemon juice. Drain cooked bacon on paper towel; crumble. Add bacon and hot bacon fat to lettuce (preferably fresh garden lettuce), toss with the buttermilk mixture. Makes 4 to 6 servings.

---

[5] Actually *Kopf* is not the same as our lettuce, but delicious little tender leaves usually served with a plain tart oil and vinegar dressing made in the German manner. Garden lettuce is the best substitute.

Kopfsalat mit Apfelsinen
(LETTUCE SALAD WITH ORANGES)

1 navel orange	1 tablespoon mustard
½ cup sweet or sour	Freshly ground black
cream	pepper
¼ teaspoon salt	4 to 6 cups salad greens

Peel orange, taking care not to discard all of white membrane. Cook peel in boiling water until tender; drain, chop. Add peel to mixture of cream, salt, mustard and pepper. Arrange orange sections over salad greens on plate, cover with the dressing. Makes 4 to 6 servings.

The Allgäu is the cheese-producing region of Germany just across Lake Constance from Switzerland. An Emmentaler cheese produced in the Allgäu is much like the cheese we call Switzerland Swiss, and either domestic Swiss cheese or Switzerland Swiss may be used in the following recipe.

Käsesalat auf Allgäuer Art
(SALAD ALLGÄU STYLE)

2 cups diced Swiss cheese	4 tablespoons olive oil
¼ cup minced onion	4 tablespoons vinegar
1 cucumber or large dill	2 tablespoons water
pickle, peeled and	Pinch of sugar
thinly sliced or diced	Salt and pepper
1 cup diced fresh fruit	
or berries[6]	

Combine all ingredients; marinate. Serve on lettuce. This is usually served with chilled white wine. Makes 4 to 6 servings.

---

[6] *Preiselbeeren* would be used in Germany. These are often called by the Germans "cranberries" but actually they are not so tart as our cranberries, are more like lingonberries.

Gefüllte Melone
(STUFFED HONEYDEW MELON)

1 large ripe honeydew
melon
1 pound tiny shrimp,
cooked
½ cup chopped walnuts

¼ pound raw
mushrooms, diced
1 cucumber, peeled and
cubed
Rote Mayonnaise

Cut melon in half crosswise. Scoop out center, leaving ¼-inch shell; make balls of the melon. Set aside some melon and some shrimp for garnish. Combine rest with walnuts, mushrooms and cucumber. Toss with ½ the recipe for *Rote Mayonnaise*. Cut a thin slice from bottom of each melon half so it will rest solidly on platter. Fill with stuffing; arrange melon balls and shrimp in pattern over top. Serve salad from the melon shells as a first course or salad entree. Pass remaining dressing. Makes about 8 servings.

Rote Mayonnaise. To 1 cup mayonnaise add ¼ cup tomato catsup or chili sauce, a very little horseradish, salt and pepper to taste. Or, use ½ cup mayonnaise and ½ cup sour cream, plus catsup, horseradish and seasonings. Makes 1¼ cups.

Geflügelsalat Emirado
(CHICKEN SALAD EMIRADO)

2 cups diced cooked
chicken meat
½ cup canned sliced
mushrooms or button
mushrooms, well drained
1 small can pineapple
cubes, drained
1 cup cooked rice

1 tablespoon brandy
½ cup mayonnaise
2 tablespoons tomato
catsup
Lettuce
2 hard-cooked eggs,
sliced
Capers

Combine chicken, mushrooms, pineapple and rice, toss with brandy. Blend together mayonnaise and catsup, stir into salad mixture. Serve on lettuce, garnish salad with slices of hard-cooked eggs and capers. Makes 6 servings.

Rindfleischsalat

(BEEF SALAD)

2 cups diced cooked beef
1 cooked potato, diced
5 sweet gherkins
1 hard-cooked egg
1 small onion, thinly sliced
2 tablespoons minced parsley

1 tablespoon mustard
Freshly ground pepper
2 tablespoons oil
2 tablespoons vinegar
½ teaspoon beef stock concentrate dissolved in ¼ cup water
Salt to taste

Place beef, potato, pickles, egg, onion and parsley in salad bowl. Make a salad dressing of remaining ingredients, pour over meat and vegetables. Marinate 1 hour before serving. Makes 4 servings of a luncheon or supper entree salad.

Nudeln mit Kümmelkäse

(CARAWAY CHEESE NOODLE RING)

1 8-ounce package egg noodles, cooked
1 cup milk, heated to scalding
3 eggs, beaten

1½ cups shredded caraway-seed cheese
1 teaspoon salt
Dash of black or cayenne pepper

Drain cooked noodles thoroughly. Slowly pour hot milk into eggs, beating with whisk until smooth. Add cheese, salt and pepper. Combine milk-cheese mixture with noodles, spoon evenly into buttered 1-quart ring mold. Bake at 325° F. until firm, about 45 minutes. Unmold. Fill center of ring with buttered mixed vegetables, or creamed chicken, or curried shrimp and fish. Serves 6.

Nudelpudding mit Käse

(BAKED NOODLES WITH CHEESE)

½ pound (8-ounce
package) egg noodles,
cooked and drained
6 tablespoons butter
4 eggs, beaten
1 cup sour cream

¼ cup grated hard cheese,
or ½ cup shredded
semi-firm cheese such
as American or German
Weisslacker

Toss hot cooked noodles with butter. Beat eggs with cream, stir in
cheese. Fold into noodles. Turn into buttered casserole and bake in
350° F. oven until firm and golden. Serve as part of a vegetable
dinner with Brussels sprouts and baked escalloped tomatoes, or
serve with cold ham or roast pork. Serves 4.

Dampfnudeln

(STEAMED DUMPLINGS)

DUMPLINGS

1 package active dry
yeast
¼ cup warm water
¼ cup milk
4 tablespoons (½ stick)
butter

¼ cup sugar
1 teaspoon salt
2½ to 3 cups flour

LIQUID

½ cup milk
½ cup butter or margarine

Dissolve yeast in warm water. Combine milk, butter, sugar and salt; bring to a boil, then cool to lukewarm. Place 2½ cups of flour in a mixing bowl, make a well in the center, add the yeast, then the cooled milk mixture. Mix until blended, then knead until smooth. Let rise in warm place about 1½ hours; when doubled, punch down, let rise again about ½ hour. Tear off pieces of dough, grease palms of your hands, roll dough to make even balls about 1 inch in diameter. Place the milk and butter in a large heavy pot or Dutch oven. Put balls of dough in the pot. Lay a cloth over top of pot, then put on cover. Bring liquid to a boil on top of stove, turn heat as low as possible, cook very slowly until you can hear the butter crackling—which means the milk is all absorbed. This takes about 30 minutes. Dumplings will be golden brown and taste much like our baked sweet rolls but are more moist. Serve with meat or stewed fruit (when they qualify as *Mehlspeisen*). Makes 12.

In Nuremberg, these are called *Karthauserklösse*. They are sometimes baked rather than steamed and then taste exactly like our sweet yeast rolls.

Zwetschgenknödel

(PLUM DUMPLINGS)

1 cup flour	½ pound very ripe blue
½ teaspoon baking powder	plums, stoned
2 large eggs, well beaten	Boiling salted water
¼ teaspoon salt	Melted butter

Put flour and baking powder in large bowl, add beaten eggs and salt, stir until well blended. Place on paper towel to dry enough to handle more easily (about 20 minutes) then roll into long "sausage." Cut ½-inch slices from roll. Grease or flour your hands, flatten each in palm of hand, pressing flat with floured fingers of the other hand until large enough to wrap around half a plum; each plum half should be carefully enclosed and edges well sealed. Drop wrapped plums into boiling salted water and cook until dumplings are puffy and airy in appearance. Remove with slotted spoon; drain well on absorbent paper. Serve hot topped with melted butter as an accompaniment to roast meat. Makes 10 to 12.

Curryreis
(CURRIED RICE)

2 tablespoons minced onion or shallot	1 cup rice
1 tablespoon butter	½ teaspoon salt
1 teaspoon curry powder	2 cups chicken broth

Cook the onion or shallot in butter with curry powder until soft. Add rice, salt and chicken broth. Bring to a boil, covered; reduce heat. Cook 20 minutes or until all liquid is absorbed and small vertical tunnels appear in rice. If fluffier rice is preferred, cover saucepan with towel, steam over very low heat 5 minutes longer. Makes 4 servings.

Griessklösschen
(SEMOLINA DUMPLINGS)

4 tablespoons butter	2 small eggs
1 cup milk	Salt
½ teaspoon salt	Pinch of grated nutmeg
½ cup Cream of Wheat or Cream Farina	Boiling salted water

Add butter to milk, heat until butter melts and milk starts to boil. Slowly add the Cream of Wheat or Farina, just as in making breakfast cereal, stirring until quite thick and can easily be shaped with hands. Add 1 egg, salt and nutmeg immediately, blending thoroughly. Remove from saucepan. When cool, add the second egg. With a spoon or your hands, shape balls 1 to 1½ inches in diameter, drop a few at a time into rapidly boiling salted water. They will rise when cooked through, in about 10 minutes. These are usually served with stewed dried fruit for *Mehlspeisen* or as dumplings in soup. Makes enough for 4 *Mehlspeise* servings, or for 6 to 8 servings of soup.

Sossen

(SAUCES)

Sauces are extremely important in the German cuisine and the kinds of sauces Germans prefer tell us much about German tastes. *Senfbutter* (Mustard Butter) and *Sahnemeerettich* (Horseradish Cream), for example, are used as frequently as other countries use white sauce (*béchamel*) and mayonnaise. The Germans use the latter two sauces also, but white sauce is likely to be made sharper with a bit of mustard, or pungent with fried onion, or tart with capers. Mayonnaise may be blended with green herbs or with tomato catsup. One of the finest of the German mustards comes from Düsseldorf, and frequently the imported Düsseldorf mustard can be found in our supermarkets and delicatessens. Most like it among our domestic mustards is the kind called "Dijon style."

Brown sauce (*Braune Grundsosse*) is used as the basis for many other sauces. I have found that canned beef gravy can be used as a shortcut in nearly every case, especially when other ingredients such as red wine or onions are added. A gourmet would find the canned product inferior to a well flavored, freshly made brown sauce, but the time saved is considerable, and for all but the most critical tastes, the results are quite satisfactory.

The German cooks use the classic French sauces such as *remoulade* and *mousseline* sauce frequently, but often they add a special German twist. *Curry Mousselinesosse,* for example, starts with coconut milk and curry powder, is then enriched with egg yolks and butter beaten into the chicken-broth base.

In their sauces, as in other German recipes, both fruit and nuts play important roles. *Apfel Meerettich* (Apple Horseradish Sauce) makes quite a delicious sauce for cold roast beef. *Haselnussbutter* (Hazelnut Butter) is excellent as a topping for hot green vegetables.

Besides the sauce recipes which appear on the following pages, other sauces appear elsewhere with the particular dishes for which they are most often used. Raisin Sauce for tongue, Dill Sauce for shrimp or lobster, Curry Cream Sauce for fish, and Fruit Sauce for puddings or other desserts may be located by consulting the Index.

Rotwein Sosse
(RED WINE SAUCE)

1 10-ounce can beef gravy
1 cup dry red wine
1 tablespoon minced parsley

1 tablespoon sugar, gravy coloring or currant jelly

Combine ingredients, simmer until well blended and reduced to desired consistency. Excellent for reheating leftover roast meat, pot roast or tongue. Makes about 2 cups.

Mostrichsosse oder Senfsosse
(MUSTARD SAUCE)

2 tablespoons butter
2 tablespoons flour
½ teaspoon salt
1 to 2 tablespoons Düsseldorf or other German mustard, or Dijon style mustard

1½ cups milk or chicken or veal broth

Melt butter, stir in flour and salt, cook until it bubbles and is golden. Add mustard (adjust amount according to taste), then slowly add liquid, cooking until smooth and of desired consistency. If broth is used instead of milk, a teaspoon each of vinegar and sugar may be added. A delicious sauce for cauliflower, green beans or poached fish. Makes 1½ cups.

Gurkensosse
(CUCUMBER PICKLE SAUCE)

3 tablespoons butter
2 tablespoons flour
1½ cups chicken or
vegetable broth
1 egg yolk

10 sweet gherkins,
sliced or chopped
2 tablespoons sour cream
1 teaspoon sugar
(optional)

Melt butter, stir in flour, then slowly add broth. Beat egg yolk until thick, add some of hot broth, then combine the two. Add gherkins, stir until sauce is creamy-smooth. Turn off heat. Add sour cream and sugar if desired. Delicious over fish balls or with fried fish or oysters. Makes 1¾ cups.

Quick Gurkensosse. Heat 1 10-ounce can condensed cream of celery soup with ½ cup broth and the chopped gherkins. Just before removing from range, stir in 2 tablespoons sour cream.

Meerettichsosse
(COOKED HORSERADISH SAUCE)

2 tablespoons butter
1 small onion or shallot,
minced
2 tablespoons flour

1½ cups milk
Salt to taste
1 to 2 tablespoons
horseradish

Melt butter, cook onion or shallot until soft. Stir in flour, cook 1 minute. Add milk slowly, cook until smooth and thickened. Add salt and horseradish. Good with fish, roast beef, chicken or green vegetables. A must with boiled beef. Makes 1½ cups.

Quick Horseradish Sauce. Add ½ cup cream to a 10-ounce can condensed cream of celery soup. Cook until smooth. Add 1 or 2 tablespoons horseradish, according to taste.

Dillsosse
(DILL SAUCE)

3 tablespoons butter
2 tablespoons flour
1½ cups stock or broth
½ cup heavy sweet or
  sour cream

1 egg yolk
Few drops lemon juice
1 tablespoon minced dill

Melt butter, stir in flour, cook until it bubbles. Slowly stir in stock or broth. Simmer until slightly thickened. Beat together cream and egg yolk; add a little of the hot broth, then combine the two, beating with a whisk over very low heat until thickened. Add lemon juice and dill, continue to beat a few seconds longer. Superb with all seafood, lamb, veal or chicken. Makes 1½ cups.

Petersiliensosse
(PARSLEY SAUCE)

¼ cup chopped parsley
1 tablespoon grated onion
2 tablespoons butter
1 tablespoon flour

1 cup beef or chicken
  bouillon
Salt and pepper to taste

Add parsley and onion to butter in saucepan, cook 1 minute. Stir in flour, then the bouillon. Season to taste. Simmer until smooth and thickened. Serve with broiled chicken, fish, almost any vegetable. Makes 1 cup.

Note: If sauce is to be used with seafood, use fish or vegetable stock instead of bouillon.

Holländische Sosse
(GERMAN VERSION OF HOLLANDAISE SAUCE)

6 tablespoons butter	4 egg yolks
1 tablespoon flour	2 tablespoons lemon juice
1½ cups fish, chicken, veal or vegetable stock	

Melt 1 tablespoon of the butter, add the flour, stir over heat until flour bubbles and is golden. Slowly add the stock, cook until well blended. In a second saucepan or top of a double boiler, beat the egg yolks vigorously until thick and light in color. Add a little of the hot sauce and 1 tablespoon of butter; beat until smooth. Add the rest of the hot sauce, place over hot water or very low heat. Beat in remaining 4 tablespoons of butter one at a time, stirring constantly. When creamy-smooth, add lemon juice, remove from heat. Keep warm until needed but do not allow to cook any more. Makes 1¾ cups.

Its uses are many, but this German version of hollandaise is especially noteworthy over asparagus, broccoli, poached eggs or seafood in any form.

Kräutersosse (Herb Sauce). Prepare *Holländische Sosse*. Separately crush in a mortar ½ cup chopped parsley, ½ teaspoon dried tarragon, 1 tablespoon chopped fresh chervil (or minced celery leaves), 1 tablespoon minced fresh or frozen dill. Blend this herb paste into warm *Holländische*. Excellent with fish or chicken. Makes 1¾ cups.

Curry Mousselinesosse
(CURRY MOUSSELINE)

½ cup hot milk	1½ cups chicken or shrimp broth
¼ cup shredded coconut	
6 tablespoons butter[1]	3 egg yolks
1 tablespoon flour	1 teaspoon lemon juice
1 teaspoon curry powder	¼ cup cream (optional)

[1] If homemade chicken broth is used, it may contain enough fat to make more than 2 tablespoons butter unnecessary.

Pour hot milk over coconut; let stand until cool, then strain into bowl, squeezing coconut to extract every bit of liquid. Melt 2 tablespoons of the butter in saucepan over very low heat. Stir in flour and curry powder, then the broth. (Use chicken broth for chicken dishes, shrimp broth made from shrimp shells for seafood.) Beat egg yolks until thick, add part of the hot sauce, return mixture to pan with remaining sauce, beating constantly with whisk. Add remaining butter 1 tablespoon at a time, beating until thick. Stir in lemon juice and, if desired, the cream. Superb with shrimp, fish balls, chicken or lamb. Makes 2 to 2¼ cups.

Senfbutter

(MUSTARD BUTTER)

4 tablespoons butter
2 tablespoons German or
  Dijon style mustard
½ tablespoon lemon juice
1 tablespoon minced
  parsley

½ cup beef, chicken or
  fish stock[2]
1 egg yolk

Melt butter, allow it to brown slightly, add mustard, lemon juice, parsley and stock. Beat egg yolk until thick, stir in a little of the hot broth, continue adding stock, beating vigorously until sauce thickens. Especially good with pork. Makes ¾ cup.

---

[2] Use beef stock if sauce is to be served over meat, chicken broth for vegetables, fish stock if it is to be served on boiled or fried fish.

Tomatensosse

(TOMATO SAUCE)

1 pound fresh tomatoes,
   or 1 1-pound can
   peeled tomatoes
1 cup (about) pork or ham
   shin
Beef bones
1 parsley sprig
1 bay leaf

1 onion, stuck with 2
   cloves
4 or 5 peppercorns
2 cups water
Salt as needed
2 tablespoons butter
1 tablespoon cornstarch
   or potato starch

Combine all ingredients but butter and starch in pot or deep pan; cook covered 40 to 45 minutes. Strain. Cool so fat will rise to top, then skim. Melt butter, stir in cornstarch or potato starch, slowly add skimmed, strained broth, cook until smooth and clear. Taste for salt. If ham shin was used in broth, no salt need be needed. Add to pot roast, use over noodles, braise pork chops in it or serve over stuffed cabbage. Makes 2½ to 3 cups.

Remouladensosse

(REMOULADE SAUCE)

1 cup mayonnaise
1 tablespoon chopped
   gherkin
1 tablespoon chopped
   capers
2 tablespoons minced
   parsley

1 teaspoon chopped fresh
   chervil or finely minced
   celery leaves
1 teaspoon Düsseldorf
   mustard
Grated rind of ½ lemon
Salt to taste

Combine all ingredients, blend well. Especially good with seafood. Makes 1¼ cups.

Tartaren-Sosse
(TARTAR SAUCE)

1 anchovy fillet, minced
¼ cup minced parsley
½ cup minced dill pickle

1 tablespoon grated onion
 or chopped chives
¾ cup mayonnaise

Combine all ingredients, blend well. Makes 1 cup.

Zerlassene Butter
(MELTED BUTTER)

Melt 1 stick (¼ pound) butter in a small pan until completely liquid but still golden—the same as what we call "drawn butter sauce." Serve over boiled fish or meat.

Braune Butter
(BROWN BUTTER)

Same as Melted Butter* but butter is allowed to get light brown.

Zwiebelbutter
(ONION BUTTER)

Sliced onions are cooked in butter until soft but not brown. (If allowed to get well browned, they become fried onions.) A nice topping for *Deutsches Beefsteak*.

Kräuterbutter
(HERB BUTTER)

2 tablespoons minced
parsley
1 tablespoon chopped
fresh tarragon, or 1
teaspoon dried tarragon
½ teaspoon minced chives
¼ teaspoon dried chervil

1 chopped shallot, or 2
tablespoons chopped
onion
¼ pound (1 stick) sweet
butter, softened
1 tablespoon lemon juice
Pinch of nutmeg
Salt and pepper to taste

Mince the herbs and onion, crush in mortar with pestle to a paste. Blend with softened butter, beating until creamy. Add lemon juice, nutmeg, salt and pepper. Form into a roll. Chill until very firm, or freeze. Slice off as needed to serve over hot steak, or melt to serve over cold meat. Makes 1 cup.

Mrs. Marion Baumann, wife of the director of the German National Tourist Association, told me she uses the cardboard center of foil or Saran Wrap as a mold for *Kräuterbutter*. She lines the cardboard roll with waxed paper, then forces the butter into it. This she freezes, so when the butter is very hard, it can be sliced into portions, rewrapped, and taken out when needed. Usually a ¼-inch slice will be served over each portion of grilled steak.

Sahnemeerettich
(HORSERADISH CREAM)

½ cup heavy cream,
whipped, or 1 cup
dairy sour cream
2 tablespoons horseradish

1 tablespoon sugar
(optional)
Few drops lemon juice

Combine ingredients, blend well. (If sour cream is used, omit lemon juice.) Use on fish, beef, chicken, almost everything. Makes ½ cup.

Apfel Meerettich Sosse
(APPLE HORSERADISH SAUCE)

1 cup apple sauce
1 or 2 tablespoons
   horseradish

Salt and sugar to taste
Few drops lemon juice or
   vinegar

Combine ingredients. Serve cold as a sauce for fish, or with cold sliced beef, pork or ham. Makes 1 cup.

Mandelbutter
(ALMOND BUTTER)

½ cup slivered blanched almonds
4 to 6 tablespoons butter

Sauté the almonds in butter until lightly browned. Serve over poached or broiled fish or chicken or green vegetables, such as green beans, broccoli or peas. Makes enough for 4 servings.

Süssspeisen

(DESSERTS)

Pastries are never served as desserts in Germany, they are eaten only with tea or coffee, as meals in themselves. Ordinarily, fruit is served for dessert, either a bowl of fresh fruit or a compote. But puddings, soufflés, custards and pancakes are also enjoyed as the sweet at the end of the meal.

The lavish use of whipped cream and the frequent appearance of apples in desserts (as in the rest of the meal) are characteristic of German *Süssspeisen*. Whipped cream lovers will drool over these.

Rumtopf
("RUM POT")

This is a first cousin to the old-fashioned brandied peaches which once upon a time were a cold-pantry item in most American households.

Fresh fruit is marinated in rum in a large stone pitcher or crock and removed as wanted. Since few of us have stone crocks or the proper sort of cellar in which to store such a crock any longer, the following may serve as an appropriate modern version.

1 1-pound can Bartlett pears
1 1-pound can peach halves
¼ cup sugar
Pinch of cinnamon

1 cup fresh or frozen berries, preferably strawberries or raspberries
1 teaspoon lemon juice
½ cup dark rum

Drain the canned fruit, setting aside ½ cup syrup altogether. Heat syrup with sugar and cinnamon to boiling; add fruit and lemon juice; cool. Add rum. Chill until time to serve. Makes 8 servings.

Backpflaumenkompott
(PRUNE COMPOTE)

1 pound large prunes	Curled peel of 1 lemon
1 cup water	¼ teaspoon cinnamon
½ cup dark rum or	Pinch of cloves
Madeira	Heavy cream

Place all ingredients but cream in saucepan, bring to a boil, simmer until prunes are tender; cool. Serve chilled. Pass heavy cream. Makes 6 servings.

Dreifruchtkompott
(THREE-FRUIT COMPOTE)

1 large can greengage plums	1 cup pitted black Emperor grapes
1 pint Bing cherries, or	Sugar to taste
1 1-pound can Bing cherries	¼ cup Kirschwasser
	Shredded toasted almonds

Drain the plums, saving ½ cup syrup. Pit the fresh cherries, sprinkle with sugar (about 2 tablespoons) and the *Kirschwasser*. (If canned cherries are used, drain, use ¼ cup of the syrup and the *Kirschwasser*.) Combine the three fruits, sweeten to taste. Marinate an hour or longer. Serve topped with almonds. Makes 6 to 8 servings.

Schwarzwälder Kirschen Flambiert
(BLACK FOREST CHERRIES FLAMBÉ)

2 cans tart red cherries
packed in heavy syrup
¼ cup sugar
2 teaspoons cornstarch or
arrowroot
Pinch of cinnamon

Pinch of nutmeg
6 tablespoons
Kirschwasser
2 tablespoons butter
1 quart vanilla ice cream

Drain cherries, putting aside 1 cup of the syrup. Combine sugar, reserved syrup, cornstarch or arrowroot, spices and 3 tablespoons of the *Kirschwasser*. Heat until mixture comes to a boil, lower heat, simmer until thickened. Pour over cherries, marinate at room temperature until serving time. Place butter in chafing dish or electric skillet, heat until butter melts, add cherries, heat to simmering, add remaining *Kirschwasser* 1 tablespoon at a time, setting each aflame. When flame has died out, spoon over ice cream. Serves 8.

Kaffee Weinschaum
(COFFEE WINE FROTH)

2 eggs, separated
½ cup sugar
1 teaspoon cornstarch
Pinch of salt
1 cup dry white wine

4 fresh peaches, chopped
and sugared, or 1
1-pound can peaches,
drained and chopped
1 pint coffee ice cream
1 teaspoon instant coffee

Beat egg yolks, sugar and cornstarch until thick and light-colored. Place in top of double boiler with salt and wine; beat with whisk over hot water until mixture thickens. Separately beat egg whites until stiff, fold into thickened sauce. Fold peaches into the sauce. Serve over coffee ice cream with instant coffee sprinkled over the top. Makes 6 servings.

Pfirsiche mit Weinsosse
(PEACHES WITH WINE SAUCE)

2 pounds fresh ripe
  peaches
Few drops lemon juice or
  brandy

½ cup sugar
6 slices spongecake
Weinsosse

Peel, stone and slice peaches; place in bowl, sprinkle with lemon juice or brandy, cover with sugar. Cover bowl tightly with Saran Wrap. Chill until time to serve. For each serving, place a slice of spongecake on a dessert plate, top with peaches, then pour *Weinsosse* over the peaches. Makes 6 servings.

Weinsosse
(WINE SAUCE)

½ cup sugar
½ tablespoon cornstarch
  or arrowroot
Grated rind of ½ lemon
1 tablespoon lemon juice
2 egg yolks

1 cup sweet white wine
  (Catawba, haute
  sauterne, cream sherry
  or Madeira)
1 egg white

In top of double boiler, combine sugar and cornstarch or arrowroot, blending well. Add grated lemon rind, juice, the 2 egg yolks and the wine. Beat constantly with a whisk over hot water until mixture thickens. Remove from heat. Beat the egg white until it forms soft peaks; carefully fold into hot sauce. Serve warm. (For a cold sauce, place cooked egg yolk-wine mixture over a bowl of ice water, fold in beaten egg white, beat with whisk until creamy-smooth.) Makes 1½ cups.

Note: When chilled, the egg white sometimes separates. If this happens, just before serving beat sauce in blender or with rotary beater until smooth.

Pumpernickel Schlagsahne
(PUMPERNICKEL CREAM)

1 cup fine dry pumpernickel crumbs	2 cups whipped heavy cream
½ cup confectioners' sugar	2 tablespoons dark rum, Kirschwasser or brandy

To make the pumpernickel crumbs, dry 5 slices of pumpernickel in a slow (250° F.) oven; when hard, break into pieces, whirl in a blender or crush with a rolling pin. Blend crumbs with sugar, the whipped cream and the rum. Chill or partially freeze (but do not permit it to become completely frozen) until time to serve. Makes 4 servings.

Makronen Schlagsahne (Macaroon Cream). Use 1 to 1½ cups crushed macaroons instead of pumpernickel. Instead of rum, strong black coffee and ½ teaspoon vanilla may be used.

Nussen Schlagsahne (Nut Cream). Use 1 cup ground almonds, hazelnuts or walnuts instead of pumpernickel.

Früchten Schlagsahne (Fruit Cream). Add 1 cup fresh raspberries, crushed and sugared red currants or chopped sweetened strawberries to the basic recipe or either of the above variations.

Schokoladencreme
(CHOCOLATE CREAM)

2 egg yolks	3 tablespoons hot black coffee
¼ cup sugar	2 cups whipped heavy cream
4 ounces German semi-sweet chocolate, melted	

Combine egg yolks and sugar, beat until thick. Blend in melted chocolate and hot coffee. Fold into stiffly beaten cream. Chill. Makes 4 servings.

(For those worried over calories, this can be made with a whipped topping mix. Not as good as with real whipped cream, but still far better than the packaged chocolate desserts.)

Bayrische Vanillecreme
(BAVARIAN CREAM)

1 envelope unflavored
  gelatine
½ cup sugar
Pinch of salt
2 eggs, separated

1¼ cups milk
½ teaspoon vanilla
1 cup whipped heavy
  cream

Combine gelatine, sugar and salt. Place in top of double boiler over hot water. Beat egg yolks until thick, stir in milk. Add this to the gelatine mixture and stir with whisk until gelatine is thoroughly dissolved. Remove from heat. Add vanilla, chill gelatine until it is consistency of unbeaten egg whites. Beat egg whites until stiff. Beat cream until thickened but not stiff. Fold cream into gelatine, then the beaten egg whites, blending well. Pour into a 4-cup mold, or 4 individual 1-cup molds, or a glass serving dish. Chill until firm.

Mit Früchten (With Fruit). Place in bowl 1 cup chopped fruit, such as peaches, apricots, pineapple, cherries or berries; sweeten to taste and marinate in ¼ cup *Kirschwasser*. Prepare Bavarian Cream as above, but use only 1 cup milk. Fold the fruit and *Kirschwasser* into the gelatine mixture after the gelatine has begun to set and just before whipped cream is added.

Kaffeecreme (Coffee Cream). Prepare as for Bavarian Cream but instead of milk, use 1 cup strong black coffee.

Punschcreme (Punch Cream). Prepare as for Bavarian Cream, but instead of milk, use ½ cup sweet white wine or cream sherry,

½ cup strained apple juice and 2 tablespoons rum. Instead of vanilla extract, use lemon extract or 1 teaspoon grated lemon rind.

Zitronencreme
(LEMON CREAM)

3 eggs, separated
2 tablespoons sugar
Grated rind of 1 lemon
2 tablespoons brandy or
  Madeira
1 package lemon-flavored
  gelatine

1 cup hot water
½ cup strained orange
  juice
2 tablespoons fresh lemon
  juice
1 cup whipped heavy
  cream

Beat egg yolks with sugar and lemon rind until thick and light. Stir in brandy or Madeira. Dissolve gelatine in hot water. Add to gelatine the orange juice, lemon juice and the egg yolk mixture. Chill until it thickens to consistency of unbeaten egg white. Beat egg whites until stiff. Beat cream until thick but not stiff. Fold whipped cream into gelatine, then the egg whites. Pour into 6-cup mold or 1½-quart glass serving dish. Chill until firm. (To unmold, dip quickly in hot water, unmold on platter.) Serve garnished with whole strawberries or black cherries. Makes 6 to 8 servings.

Apfelreis
(APPLE RICE PUDDING)

½ cup rice
1¼ cups milk
Grated rind of ½ lemon
½ cup sugar
½ teaspoon salt
6 to 8 apples (2 pounds),
  peeled and sliced

2 tablespoons butter
½ cup sweet cider or
  apple juice
2 tablespoons confectioners'
  sugar
2 egg whites, stiffly beaten

Cook the rice in the milk with lemon rind, sugar and salt until soft. Place a layer of rice in a deep (1½-quart) baking dish, add half the apples, dot with 1 tablespoon butter, add remaining rice and top with apples. Dot with remaining butter. Pour cider or apple juice over all. Bake 45 minutes in 350° F. oven. Blend sugar into the beaten egg whites, spread over apples, bake until meringue is golden. Serve warm. Makes 6 servings.

* * *

This popular German dessert is basically the same as the Danes' red fruit pudding, *Rodgrod*. It is also similar to the cornstarch fruit puddings the English call flummery.

Rote Grütze
(RED FRUIT PUDDING)

1 1-pound can tart red pitted cherries packed in heavy syrup	1 tablespoon lemon juice
	1 tablespoon currant jelly
	Few drops red food coloring
1 10-ounce package frozen raspberries, defrosted	1 cup whipped and sweetened heavy cream
1½ tablespoons cornstarch	

Drain the fruit, saving and measuring juice. In saucepan, blend cornstarch with a little of the juice, add the rest, bring to a boil, stirring, until juice bubbles and is thickened. Add lemon juice, currant jelly and food coloring. Fold in the fruit. Cool, then chill. Serve in a glass bowl or in individual sherbets, topping each serving with whipped cream. Makes 5 or 6 servings.

Note: If you have a blender, purée fruit and juices in it, then force through sieve to remove raspberry seeds. Thicken with cornstarch, add lemon juice and jelly, cook until thickened.

Fruchtreis

(FRUIT RICE MOLD)

1 envelope unflavored
gelatine
3 tablespoons sugar
2 tablespoons rum or
brandy
1 egg yolk
1 cup milk
1½ cups cooked rice
1 teaspoon grated lemon
rind

1 teaspoon vanilla
½ cup slivered almonds
1 cup drained canned fruit
(apricots, peaches or
pineapple)
1 cup whipped heavy
cream

Blend gelatine with sugar, add rum. Beat together egg yolk and milk, place with gelatine in top of double boiler, cook, stirring constantly, until gelatine is dissolved and sauce slightly thickened. Add to rice with lemon rind, vanilla and almonds. Fold in the fruit and the whipped cream. Spoon into rinsed 1-quart mold or glass serving dish. Chill until firm. Serve topped with defrosted frozen raspberries or strawberries as a sauce. Makes 6 servings.

Arme Ritter

("POOR KNIGHT")

This is another version of what we call "French toast." The only difference—chopped almonds are added to the batter and it is served as a dessert topped with a fruit sauce or fruit preserves.

3 eggs, beaten
1 cup milk
½ teaspoon salt
¼ cup coarsely chopped
almonds

6 slices white bread or 12
thin slices Vienna bread
Shortening for frying
Fruit Sauce

Beat eggs, milk, salt and almonds together. Dip bread in the mixture, fry on both sides until golden. Serve topped by Fruit Sauce. Makes 6 servings.

Fruit Sauce. Purée a 10-ounce package of defrosted frozen raspberries, peaches or strawberries in blender. Add a tablespoon of cornstarch (thinned with a little of the juice), simmer until thickened. Cool.

Apfelpfannkuchen
(APPLE PANCAKES)

1 cup sifted all-purpose flour
1 tablespoon sugar
¼ teaspoon salt
2 eggs, beaten
1 cup milk

8 tablespoons (1 stick) butter
3 tart firm apples, peeled and sliced
Cinnamon-sugar mixture
Confectioners' sugar

Combine flour, sugar and salt in bowl. Make a well in the center, add eggs and milk, beat until batter is smooth. Let stand while cooking apples.

Place 3 tablespoons of the butter in a skillet, sauté the apple slices in the butter until golden and tender but not soft. Remove; sprinkle with cinnamon-sugar (mixture used for cinnamon toast). Keep warm.

In an omelet pan or crepe pan, melt remaining butter, add the thin batter for one pancake at a time, tilting pan so batter spreads evenly. Cook until lightly browned on one side, turn over. As pancakes are finished, pile some of the apple mixture on each, roll up. Sprinkle tops of rolled pancakes with confectioners' sugar while warm. These may be kept in a warm (250–275° F.) oven until dessert time, or may be reheated in foil. Makes 12 pancakes, enough for 6 servings. Serve topped with whipped cream or sour cream.

Zwetschgenpfannkuchen (Plum Pancakes). Use 6 to 8 chopped stoned red or blue plums, sweetened, instead of apples, for the filling.

Kirschpfannkuchen (Cherry Pancakes). Use 1 quart pitted tart red cherries, sweetened to taste, or a 1-pound can tart red cherries, packed in heavy syrup (drained), instead of apples, for the filling.

Kaiserschmarren (Scrambled Pancakes). Prepare the batter as for *Apfelpfannkuchen,* but separate the eggs. Prepare the batter with flour, egg yolks, sugar, salt and milk, then fold in the stiffly beaten egg whites. Cook the apples or other fruit in butter, add the pancake batter all at once, cook until lightly browned in bottom, then turn over with spatula, as for scrambled eggs. Pancake will break into pieces, but this does not matter. Let cook until lightly browned on the moist side, then remove to warmed plate or platter, sprinkle with confectioners' sugar. Add additional sautéed fruit over top, if desired, or serve topped with sour cream.

Gebäck, Kuchen und Torten

(BAKED GOODS, PASTRIES AND TORTES)

The art of the *Konditorei* is the glory of the German cuisine. German pastry shops produce fabulous cakes and pastries, intricately decorated, lavish with whipped cream, and this sweet-toothed race consumes them in fantastic quantities. Both in late morning and mid-afternoon, customers throng to the *Konditorei* to sit at tables and indulge in one or more sweets along with strong coffee. Most people will carry out a box of pastry with them when they leave.

Some of the *Konditoreien* are huge establishments occupying several floors. Kurfürstendamm (or "Ku-damm" as it is affectionately called) in West Berlin has several such *Konditoreien* in every block. When weather permits, chairs are placed on the wide sidewalks so that customers may bask in the sun while nibbling on cream-swathed tortes and nut-crusted *Kuchen*. In cooler weather, a view of the elegant boulevard is still possible, for the balconies are enclosed with glass and heated, and customers may sit here looking out on the thronged boulevard below. In the midst of winter, the carpeted interiors are more gay, with waiters balancing trays of pastry and coffee above the heads of the chattering customers, trying to weave their way through the throngs crowding in on the lookout for empty chairs.

Besides the large, elegant pastry houses, there are dozens and dozens of smaller *Konditoreien* in every city and town. Yet small as the shop may be, the variety of its pastries is always spectacular. I brought home with me a menu from one such small café in Cologne, a room with perhaps a dozen tables, yet its menu lists fifty-seven kinds of pastries, cakes and sweets (plus a few *Vor-*

speisen, two kinds of soup, twelve coffee drinks and several breakfast suggestions available at all hours).

Since each shop boasts its own specialties, and there is no end to the variety of sweets available in Germany, I can only include here a few samples. What's more, each pastry cook seems to make her own version of the classic pastries. *Schwarzwälder Kirschtorte,* for example, is listed on virtually every *Konditorei* menu, yet it never seems to be made the same way twice.

Gebäck means "baked goods" and includes yeast breads and sweet rolls as well as pastries. I was surprised to learn that home bread-making is rather rare, except on the farms. Most German women today buy bread from commercial bakeries or from the farmers' markets. But conversely, the German women I talked to were surprised to learn that American women did any yeast-baking at all. When some recipes calling for yeast were given to me, one woman remarked, "But you couldn't do this in America. American women don't use yeast in baking, do they?" (Fleischmann's would be astonished to hear this, I'm sure!)

Pumpernickel cannot be made at home, because it must bake in specially constructed ovens for twenty-four hours. It is the long, slow baking that gives the German pumpernickel its particular flavor, and the Germans prefer it to be a little dry, with a special sour-sweet pungency. I was told that in "olden times" in Westphalia, the dough for making pumpernickel was worked with the feet, a ceremony comparable to the pressing of grapes for making wine. That was long ago, however, and machines have long since been perfected for kneading the dough in exactly the right manner.

(The name *Pumpernickel,* incidentally, is one of those strange mysteries no one has been able to solve. I've heard half a dozen different explanations of the name, each more ridiculous than the one before. It is probably an old Saxon or Frankish word whose original meaning has long since been forgotten.)

Black bread (*Schwarzbrot*), *Roggenbrot,* which is made with cornmeal and rye, and *Bauernbrot,* round crisp loaves baked in country stone ovens, are a few of the wonderfully flavorful breads which can be purchased in German bakeries and enjoyed in German restaurants. But even German cookbooks rarely include recipes for these breads to be made at home.

The names for baked goods are quite as confusing as other German food names. The word *Kuchen,* for example, does not mean "cake" at all. In most cases, a *Kuchen* is made with a dough quite similar to our pie crust dough but much richer (made entirely with butter). Sometimes a *Kuchen* will be made with sweet yeast dough, but almost never of a batter like our cake batters. *Torte* is an all-encompassing word, impossible to define in a sentence, for some tortes resemble our pies, others resemble many-layered cakes. Some are lathered with whipped cream, others may have a buttercream filling and a meringue-nut topping. Among the most interesting were the tortes topped with a layer of fruit salad in gelatine! These are called *Obstsalattorten,* literally "fruit salad tortes."

Several cookie recipes and a recipe for marzipan have been included in this chapter. But both marzipan and the world-famous *Lebkuchen* of Nuremberg are usually purchased from confectionary shops or *Konditoreien* rather than made at home. I was in Germany when the Christmas season was approaching, and the marzipan figures in the shop windows were absolutely fascinating. I brought quite a selection home to my daughter, but she could not bring herself to eat them—they were too enchanting to look at, she felt they should be preserved.

Strudel

The making of strudel dough at home is a tedious and difficult technique and one that few German women attempt any longer in their modern tiny kitchens. A first requirement is a sturdy kitchen table, or adequate substitute, on which a floured sheet or linen cloth can be spread, and space enough around the table to move freely. This in itself is a deterrent for most of us. But even with a table top of proper size, a courageous heart and fingers that are clever at kneading and manipulating the dough, the task is formidable, for the dough must be stretched to paper-like fragility.

My friend Helen Feingold, Food Editor of *TV Guide* magazine, is an expert at strudel-making, for her mother was Austrian and she learned this most difficult of pastry techniques quite literally at her mother's knee. I am indebted both to Helen and her late mother, Helene Krainer, for the following recipe, for I confess I have never had the courage to try stretching strudel dough myself.

There are many bakeries that sell strudel leaves ready to use, and packaged strudel or phyllo leaves can be purchased in certain delicatessens and food specialty shops. (Phyllo pastry will be found in Greek groceries. The dough is different from that of strudel, but the resulting pastry has the same fragile, buttery crispness.) The filling as given in Helene Krainer's *Apfelstrudel* may be used inside prepared leaves, following package directions for moistening and buttering the leaves of dough.

Helene Krainer's Apfelstrudel
(APPLE STRUDEL)

Strudelteig (STRUDEL DOUGH)

2 cups sifted all-purpose flour	**2 tablespoons oil**
½ teaspoon salt	**½ cup lukewarm water**
1 egg, well beaten	**¾ cup melted butter**

Put flour mixed with salt into a bowl. Make a hole in the center of the flour and add egg, oil and water. Stir until a soft dough is formed that comes clean away from the sides of the bowl (it does not matter if some flour is left in the bowl). Knead dough on a lightly floured board for 15 minutes or until it is of much the same consistency as bubble gum. Cover it with an inverted warm bowl and let it rest in a warm place for 1 hour.

Cover a large kitchen table, or a *sturdy* card table, with a sheet. Rub the sheet with flour. Roll out the dough as large as possible with a *warm* rolling pin, lifting up dough frequently to prevent sticking. Brush dough lightly with a little of the melted butter. Now remove any rings that may be on your fingers and dust your hands with flour. Place your floured hands palm side down *under* the dough. Now with your knuckles gently pull the dough from the center out, gently stretching and stretching until it is as thin as note paper. When finished, it should be about 30 × 40 inches in size and some will hang over the edge of the table. If any holes have formed, these may be patched with small pieces of dough pressed firmly into place. Brush again with melted butter, generously this time; about half the ¾ cup of melted butter should be used. (Save the remainder to brush over the outside of rolled-up strudel.) With scissors trim the edges of the dough. Add the filling.

FILLING

1 cup toasted bread crumbs	1 cup broken walnut meats
6 apples, preferably Greenings or Rome Beauties, peeled, cored and thinly sliced	½ cup sugar
	1 teaspoon ground cinnamon
¼ cup raisins	Grated rind of 1 lemon

Sprinkle the crumbs over the strudel dough, keeping a 2-inch margin around all sides. Combine apples, raisins, walnuts, sugar, cinnamon and lemon rind. Pat this mixture into a long mound on the 30-inch side of the dough, 2 inches from the end. Fold over the 2-inch end margin. Now fold over the dough lengthwise on both sides. Gradually lift the sheet and very carefully roll up the strudel, taking care that the fragile dough does not break. Shape with your fingers as you roll up the strudel. Place the rolled strudel in a horseshoe shape on a buttered baking sheet. Brush with remaining melted butter. Bake in an oven preheated to 375° F. for 45 to 50 minutes until richly golden and flaky-crisp. Cool slightly after removing from oven and while warm sprinkle with confectioners' sugar. Serve while still warm. Makes 8 to 10 servings.

Note: If desired, canned sliced apples may be used instead of fresh apples, omitting sugar in above filling recipe.

Mürbeteig
(SWEET PASTRY)

2 cups sifted all-purpose
  flour
Pinch of salt
1 teaspoon baking powder
2 to 4 tablespoons sugar
¾ cup butter (1½ sticks)

1 medium egg, beaten
1 to 2 tablespoons liquid
  (milk, cream, water or
  rum)
Grated lemon rind
  (optional)

Combine flour, salt, baking powder and sugar. Chop in butter until
very fine. Add beaten egg and liquid and the lemon rind (if used).
Work with fingers until smooth like pie dough. Press evenly, using
fingers and heel of palm, over bottom and sides of 9-inch round
cake pan, fluting above rim. (Or shape as indicated in recipe.)
Or, chill the dough several hours, then roll out between waxed paper
to ¼-inch thick. Add filling; bake in oven preheated to 400° F.
until golden and flaky-crisp.

Zwetschgenkuchen
(PLUM PASTRY)

1 recipe Mürbeteig (Sweet
  Pastry)*
2 pounds blue plums
  (fresh prunes) or red
  plums, pitted

¾ cup sugar
1 teaspoon cinnamon
2 tablespoons flour
¼ cup slivered blanched
  almonds (optional)

Fit pastry over bottom and up sides of 9-inch round cake pan.
Place pitted plum halves over bottom; sprinkle ½ cup of the sugar
over plums. Combine remaining ¼ cup sugar with cinnamon, flour
and almonds; sprinkle over top. Bake in oven preheated to 400° F.
about 40 minutes until pastry is flaky-crisp and golden and plums
bubbling with syrup. Makes 6 servings.

Kirschkuchen
(CHERRY PASTRY)

1 recipe Mürbeteig (Sweet
  Pastry)*
1 quart tart pie cherries or
  black Bing cherries,
  pitted
½ to ¾ cup sugar

2 tablespoons Kirsch
2 eggs, well beaten
½ cup heavy sweet cream
  or sour cream
¼ cup confectioners' sugar

Line 9-inch round cake pan with the pastry over bottom and up sides. Combine the cherries with sugar and *Kirsch* (use ½ cup sugar for Bing cherries, ¾ cup for pie cherries); spread over pastry. Bake in oven preheated to 400° F. for about 25 minutes. Combine the eggs, cream and sugar; pour over the fruit in the pastry, reduce oven heat to 350° F. Bake until custard is set, about 20 minutes longer. Cool. Serve while still slightly warm but at room temperature. Makes 6 servings.

With Canned Pie Cherries. Use tart red cherries packed in heavy syrup; drain well, add ¼ cup of the syrup, ½ cup sugar, ½ teaspoon cornstarch and 2 tablespoons *Kirsch*. Bake as above, adding the custard mixture halfway through baking.

Apfeltorte
(APPLE TART)

1 recipe Mürbeteig (Sweet
  Pastry)*
4 or 5 tart apples, peeled
  and sliced
¼ cup sugar
¼ teaspoon cinnamon
  (optional)

½ cup raisins or currants
½ cup slivered blanched
  almonds
2 tablespoons butter
Confectioners' sugar

Line bottom and sides of 9-inch round cake pan with pastry. Lay apple slices across the bottom. Combine sugar and cinnamon, sprinkle over apples. Add raisins or currants, butter and almonds. Bake in oven preheated to 400° F. until pastry is golden-crisp and fruit mixture bubbling. Remove from oven, promptly shake confectioners' sugar over top. Makes 6 servings.

Apfelkuchen

(APPLE CAKE BAVARIAN STYLE)

1 recipe Mürbeteig (Sweet Pastry)*	1 cup sour cream
4 or 5 tart apples, peeled and sliced	2 eggs, beaten
½ cup sugar	2 tablespoons rum or brandy
1 teaspoon cornstarch	2 tablespoons sifted confectioners' sugar

Line bottom and sides of 9-inch round cake pan with pastry. Lay sliced apples over bottom. Blend together sugar and cornstarch, sprinkle over apples. Bake in oven preheated to 400° F. about 25 minutes. Combine sour cream, eggs, rum or brandy and sugar. Spoon over apples in the pastry. Lower heat to 350° F. Continue baking until custard is set. Cool. Makes 6 servings.

Obstsalattorte

(FRUIT SALAD TORTE)

1 3-ounce package lemon-flavored gelatine	Buttercreme Filling
½ cup boiling water	1 cup whipped heavy cream
1 large (1-pound 12-ounce) can fruit cocktail	1 teaspoon vanilla
1 recipe Mürbeteig (Sweet Pastry)*	2 tablespoons confectioners' sugar

Dissolve gelatine in boiling water. Drain fruit cocktail, saving 1 cup of the juice. Add juice to the gelatine, chill until it begins to set, then add the drained fruit. Pour into 9-inch round cake pan. Chill until firm.

Prepare the pastry; roll out to make 2 layers to fit 9-inch round cake pan. Bake in oven preheated to 400° F. until golden and crisp.

Prepare the Buttercreme Filling. Spread between the two pastry layers.

When gelatine is firm, unmold by dipping pan quickly in water, hold a plate over the top, and invert. Slip molded fruit onto the torte. Whip the cream until stiff, add vanilla and sugar, spread around the edge of the cake. Keep chilled until time to serve. Makes 6 to 8 servings.

BUTTERCREME FILLING

12 tablespoons (1½ sticks) butter, softened
2 egg yolks
1 cup sifted confectioners' sugar

2 to 3 tablespoons milk
1 tablespoon rum, or 1 teaspoon vanilla

Cream butter until fluffy; add egg yolks and sugar, beat to a froth. Add milk, rum or vanilla; beat until smooth and creamy.

Haselnusstorte
(HAZELNUT TORTE)

½ cup fine dry bread crumbs
½ cup milk
1 tablespoon dark rum
4 tablespoons butter
½ cup granulated sugar
5 or 6 eggs, separated

1 cup ground hazelnuts
2 cups heavy cream
2 tablespoons confectioners' sugar
1 tablespoon rum (optional)
¼ cup chopped hazelnuts

Soak the crumbs in milk and rum. Beat butter until creamy; add sugar, beating to a froth. Add yolks of eggs to soaked crumbs, then the butter mixture. Beat egg whites until stiff; fold in. Stir in ground hazelnuts.

Grease 3 8-inch round cake pans. Divide batter evenly in the 3 pans. Bake in oven preheated to 350° F. for 30 to 40 minutes or until it springs back when touched. Let cool in pans 5 minutes, then turn out on racks.

Beat the cream until stiff; fold in sugar and rum. Spread the cream between the layers and over the top. Sprinkle chopped nuts over top. Makes 10 to 12 small but very rich servings.

Note: For a less rich torte, bake in 2 9-inch layers, use only 1 cup cream for the whipped cream filling and topping.

Walnuts may be used instead of hazelnuts, if the latter are not locally available.

Mandeltorte (Almond Torte). Use almonds instead of hazelnuts in the basic recipe. Bake in one 9 × 13-inch pan. Serve plain, cut into squares, omitting whipped cream. This makes a more delicate torte, not so rich and heavy, and is excellent with tea.

Linzer Torte

1 cup butter, softened	Pinch of salt
1 cup sifted confectioners' sugar	½ teaspoon cinnamon
1 egg	1 egg white
2¾ cups sifted all-purpose flour	Grated rind and juice of 1 lemon
1½ cups ground hazelnuts or almonds	1½ cups raspberry jam or currant jelly
	Confectioners' sugar

Beat butter until creamy; beat in sugar to a fluff, add the egg, beat until frothy; then add flour, nuts, salt and cinnamon. Chill thoroughly, then roll out two-thirds of the dough large enough to cover the bottom and sides of a 9-inch round cake pan, preferably one with removable bottom. Brush egg white over the bottom; let it dry. Roll out remaining dough, cut into lattice strips. Blend the lemon rind and juice with the raspberry jam or currant jelly, spread this filling over the pastry dough. Place lattice pastry strips over the top. Bake in oven preheated to 400° F. for 45 minutes. When torte is removed from oven, immediately sprinkle top with confectioners' sugar. Spoon additional jam into squares formed by the lattice if filling has shrunk noticeably. Makes 6 to 8 servings.

* * *

Schwarzwälder Kirschtorte is one of the most famous tortes of Germany. It originated in Swabia, the Black Forest region, but is listed on menus in *Konditoreien* throughout West Germany. It is rarely made the same way twice, but always is a combination of chocolate and cherry with a wicked amount of *Kirsch*-flavored whipped cream.

Schwarzwälder Kirschtorte

(BLACK FOREST CHERRY TORTE)

TORTE

2 cups cake flour	2 cups granulated sugar
2 teaspoons double-acting baking powder	4 teaspoons lemon juice
6 eggs	¾ cup hot milk

Sift flour and baking powder together 3 times. Beat eggs until light and thickened (about 10 minutes). Gradually add sugar to eggs, beating constantly. Add lemon juice. Fold in flour a little at a time. Add the hot milk, mixing quickly until batter is smooth. Lightly grease and flour 3 9-inch round cake pans, preferably pans with removable bottoms. Divide the batter evenly between the 3 pans. Preheat oven to 350° F.; bake cake layers for 25 minutes or until tester comes out clean. Remove from oven and invert pans until cake is cool. Remove from pans and slice each layer crosswise into 2 layers, making 6 layers.

CHERRY FILLING

1 1-pound 4-ounce can tart red cherries in heavy syrup
2 tablespoons arrowroot or cornstarch
8 to 10 drops red food coloring

Combine in saucepan, cook, stirring constantly, over medium heat until smooth, thick and clear. Remove from heat; cool.

CHOCOLATE FILLING

1 bar German sweet chocolate
1 cup heavy cream, whipped

Melt chocolate over hot water; cool to room temperature. Fold into the whipped cream. Chill 15 to 20 minutes.

KIRSCHCREME (*Kirsch-flavored whipped cream*)

Pinch of salt
2 cups heavy cream, whipped
3 tablespoons Kirschwasser

Add salt to cream as you beat it. When cream stands in peaks, fold in the *Kirschwasser*.

Place one cake layer on a large round cake plate. Spread with half the chocolate filling. Add the second cake layer; spread with a scant cup of the whipped cream. Add the third layer; spread with remaining chocolate filling. Add the fourth layer; spread this with another scant cup of whipped cream. Over the fifth layer spread the cherry filling. Top with sixth layer. Spread remaining whipped cream over top and sides. Garnish with maraschino cherries and shaved curls of German sweet chocolate. Refrigerate at least an hour before serving. Makes 12 to 14 very rich servings.

Bienenstich
(BEE STING CAKE)

1¾ cups sifted all-purpose
    flour
3 teaspoons baking powder
½ teaspoon salt
8 tablespoons (1 stick)
    butter
⅔ cup granulated sugar
2 eggs, unbeaten

1 teaspoon vanilla
6 tablespoons milk
½ cup slivered blanched
    almonds
⅓ cup sugar
¼ cup (4 tablespoons)
    butter
1 tablespoon milk or cream

Preheat oven to 375° F. Grease and flour a 9-inch spring-form pan. Sift together flour, baking powder and salt. Cream the butter until fluffy, add sugar gradually, beating until light. Add eggs one at a time, beating well after each addition. Add vanilla. Add dry ingredients one-third at a time, alternately with the 6 tablespoons milk. Stir only enough to blend thoroughly. Pour into the spring-form pan.

Heat together almonds, sugar, butter, and milk or cream until sugar dissolves. Pat a spoonful of flour over the top of the cake batter, using the back of a spoon. Pour the almond mixture evenly over the batter. Bake 25 minutes or until cake tester comes out clean. Cool while preparing filling.

FILLING

2½ tablespoons sugar
2 tablespoons cornstarch
3 eggs yolks, lightly beaten
1 cup milk

½ teaspoon almond extract
3 egg whites, stiffly beaten
Pinch of salt

Combine sugar, cornstarch and egg yolks in top of double boiler. Separately heat milk to scalding, slowly pour over egg-yolk mixture, stirring constantly and quickly with whisk. Place over hot water, cook, stirring constantly until smooth and thick. Do not allow to boil. Stir in almond extract. Beat egg whites, adding the salt, until stiff peaks form. Fold egg whites into the yolk mixture. Place a piece of waxed paper over the top, chill.

When the cake has cooled, slice in half crosswise to make 2 layers. Place bottom layer cut side up on cake plate. Spread with filling. Top with second layer with the almond-glazed side up. Refrigerate until time to serve. Makes about 10 servings.

Mohnkuchen

(POPPY SEED CAKE)

1 recipe Mürbeteig (Sweet Pastry)*	½ cup grated or ground almonds
4 tablespoons milk, scalded	¼ cup raisins
7 ounces poppy seeds (2 3½-ounce jars)	8 tablespoons butter
⅓ cup sugar	½ cup flour
1 egg yolk	3 tablespoons sugar

Prepare the pastry. Roll out to a rectangle on lightly floured pastry cloth, using a pastry sock over the rolling pin. Or, chill ½ hour, roll out between sheets of waxed paper. Place in jelly-roll pan or on baking sheet.

Add hot milk to the poppy seeds; let stand 10 minutes. When cool, add sugar, egg yolk, almonds and raisins. Beat to blend well. Spread mixture over the unbaked pastry. Combine 4 tablespoons of the butter, flour and sugar to make a crumb topping. Sprinkle over poppy-seed mixture. Dot remaining butter over crumb topping.

Preheat oven to 375° F. Bake until pastry is crisp, about 45 minutes. When cool, cut into squares to serve. Makes about 16 squares.

Mokka-Nusstorte
(MOCHA NUTCAKE)

5 eggs, separated
1 cup sugar
1 tablespoon instant coffee powder

½ cup sifted all-purpose flour
½ cup hazelnut or walnut meats, finely ground

Beat egg whites until soft peaks form. Add sugar gradually until mixture is stiff. Beat egg yolks separately until thick and light; fold in. Blend together coffee, flour and nuts; gently but thoroughly fold into egg-white mixture until no white streaks remain. Spoon into 9-inch tube pan (preferably one with removable bottom) which has been greased then floured. Stir once more to remove air bubbles. Bake in oven preheated to 325° F. for 50 to 55 minutes. Cool on rack. Split cake in 4 layers. Fill with *Mokkacreme*. Sprinkle confectioners' sugar over top.

MOKKACREME

2 cups (1 pint) heavy cream
2 tablespoons confectioners' sugar
1 tablespoon instant coffee powder dissolved in 1 tablespoon rum or brandy

Beat cream until thick, blend in sugar, then the coffee dissolved in rum or brandy. Stir until smooth. Makes 4 cups.

Frankfurter Kranz
(FRANKFURT CROWN COFFEECAKE)

3½ cups sifted all-purpose flour
4 teaspoons baking powder
1 cup butter or margarine
1½ cups granulated sugar

6 eggs, separated
1 teaspoon vanilla extract
Buttercreme Filling*
Krokant (Sugar-coated Almonds)

Sift flour with baking powder, place in large mixing bowl. With electric mixer, beat butter with sugar until light and fluffy. Add egg yolks one at a time with mixer in motion; add vanilla. Add this mixture to the flour, stir just until well blended. Beat egg whites until stiff, fold into batter, taking care to remove all air bubbles.

Grease a Turk's head mold (with tube in center). Pour batter into mold. Bake in oven preheated to 275° F. for 1 hour or until toothpick inserted in center comes out clean.

Remove from pan immediately; cool on cake rack.

Split cake into 3 layers. Spread Buttercreme Filling between layers and over the top. Sprinkle the sugar-coated almonds over the frosting.

Keep cake chilled until time to serve.

Krokant (Sugar-coated Almonds). Place ⅓ cup sugar, ½ cup butter, 1 tablespoon milk and 1 cup slivered blanched almonds in saucepan; cook over low heat until nuts are coated with syrup and lightly browned. Turn out onto waxed paper; cool. Separate into pieces with 1 or 2 slivers of almond in each piece. Sprinkle over the frosting.

Butterkuchen

2 envelopes active dry yeast	½ cup butter
½ cup warm water	4 cups sifted all-purpose
¾ cup milk	flour
½ cup sugar	Grated rind of 1 lemon
1 teaspoon salt	3 eggs

BUTTER TOPPING

½ cup (1 stick) butter	⅓ cup slivered blanched
1 cup sugar	almonds
½ teaspoon cinnamon	

Sprinkle the yeast over warm water. Heat milk, sugar, salt and the ½ cup butter together until sugar is dissolved and butter melted. Cool to lukewarm. Add dissolved yeast. Place the flour blended with lemon rind in large mixing bowl; form a well in the center. Add yeast-milk mixture and the eggs. Stir until blended and smooth. Pour into a buttered 9 × 13-inch baking pan, spreading dough evenly. Let rise in warm place about 45 minutes.

Chop the butter into the mixed sugar and cinnamon to form fine particles. Sprinkle over top of risen batter. Add the almonds. Bake in oven preheated to 375° F. for 30 minutes or until top is golden and syrupy. Makes about 12 servings.

Streuselkuchen. This is much the same as *Butterkuchen* except that the lemon rind is omitted from the batter and a crumb topping of 1½ cups flour, ¾ cup sugar, ¼ cup ground almonds and 8 tablespoons (1 stick) butter are sprinkled over batter. If desired, ¼ teaspoon cinnamon may also be added to the topping mixture.

Apfelbutterkuchen (a Bremen specialty). Prepare as for *Butterkuchen,* place sliced peeled apples over top of dough before placing in oven. Cover apples with same Butter Topping. Almonds are an optional addition (and very good!).

Bremer Klaben
(BREMEN SWEET BREAD)

'A Christmas specialty in Bremen.

2 packages active dry yeast	1 cup raisins
½ cup warm water	½ cup currants
1½ cups lukewarm milk	¾ cup slivered blanched
½ cup sugar	almonds
1 teaspoon salt	Grated rind of 3 lemons
½ cup (1 stick) butter,	½ teaspoon ground
softened	cardamom
7 to 7½ cups sifted all-	Melted butter
purpose flour	

Sprinkle the yeast over the warm water; stir until dissolved. Add milk (scalded then cooled to lukewarm), sugar, salt, butter and half the flour. Add 1 cup of remaining flour to fruit and half the nuts; toss to coat. Add this and remaining flour to batter, along with lemon rind and cardamom. Beat to blend into a soft dough. Turn dough onto floured board; knead until smooth and elastic. Place in greased bowl, brush top with melted butter, let rise until doubled. Punch down, knead again on floured board, form into one long roll. Place in buttered jelly-roll pan or baking sheet, let rise again until doubled. Press remaining almonds over top. Bake in oven preheated to 375° F. for 1 hour or until top is crusty gold. Remove from oven. Brush with melted butter; or dust with confectioners' sugar while warm. This is a year-round specialty of Bremen, but especially at Christmastime it is made in every home and served in all the *Konditoreien* with good Bremen coffee.

Dresdener Stollen

(CHRISTMAS YEAST BREAD OF DRESDEN)

½ cup seedless raisins
¼ cup chopped citron
¼ cup chopped candied
  orange peel
¼ cup dark rum
1 package active dry yeast
¼ cup warm water
¾ cup milk
¼ cup sugar
½ teaspoon salt
4 tablespoons (½ stick)
  butter

2¾ to 3 cups unsifted all-
  purpose flour
⅛ teaspoon ground
  cardamom
2 eggs, beaten
1 teaspoon grated lemon
  rind
½ cup (about 6 ounces)
  shredded blanched
  almonds
2 to 3 tablespoons melted
  butter
Confectioners' sugar

Soak the fruit in rum while preparing the dough. Dissolve the yeast in warm water. Combine milk, sugar, salt and butter, heat until sugar is dissolved and butter melted. Cool to lukewarm. Place 2 cups flour mixed with cardamom in large bowl, forming a well in the center. In the well, place the dissolved yeast, the lukewarm milk mixture and the eggs. Stir to blend, then beat until smooth and dough easily comes away from bowl. Drain the fruit, add with lemon rind and ¼ cup of the almonds to the ¾ cup flour, toss until fruit and nuts are well coated. Add coated fruit and nuts to the dough, work with fingers until fruit and nuts are well distributed in the dough. Knead on lightly floured board until smooth and elastic, about 5 minutes. If too sticky, work in a little more flour. Place in greased bowl, turning to grease top. Cover; let rise in warm place until doubled in bulk, about 1 hour.

Turn out on board, roll dough into oblong shape ½-inch thick. Brush melted butter over the top. Fold in half lengthwise in pocketbook shape, so that upper half does not quite cover the lower edge. Form into a crescent. Place on greased baking sheet. Brush top with more melted butter. Let rise again until doubled (35 to 45 minutes). Press remaining almonds into dough. Preheat oven to 350° F., bake the *Stollen* at this temperature about 40 minutes until golden and firm. Remove. Brush with a generous amount of melted butter. Dust with confectioners' sugar while warm.

Hutzelbrot
(FRUIT BREAD)

2 cups mixed dried fruit, soaked

2 envelopes active dry yeast

½ cup warm water

½ cup sugar

6 to 7 cups sifted all-purpose flour (or use ½ all-purpose flour, ½ rye flour)

¼ teaspoon ground cardamom

½ teaspoon powdered coriander

¼ teaspoon powdered anise or fennel

⅛ teaspoon powdered cloves

1 teaspoon salt

½ cup butter or shortening

1 cup shredded almonds

1 cup chopped hazelnuts or walnuts

1 cup golden raisins

⅓ cup chopped candied orange peel

¼ cup Kirschwasser, brandy or rum

Cook the dried fruit in water to cover until soft; drain, saving 1 cup of the liquid. Chop the fruit finely, discarding any hard bits of the fruit or pits.

Dissolve yeast in warm water with sugar. Sift and measure the flour; if using part rye flour, thoroughly blend the two. Add spices and salt to the flour. Place half the flour in a large mixing bowl, make a well in the center, add the dissolved yeast and the reserved liquid from fruit which has been heated, then cooled to lukewarm. Add melted butter or shortening. Mix until well blended; let rise 15 minutes in warm place to form a light sponge. Toss 1 cup of remaining flour with chopped fruit and nuts. Add this and rest of flour to the sponge along with the *Kirschwasser*. Beat until smooth; turn out onto floured board, knead until smooth and elastic. Place in greased bowl, let rise in warm place 45 minutes to an hour until doubled. Punch down, knead again, divide dough in half. Shape into 2 round balls. Place on greased baking sheet, let rise again.

Preheat oven to 375° F. When loaves are again doubled, place in oven, bake until crust is golden and crisp, 45 minutes to 1 hour. After removing from pans but while bread is warm, brush with a little of the liquid from the dried fruit. Makes 2 loaves.

* * *

Only in Berlin are these called *Pfannkuchen*. In the rest of Germany they are called *Krapfen*. They used to have still another name, "Bismarcks," because the famous unifier of Germany was so fond of them.

Berliner Pfannkuchen oder Krapfen
(JELLY DOUGHNUTS)

1 envelope active dry yeast	½ cup melted butter
1 cup milk, scalded, cooled to lukewarm	Grated rind of ½ lemon
3½ cups sifted all-purpose flour	Currant jelly or apricot jam
½ cup sugar	1 unbeaten egg white
3 eggs, beaten	Deep fat for frying
	Confectioners' sugar

Sprinkle the yeast over ¼ cup of the lukewarm milk (105–115° F.). When yeast is dissolved, add remaining milk, stir to blend, then add half the flour, work into a soft dough. Cover lightly with a towel, let stand in a warm place free from drafts about 1 hour.

Combine sugar, eggs, melted butter and lemon rind. Add to the risen sponge with remainder of flour. Beat thoroughly. Let dough rise again for ½ hour. Punch down, roll out on lightly floured board to ½-inch thick. Cut in rounds with 3-inch cookie cutter (it should make 32). Place a heaping teaspoonful of jelly or jam on half the rounds. Brush around edges with egg white. Place remaining rounds on the top, press to seal. Where a bump shows the jelly to be, cut a hole so that jelly is exposed.

Fat or oil should be 2 inches deep in heavy pot or deep-fat fryer. Heat to 375° F. Drop doughnuts into the fat, a few at a time—do not crowd fryer. When doughnuts rise to top and are brown on each side, remove with slotted spoon, drain on absorbent paper. Sprinkle confectioners' sugar over the top. Makes about 30.

*   *   *

Few German *Hausfrauen* make *Lebkuchen* at home any longer for they can be purchased in tins at any market at Christmastime. The flavor is much like that of our gingerbread.

Nürnberger Lebkuchen
(NUREMBERG SPICE COOKIES)

1 cup honey
1 cup sugar
4 eggs
2 tablespoons cocoa
1 cup milk (or 1 cup black coffee)
3 cups sifted all-purpose flour
½ teaspoon baking soda
¼ teaspoon cloves
¼ teaspoon cardamom or nutmeg
¼ teaspoon powdered ginger
½ teaspoon cinnamon
½ cup finely chopped citron or candied orange peel (optional)
Sugar glaze
Whole blanched almonds
Citron pieces

Combine honey, sugar and eggs; beat until thick. Add cocoa and milk or coffee. Sift together flour, soda and spices. Combine with egg mixture, blend thoroughly. Fold in candied fruit peel. Grease 2 baking sheets. Preheat oven to 400° F. Spoon batter over the sheets evenly, to ½-inch thick. Bake 10 to 12 minutes until no imprint remains when touched. Prepare the glaze as *Lebkuchen* bakes. Spread the glaze over the *Lebkuchen* while warm, arrange almonds and cut pieces of citron over the top. When cold, cut into squares. These should be soft and sweet, similar to gingerbread but more delicately spiced. If stored in an airtight container they will keep for weeks. Makes about 35 squares.

Sugar glaze. Place in small bowl ½ cup sifted confectioners' sugar. Add ½ teaspoon vanilla and 1 tablespoon of water. Stir until smooth; add more water 1 teaspoon at a time until mixture is consistency of cream. Spread at once over *Lebkuchen*. (This glaze can also be used on cookies, coffeecake or baked sweet yeast breads.) Makes about ⅓ cup glaze.

Spitzbuben
("URCHINS")

2 cups sifted all-purpose
   flour
12 tablespoons (1½ sticks)
   butter, softened
1 cup sugar

½ cup coarsely grated or
   chopped almonds
Jelly or jam
Confectioners' sugar

Beat together flour, butter, sugar and almonds to a smooth dough. Chill. Roll out on very lightly floured board to ⅛-inch thickness. Cut into circles with 2-inch biscuit cutter. Cut out centers of half the circles. Bake on ungreased baking sheet in oven preheated to 350° F. for 12 to 15 minutes until delicately browned. Remove. Put jam on the circles, top with the rings so that jam shows in center. Sprinkle with confectioners' sugar. Makes about 20.

Pfeffernüsse
(PEPPER "NUTS")

2 eggs, beaten
1 cup sugar
¼ cup ground almonds
¼ cup candied orange peel and citron, finely chopped
1 teaspoon cinnamon
⅛ teaspoon cloves
¼ teaspoon black pepper
¼ teaspoon ground ginger
Grated rind of 1 lemon
3 cups sifted all-purpose flour
Rum (about ¼ cup)
Confectioners' sugar

Beat eggs and sugar together until frothy. Add almonds, orange peel and citron (if you have an electric blender, it will quickly grind the almonds and mince the candied fruit). Add spices and lemon rind to flour; combine with egg mixture, knead to firm smooth dough. Shape into a long roll, about 1½ inches in diameter. Chill, then cut into ½-inch slices. Place slices on greased baking sheets, let stand uncovered overnight. Next day, turn over the "nuts," then bake in 300° F. oven 20 minutes or until lightly browned. While still warm, sprinkle with rum and confectioners' sugar. After they are completely cold, store in airtight container. Makes 50 or more hard little "nuts" that become more chewy and flavorful with age.

* * *

American children raised on soft cookies simply won't understand *Springerle* because they are hard and without a great deal of flavor. They are intended to be looked at rather than eaten and some are as fanciful as lacy Valentine cards.

Springerle
(PRESSED ANISE COOKIES)

2 eggs
1 cup granulated sugar
2 cups sifted all-purpose
flour

2 to 4 teaspoons anise
seed

Beat eggs in electric mixer until very light and pale-colored. Gradually add sugar. (Beat for 10 to 15 minutes with electric mixer, 30 minutes by hand.) Add flour; knead to a stiff dough, adding more flour if necessary. Roll to ⅛-inch thick on lightly floured board. Flour *Springerle* molds or patterned rolling pin. Press mold or pin firmly onto dough to get a good imprint, then gently pull away and cut into indicated shapes. Grease baking sheets and sprinkle each with anise seed. Place the cookies on the sheets. Let stand uncovered in a cool place at least 12 hours—24 hours is even better. Bake at 300° F. with oven door slightly ajar for 8 to 10 minutes until cookies are a pale yellow in color. Let cool completely before touching. These will be hard and brittle. The number of cookies the recipe makes depends on size and shape of the molds—some molds are as large as 6 × 6 inches.

*   *   *

Nothing expresses the German love of edible art more succinctly than marzipan candies which are shaped into piglets, cats, poodles, flowers, fruit and all sorts of other objects. They are delicious to eat, too.

Marzipan

1 pound shelled blanched
almonds
1 1-pound box 10-X
confectioners' sugar

1 egg white, unbeaten
3 or 4 tablespoons
rosewater or orangewater

-237-

Carefully dry the shelled almonds, then grind to a powder in an electric blender, if you have one. Blend almonds, the sugar, the egg white and just enough rosewater or orangewater (available from pharmacies) to make a pliable stiff dough. Knead with fingers, then place on board dusted with confectioners' sugar and form into desired shapes, to resemble miniature apples, peaches, strawberries or, if you have an artist's touch, little pigs or birds. Tint with food coloring. Balls of marzipan may be rubbed in chocolate dots or colored sugar. If dough becomes too stiff, work in a little lemon juice, rosewater or orangewater, adding drop by drop.

When candies are shaped, dry thoroughly in a cool, airy place for 24 hours, then wrap separately or place in a container (such as a little straw basket for fruit) and cover completely with Saran or other plastic wrap. Makes 2 pounds of candy.

Käsekuchen

(CHEESECAKE)

2½ cups zwieback crumbs (6-ounce package)	1½ tablespoons lemon juice
½ cup sugar	Grated rind of ½ lemon
1 teaspoon cinnamon	1 cup light cream
½ cup melted butter	1½ pounds cottage cheese (2 12-ounce packages)
4 eggs	¼ cup all-purpose flour
1 cup sugar	¼ cup chopped nuts
⅛ teaspoon salt	

Generously butter a spring-form mold or large cake pan with removable bottom. Mix zwieback with ½ cup sugar, cinnamon and melted butter; reserve ½ cup of mixture. Spread remaining mixture on bottom and sides of mold, pressing to form crust. Beat eggs until light, add 1 cup sugar, salt, lemon juice and rind; stir in cream, cottage cheese and flour; beat in electric blender or mixer until smooth. Pour into crumb-lined form and cover with reserved zwieback mixture and nuts. Bake at 350° F. for 1 hour until center is set (test with cake tester). Turn off heat, open oven door, let stay in oven 1 hour longer. Makes 10 to 12 servings.

Appendix

SOME OF GERMANY'S OUTSTANDING
RESTAURANTS

(The following is not in any sense an inclusive list. I have
mentioned only those restaurants which I have personally visited
plus some others so renowned I regret I could not have sampled
their fare.)

Berlin
 Aben, Kurfürstendamm 103
 Bristol Grill, Kurfürstendamm 27
 Ritz, Rankestrasse 26
 Rollenhagen-Stube, Kurfürstendamm 229
  (Noted for its delicious snacks.)
 Schlichter, Lutherstrasse 33

Bremen
 Essighaus, Langenstrasse 19
  (Be sure to have *Bremer Kükenragout* here.)
 Ratstube, Deutsches Haus, Market Square
  (*Scampis Rolandia* is a delectable creation of the chef.)
 Schnoor 2
  (An especially delightful spot for late suppers, located at Num-
  ber 2 Schnoor Street, a quaint winding street full of antique
  shops.)
 S & K, Bennigsenstrasse 14

Cologne
 Bastei, Kaiser Friedrich-Ufer
  (Enjoy a lovely view of the Rhine while dining on superb food.)
 Kuckuck, in the Stadtwald

Wirtshaus im Spessart, Kleine Budengasse 1
(This is located above a 2000-year-old Roman sewer, near the Town Hall. Small rooms, candlelit, charmingly decorated with objects from an old wine house. Grilled specialties cooked to order.)
Weinhaus Wiesel, Domkloster 2
Im Wallfisch, in the Salzgasse
Kölner Hof, Bahnhofstrasse 5–7

Diedesheim
Gasthaus zur Kanne
(This is located in a building which is said to have housed an inn or restaurant continuously since the twelfth century. Snails are particularly good here.)

Düsseldorf
Breidenbacher Hof, Alleestrasse 34
KD, Königsallee 12
Müller & Fest (M & F), Königsallee 14
Walliser Stuben, Adersstrasse 46

Ettlingen
Erbprinz Hotel dining room
(This is rated by French gourmets as one of the ten best dining rooms in Europe.)

Frankfurt
Brückenkeller, Schützenstrasse 6
(An elegant underground establishment in an ancient wine cellar. Excellent food and service; music by strolling minstrels.)
Kupferkanne (The "Copper Pan") Opernplatz 2
(Specialties cooked at your table in copper pans.)
Rotisserie 5 Continents, at the airport
(International foods prepared by visiting foreign chefs.)
Hopfengarten, in Dornbusch section

Murrhardt
Gasthaus Sonne-Post
(Spotlessly clean restaurant with such excellent food it attracts customers from many miles away.)

Hamburg
Alsterschiff
(A boat turned into a restaurant on the Alster lake. You dine on the water, watching gulls sweep nearby.)
Ehmke, Am Gänsemarkt 50
(Wine restaurant specializing in seafood.)
Schumanns Austernkeller, Junfernsteig 34
(Another seafood house, very elegant.)
Ratsweinkeller, in the Town Hall
(Elegant, hushed atmosphere, superb wines and service.)
Vier Jahrszeiten, on the Alster.
(Three fine dining rooms.)

Havexheim
Droste zu Hülshoff, located in family castle of Baron von Hulshoff

Münster
Bei Pinkus Müller
(A tavern favored by students who often make the rafters ring with drinking songs.)

Munich
Böttner, Theatinerstrasse 8
(Especially noted for its snacks.)
Chesa Rügg, Wurzerstrasse 18
(Grilled specialties.)
Humplmayr, Maximiliansplatz 17
(Dark-paneled elegance, superb food and service.)
Walterspiel, in Vier Jahreszeiten Hotel, Maximilianstrasse 4
(Named after one of Germany's truly great chefs.)
Zur Kanne, Maximilianstrasse 36
(A favorite after-theater spot, but closed on Saturday nights.)

Stuttgart
Alte Post, Friedrichstrasse 43
Exquisit, Karlstrasse
Alte Kanzlei, Schillerplatz 5

APPENDIX

Weinstube zur Schreinerei
(This is across the river in the suburb of Bad Kannstadt, a simple place where the food is cooked by the owner and his wife. Be sure to have *Zwiebelkuchen*.)

Wildbad

Hotel Sommerberg
(A luxurious resort hotel on the edge of the Black Forest which prepares Swabian specialties magnificently.)

Index

INDEX

INDEX

salad or cole slaw, 177
stuffed, 146–47
white, in sour cream sauce, 176
Cakes and cookies:
  apfelbutterkuchen, 230
  apple, Bavarian style, 221
  bee sting, 226–27
  Bremen sweet bread, 230–31
  butterkuchen, 229–30
  cheesecake, 338
  coffeecake, Frankfurt crown, 228–29
  fillings and toppings:
    buttercream, 222
    butter topping, 229–30
    cherry, 225
    chocolate, 225
    mokkacreme, 228
    sugar glaze, 235
  fruit bread, 232–33
  jelly doughnuts, 233–34
  lebkuchen, 85, 90, 91
  mocha nut, 228
  Nuremberg spice cookies, 234–35
  pepper "nuts," 236
  poppy seed, 227
  pressed anise cookies, 237
  spice (*lebkuchen*), 85, 90, 91
  stollen, 231–32
  streuselkuchen, 230
  "urchins," 235
  See Tortes
Calf's tongue:
  with horseradish sauce, 99
  with mushrooms, 98–99
  with raisin sauce, 99
Camembert canapés, 50–51
Canapés. *See* Appetizers
Candy: marzipan, 237–38
Caper sauce, 76, 116–17
Capon with mushrooms, 124
Caraway: cheese noodle ring, 129, 189
  cheese twists, 45
  crisps, 44
  potatoes, 169
Carp, 70
  blue, 71
  for New Year's Eve, 70–71
Catsup, 86
Caviar, stuffed eggs, 49
Celeriac. *See* Celery root
Celery punch, 31
Celery root, 181–82
  salad, 182
Champagnerkraut (sauerkraut cooked in white wine), 152, 157, 176–77
Cheese:
  baked noodles with, 190
  cake, 238
  camembert: canapés, 50–51
  caraway, noodle ring, 189
  cream:
    plate, Palatinate, 50
    truffles, 48
  hand, with chopped onion, 49–50
  noodles, 148
  plate, Palatinate, 50
  quark, 127
  salad Allgäu style, 187
  soup with egg, 59

truffles, 48
twists, 44–45
Cherry(ies):
  filling, 225
  flambé, Black Forest, 205
  pancakes, 213
  pastry, 220
  torte, Black Forest, 224–25
Chicken, 119–20
  capon with mushrooms, 124
  liver pâté, 51
  queen's pastries, 122
  ragout, Bremen style, 121
  salad Emirado, 188–89
  young cockerels or broilers South German style, 122–23
  young hen hunter's style, 123
Chocolate: cream, 207–8
  filling, 225
Christmas yeast bread of Dresden, 231–32
Clear broth, 54–55
Codfish:
  balls with spinach, 75
  poached, 76
Coffee, 28–29
  cream, 208
  wine froth, 205
Coffeecake, Frankfurt crown, 228–29
Cold potato salad, 175
Cole slaw, 177
Cooked horseradish sauce, 195
Cooked potato dumplings, 173–74
Corned beef. *See* Labskaus
Cornish hens, 129
Crab salad Helgoland style, 36
Crayfish, 36n
Cream cheese:
  plate, Palatinate, 50
  truffles, 48
Creamed spinach, 181
Croquettes, potato, almond-studded, 168
Croutons, pumpernickel, 61
Cucumber: pickle sauce, 195
  punch, 31
  salad, 186
Cured pork rib, 96
Currant juice (red), 28
Curried rice, 192
Curry: cream sauce, 74–75
  meats, 86
  mousseline, 197–98
Curry Mousselinesosse (curry mousseline), 75, 83, 193, 197–98
Curryreis (curried rice), 192
Curry Sahnensosse (curry cream sauce), 74–75
"Curry" *wurst,* 87
Custard cubes for soup, 56

Dampfnudeln (steamed dumplings), 190–91
Desserts, 203–13
  apple pancakes, 212
  apple rice pudding, 209–10
  Bavarian cream, 208–9
  Black Forest cherries flambé, 205
  cherry pancakes, 213
  chocolate cream, 207–8
  coffee cream, 208
  coffee wine froth, 205

INDEX

INDEX